"We are now more than two decades out from the groundbreaking and world-changing reporting by the "Spotlight" team at the *Boston Globe* that brought the crisis of clergy sexual abuse and its insidious cover-up by church leaders to light. While much has been done during these decades to address the harm caused, still much more is needed. This volume brings together a wide range of expertise and insight to help in this effort, especially as it relates to ministry in the church today. I recommend this book to everyone engaged in pastoral ministry in the Catholic Church today, especially those entrusted with leadership of dioceses, religious congregations, and parishes. It should also be required reading in seminaries and graduate schools of theology and ministry."

— Daniel P. Horan, professor of philosophy, religious studies, and theology, Saint Mary's College, Notre Dame, Indiana

"If you wonder what the clergy sexual abuse crisis is all about, let this book explain it to you. Although you can never fully understand sexual abuse unless you have lived it, the loss is so profound that the very essence, identity, spirituality, and relational ability is forever changed in the victim and will never be the same as it was before the abuse took place. Within these pages is an insightful overview of this crisis with an emphasis on the effect it has had on the people of God—parish, faith, religious communities, the priesthood, and the entire faithful. Hopefully, these pages will give you a deeper look than you have had, and you will be changed, for the better, knowing what you can do to help transform our Church into a haven of justice and peace."

— Paula Kaempffer, coordinator for restorative practices and survivor support, Archdiocese of Saint Paul and Minneapolis

"This collection of essays makes common cause with numerous recent initiatives stemming from Catholic universities and theologians across the globe, all making constructive response to the challenges posed by the phenomena of clergy sexual abuse. Increasingly, Catholic universities are where the church is doing its thinking on this issue. This volume will benefit ground force actors responsible for safeguarding in dioceses, schools, parishes, and seminaries, and it will contribute helpful resources to church leadership, not only to bishops but to priests, principals, administrators, and teachers in all settings, even as the work of protection and healing belong to all in the church. *Accountability, Healing, and Trust* joins a number of recent volumes that, together, show us how to bridge the work of church and academy and, still together, disrupt patterns of vulnerability and promote the flourishing of all."

— John N. Sheveland, professor of religious studies, Gonzaga University; editor of *Theology in a Post-Traumatic Church*

"As there can be no authentic celebration of resurrection hope that bypasses the crucifixion, the Catholic Church, in all of its expressions, cannot be a source of safety and healing by bypassing the grim reality of sexual abuse within the church. *Accountability, Healing, and Trust* does engender hope, doing so through respect for the needs of survivors, honest confrontation with the sinfulness and failure that blight many aspects of the ecclesial community, and a commitment to the conversion that the church's prayer and worship engender. This is a challenging book, but a necessary one."

— Richard Lennan, professor of systematic theology, Boston College— Clough School of Theology and Ministry

"At a time when some in the church advocate for leaving discussions of abuse behind, this book offers a vital reminder: Our work to address the systemic roots of abuse and institutional betrayal is far from over. The thought-provoking essays in this collection challenge us to work toward a future where accountability, justice, and authentic accompaniment permeate the life of the church at every level. Most importantly, this volume encourages an approach that amplifies the voices, stories, and wisdom of abuse survivors—reminding us that their insights are indispensable for the healing and transformation of the church."

— Sara Larson, executive director, Awake

Accountability, Healing, and Trust

Interdisciplinary Reflections for Ministry
in the Midst of the Catholic Sex Abuse Crisis

Edited by

Kimberly Hope Belcher

and

David A. Clairmont

LITURGICAL PRESS
Collegeville, Minnesota

litpress.org

Library of Congress Cataloging-in-Publication Data

Names: Belcher, Kimberly Hope, editor. | Clairmont, David A., editor.
Title: Accountability, healing, and trust : interdisciplinary reflections for
    ministry in the midst of the Catholic sex abuse crisis / edited by Kimberly
    Hope Belcher and David A. Clairmont.
Description: Collegeville, Minnesota : Liturgical Press, [2025] | Summary:
    "Organized around three themes: accountability, healing, and trust, the
    contributors to this volume probe the understanding of the church's mission
    and name the most significant divisions in the response to the sexual abuse
    crisis. This volume focuses on ways forward and treats clergy and lay people,
    scholars, and ministers as partners in the work of creating an atmosphere
    of accountability, healing, and trust in the post-abuse-revelation church"—
    Provided by publisher.
Identifiers: LCCN 2024033190 (print) | LCCN 2024033191 (ebook) |
    ISBN 9780814688977 (trade paperback) | ISBN 9780814688991 (epub) |
    ISBN 9780814689646 (pdf)
Subjects: LCSH: Catholic Church—Clergy—Sexual behavior. | Child sexual
    abuse by clergy—United States. | Responsibility—United States.
Classification: LCC BX1912.9 .A33 2025 (print) | LCC BX1912.9 (ebook) |
    DDC 282/.73—dc23/eng/20240814
LC record available at https://lccn.loc.gov/2024033190
LC ebook record available at https://lccn.loc.gov/2024033191

Contents

PART ONE
Accountability—Listening to the Words of Survivors

PART THREE
Trust—Re-forming the Body of Christ

Appendixes
Liturgical Resources to Promote Accountability, Healing, and Trust

Preface

The papers in this volume originated as contributions to a conference held at the University of Notre Dame on March 3–5, 2022. "Accountability, Healing, and Trust: Conversations in Theology, Psychology, and Law for the Life of the Church" initially began as discussions among faculty and graduate students in the Department of Theology at Notre Dame, part of a university-wide initiative to envision both academic and pastoral responses to the clergy sexual abuse crisis in the Roman Catholic Church. In March 2019, Notre Dame President Rev. John Jenkins, CSC, announced that the Office of the President would fund a series of research projects that "address issues emerging from the Church sexual abuse crisis." In April 2019, at the urging of our chair Timothy Matovina, faculty and graduate students in the Department of Theology gathered to discuss the abuse crisis and to discern the various ways the department might respond. At the conclusion of that meeting, several faculty and graduate students volunteered to serve on a department committee that formulated a grant proposal, in conversation with members of other departments and with psychology and law professionals in the community. We both served on that committee, as did our colleagues Anselma Dolcich-Ashley (whose contribution appears in this volume) and Jean Porter from the Department of Theology; Susan St. Ville from the Keogh School of Global Affairs; Kristin Valentino from the Department of Psychology; John Robinson and John Maciejczyk from the Law School; Susan Feathergill of Feathergill and Associates in Mishawaka, Indiana; and Amanda Zelechoski of Purdue University. The committee received additional assistance from Michael Rubbelke, Casey Mullaney, Marie-Claire Klassen, and Brian Boyd. The grant received funding through the Office of Research program and was later supported by another major grant from the College of Arts and Letters. After a number of delays, due in part to the pandemic, the work of that committee, in collaboration with individuals and units from across the university, yielded the conference on which this volume is based.

It is important to note that the conference organized by the Department of Theology was only one of many initiatives supported by the Office of the President through the Office of Research grant program. Our Notre Dame colleagues Mark Doerries, Amanda McKendree, Kathleen Cummings, Richard Garnett, Daniel Hungerman, Katy Lichon, Daniel Philpott, Clemens Sedmak, and Kristin Valentino all advanced projects investigating the abuse crisis through the same program that supported this conference.[1]

In our invitation to our conference speakers, we stated that the goal of the conference was

> to explore practical strategies to increase accountability, promote healing, and rebuild trust in the life of the Catholic Church in the aftermath of the clergy sexual abuse crisis. Its focus will be on the needs of local parishes, their leaders and staff, including educators in Catholic schools. The conference will also explore the intersection of parish life and the formation of ordained and lay ecclesial ministers in seminaries, dioceses, and Catholic universities. Scholars of theology, psychology and law will present recent research on these issues in conversation with those working in ministerial settings who have developed approaches and practical programs to address the needs of Catholic parishioners, students, and Church leaders during these challenging times.

Although the papers gathered in this volume are closely connected to the original aims of the conference and the presentations offered there, it became clear that the ensuing conversations and the subsequent paper revisions all focused in one way or another on ministry in the church, broadly understood—parishes, Catholic schools, dioceses, social service organizations—for both those actively working in ministry and those preparing for ministry. Indeed, many of the questions of, conversations with, and insights by students in our ministry program at Notre Dame helped us to envision the panel topics for the conference. Not all who presented at the conference

---

[1] Joanne Fahey, "Notre Dame Faculty Advance Research Related to the Church Sexual Abuse Crisis," Notre Dame Research, June 1, 2022, https://research.nd.edu /news-and-events/news/notre-dame-faculty-advance-research-related-to-the-church -sexual-abuse-crisis/.

elected to have their papers included in the volume, but we are grateful to all who presented their research: Rev. Gerard McGlone, SJ; Myriam Wijlens; Jennifer Beste; Marcus Mescher; Elizabeth Pulido Hernandez; Sarah Gallagher; Rev. Kevin Grove, CSC; Anselma Dolcich-Ashley; Eric T. Styles; Deborah Organ; Rev. Ronald Raab, CSC; Rev. Kenneth Schmidt; Bishop Kevin C. Rhoades; Stacey Noem; Deacon James Keating; Sara Larson; Michael Rubbelke; Melanie Susan Barrett; Mary Catherine McDonald; Rev. Bruce Morrill, SJ; J. J. Wright; Elisabeth Rain Kincaid; Hilary Jerome Scarsella; Mark Roosien; Patrick J. Wall; Mary Glowaski; Rev. John Paul Kimes; Susan Feathergill; Br. John Mark Falkenhain, OSB; Julia Feder; and Peter Capretto. More information about their presentations is available through the conference website.[2]

We are grateful to our original conference sponsors: the Notre Dame Office of Research, the College of Arts and Letters' Institute for Scholarship in the Liberal Arts, the McGrath Institute for Church Life, Notre Dame Campus Ministry, Liturgical Press, and the Department of Theology, among others. We also thank Amber Kirk and Kaylee Wolf from University Events, Patrick Deegan from the Office of Research, and Kate Gary and Heidi Henke from the College of Arts and Letters communication office whose work has allowed ideas for a conference to become the reality of a conference. We express our gratitude to our colleagues in the Theology Department, especially our then-chair Timothy Matovina and department administrator Melody Kesler; our conference panel conveners Stacey and Josh Noem, Susan and Jeff Feathergill, Mary Catherine Hilkert, OP, John Fitzgerald, Lindsey Barrett, Susan St. Ville, and Brian Boyd; the members of the Holy Cross community at Notre Dame, especially Rev. Michael Connors, CSC, for their constant encouragement; to Mary Heaton for her work with the conference staff and her care of those in attendance; and finally our families for their support of the conference and our efforts to bring the insights of our conference presenters to a wider audience through the essays in this volume.

Kimberly Hope Belcher and David A. Clairmont
Notre Dame, Indiana

---

[2] Conference: Accountability, Healing, and Trust, "Conversations in Theology, Psychology, and Law for the Life of the Church," March 3–5, 2022, University of Notre Dame, https://theology.nd.edu/news-events/conferences-seminars/conference-accountability-healing-and-trust/.

Introduction

Listening, Witnessing, and Re-forming in Church

Kimberly Hope Belcher and David A. Clairmont

The wounds inflicted by sexual abuse and the ensuing crisis in the Roman Catholic Church cut deep and have not healed. Even as the Charter for the Protection of Children and Young People (often referred to as the Dallas Charter), passed by the United States Conference of Catholic Bishops in June 2002 and subsequently revised three times (2005, 2011, and 2018), provides an important set of safeguards to prevent future instances of sexual abuse in the church, it is directed toward one element of a much larger problem.[1] The problem has deep historical roots in Catholic culture and practice, in certain (but certainly not all) theologies of the nature of the church and of church teachings on human sexuality, in the intersection of human psychosocial development and formation for ministry, and in the sometimes varied expectations for disclosure and accountability in canon law and civil law.

This book is one of many recent attempts to put academic resources—in psychology, law, and theology, among many others—in service to the church at a time when those resources are sorely needed,

---

[1] United States Conference of Catholic Bishops (USCCB), Charter for the Protection of Children and Young People (June 2018), https://www.usccb.org/offices/child -and-youth-protection/charter-protection-children-and-young-people.

whether or not they are uniformly welcomed.[2] The essays in this volume draw on many different such resources in an attempt to describe the problem of clergy sexual abuse and ongoing efforts to hide it, the culture that gave rise to it and fostered complicity in it among church leaders and ordinary churchgoing Catholics, and the profound pain and alienation that the abuse crisis has caused for so many in the church today.

There is probably no single "best" way to address the great range of problems occasioned by the abuse crisis, but all of the contributors to this volume recognize that the abuse crisis has affected the work of ministry in profound ways. From the training of future ministers—lay and ordained—to the exercise of the church's various ministries in parishes, education, and direct service, the abuse crisis calls out for a response to the questions posed by abuse survivors and those who accompany and hope to serve them.

The essays in this collection are organized around three themes: accountability, healing, and trust. We selected these themes to organize the volume because they seemed to us the ones most important for those working in ministry in the church today. These themes also resonated with us as among the most in need of prayerful consideration by all the Catholic faithful since they touch on the deepest understanding of the church's mission and also, sadly, name the church's most significant divisions in the response to the abuse crisis. For example, we read in the Gospel of Matthew that we will be called to account for the treatment of our neighbors and that Jesus will see in our works of mercy to care for our neighbors our treatment of Jesus himself (Matt 25:31-46). When, in the Gospel of Luke, we listen to the

---

[2] Many of these resources are cited in the following chapters, but among those that have been important for our own thinking about the crisis are *Sexual Abuse in the Catholic Church: A Decade of Crisis, 2002–2012*, ed. Thomas G. Plante and Kathleen L. McChesney (Santa Barbara: Praeger, 2011); *Church Ethics and Its Organizational Context: Learning from the Sex Abuse Scandal in the Catholic Church*, ed. Jean M. Bartunek, Mary Ann Hinsdale, and James F. Keenan (Lanham, MD: Sheed & Ward, 2006); and most recently *Doing Theology and Theological Ethics in the Face of the Abuse Crisis*, ed. Daniel J. Fleming, James F. Keenan, and Hans Zollner (Eugene, OR: Pickwick Publications, 2023). We also benefitted greatly from the leadership of and the participants in the Taking Responsibility project at Fordham University (https://takingresponsibility .ace.fordham.edu/project-description-and-goals/) and to the other Jesuit institutions that worked with Fordham to host meetings.

story of the Good Samaritan, we are called to "do likewise" in healing the bodies of those who have been violated (Luke 10:25-37). The Gospel of John tells us that Jesus invites trust in him as "the way and the truth and the life" (John 14:6) and promises that he will not leave us orphaned (John 14:18) because he will send us the "Spirit of truth" (John 14:16-17) who will be our advocate. Jesus calls us to account for our own actions and the treatment of our suffering neighbors; he counsels us to act with creativity and courage to bring healing when our neighbors are violated; he assures us that we can trust in him because his Spirit of truth will not hide suffering in shadows or allow cries to fade behind closed doors.

The contributors to this volume come from a range of backgrounds, experiences, and ministries in the church. Some work directly in parishes; others in education; still others in direct service to those whose daily needs go unmet. Some contributors have been moved to write through their encounters with the abused and with abusers; others write from the experience of abuse. All write out of their love of God and in service to the church—sometimes strained, often pained, occasionally angry, always sincere. Most are practicing Catholics; others share their observations about what has happened in the Catholic Church from the perspective of other Christian communities that are also contending with sexual abuse among their members. All the contributors hope that their essays can be of some assistance to those working in ministry.

The essays are organized into parts along the three organizing themes. In part 1, we explore the theme of accountability through the work of listening to the words of survivors. Gerard McGlone's essay sets the theme for this section by calling our attention to the preeminent place that listening must hold in any effort by any member of the church to give an account of what has happened and hold accountable those who allowed a culture of abuse to flourish. Exploring the biblical scene of the disciples gathered in the upper room after the crucifixion, McGlone invites us to think about the connections between the trauma of the crucifixion and the disciples' decision to speak out of that turmoil, and those who speak from the trauma of abuse today. Jennifer Beste takes up the theme of justice, pushing us to consider both the scope of abuse and the depth of harm it has caused while also urging us to consider how the culture and structure of Catholic leadership has prevented us from appreciating the scope of abuse and the depth of harm. Reflecting on her own conversations with survivors over the past fifteen years, Beste reminds us that there exist model practices that the church can emulate if it is willing to do so and that these practices focus first on listening to and believing those who have been abused. Sarah Gallagher focuses on one particular context where sexual abuse intersected with the efforts by Catholic schools to disrupt Native American families and erase Native American culture. Through her work with the Truth and Healing Committee of the American Indian Catholic Schools Network, Gallagher suggests that the practice of Native-led listening sessions, as a foundational aspect of restorative justice, holds great promise for healing from the abuse suffered by Native American communities and may offer an important model for the listening practices of the wider church. Hilary Jerome Scarsella offers an analysis of how the Catholic Church responded to the abuse crisis from the perspective afforded by her work in survivor advocacy with Into Account. Contextualizing the Catholic response with respect to other Christian traditions' responses, she counsels Catholic Christians to prioritize both listening to the stories of survivors but also making resources available to survivors so they can navigate whatever approach to healing and possible reconciliations make sense to them. Marcus Mescher explores the question of how the church can be a source of healing even as it has also been the locus of terrible abuse. Focusing on the betrayal, shame and futility, weaponization of faith, isolation, and institutional failure experienced by those who have been abused, Mescher argues for an approach to ministry that focuses on listening, solidarity, and building relationships with survivors.

In part 2, we explore the theme of healing through the work of witnessing to the lives of survivors. Anselma Dolcich-Ashley examines how narrow interpretations of the Sixth Commandment's prohibition of adultery have obscured the abuse crisis as not only a moral failure of individuals but also a structural injustice. Dolcich-Ashley reminds us that the authority in the church rests not only with bishops but with all the faithful as a result of their baptism, especially in those instances where the faithful grasp the nature of the injustice better than those with episcopal authority who have failed to protect them. Bruce Morrill examines the relationship between the church's sacramental life and its clerical culture, highlighting how the symbolic power of the sacraments has often been linked with the moral authority of church leaders. Offering a critique of what he calls "sacramental clericalism," Morrill cautions that a "false sacrality" in the performance of rituals obscures the sacramental nature of the people of God and the possibility that the liturgy might itself be an occasion for healing rather than further wounding of the abused. Kimberly Hope Belcher introduces the work of ritual theorists to help make sense of the ways that the sacraments, other liturgical celebrations, and newly envisioned rituals in the Christian community might help the church to address its reticence in responding to the abuse crisis in a creative ritual mode. Taking as an example the raising of Lazarus recounted in the Gospel of John, Belcher brings the reader into a process of envisioning the phases of healing from abuse and returning to the community that was the site of abuse. Patrick Wall offers insights from his legal work with survivors, reminding us that there is a long history of church deliberations—in canon and civil law—about abusive priests and that there are lessons we can learn from studying this history. Reflecting on the ability of the law to change the approach and behaviors of sometimes reluctant church leaders, he discusses the relationship between putting the well-being of survivors first and avoiding practices—even if well-meaning—that can further harm the abused. Kenneth Schmidt explores the effects of trauma in the life of the church, considering especially the challenge of preaching in a traumatized community. As preaching is an act that helps those who listen to recall, interpret, understand, and find meaning, Schmidt describes the preacher as a "wounded healer" whose words have the potential to help those gathered to recall, interpret, understand, and find meaning in the gospel and in their own wounds.

In part 3, we explore the theme of trust through the work of re-forming the Body of Christ while taking seriously our devastating knowledge of abuse and cover-up. This work of re-formation addresses several communities: current and future ministers in the church, lay and ordained; those who work with abuse survivors, such as lawyers; and those who work with young people who are raising important questions and taking responsibility for the church in various ways. Stacey Noem reflects on the experience of working with people preparing for ecclesial ministry in all four kinds of formation required in their training: intellectual, pastoral, human, and spiritual. Noem explains how excessive attention to one pillar of formation (the intellectual, for example) at the expense of other pillars (human formation, for example) frustrates the goal of a holistic, integrated formation of ministers, further complicated by the relatively few number of formation programs in the United States that train lay and ordained ministers together in the same program. Kevin Grove also discusses the challenges arising in ministry formation, arguing that the professionalization of ministry is an important recent development in seminary education. Grove goes on to say that the developing professionalization of clerical and lay ministers provides hope for the future, but is not matched by an equal accountability among high level authorities. He calls for a renewed attention to the whole Christ, who laments with us and will accompany the church in this work. Envisioning the nature and practice of spiritual care for sexual violence, Peter Capretto diagnoses a problem in education for ministry. Noting a tendency in ministry education to equate what is acceptable training to what minimizes liability, Capretto argues instead that ministry education should focus on revisioning the community in ways that will make "unrepentant abusers afraid to enter it." Melanie Barrett considers historical examples of deficient moral formation both within and outside the church in order to articulate virtues that ought to characterize the church community. Barrett argues that the kind of moral formation needed to prevent future abuse and cover-ups must be based on a use of language that "corresponds truthfully to reality" and on the development of the virtues that promote justice in the community. David Clairmont considers the challenges that attend the moral and spiritual education of young people in the church in light of the qualities of their social environments and their awareness of the abuse crisis. Clairmont argues for a reframing of the discussion of safety in terms of the practice of mercy to help form young people as agents for mercy for the present and future church. Tristan Cooley and J. J. Wright introduce their work with students to create an original musical composition of the passion narrative. They consider both the creative process and the community discernment needed to join the gospel narrative, the experience of abuse in the church, and the shared work involved in creating, in and for a faith community, a beauty that might heal.

The Appendixes contain liturgical resources that might begin to promote accountability, healing, and trust. The *visio divina* and the morning and evening prayer composed by Kimberly Hope Belcher, Julia Canonico, and Eric T. Styles were used at the conference and are offered here with the hope that these resources will be useful in other settings as well. Ronald Raab has written a litany reflecting the movement of individuals and their communities from anguish toward justice. With Paul Turner, Raab also published *The Stations of the Cross in Atonement for Abuse and for the Healing of All*, for which he contributed fourteen original paintings.[3] Those who gathered for the conference were given the opportunity to pray together with Raab's art, considering how each person working in various ministries in the church might join their work "in atonement for abuse and for the healing of all."

Many of the essays contained in this book are reflections on the ways that the faith community at the University of Notre Dame has struggled with how to respond to the abuse crisis, but all who contributed to the original conference and to this volume offered their time, thought, and courage in service to survivors and to those who minister with them through listening, giving voice, and bearing witness to the wounded Body of Christ.

---

[3] Paul Turner, *The Stations of the Cross in Atonement for Abuse and for the Healing of All*, illustrated by Ronald Patrick Raab (Collegeville, MN: Liturgical Press, 2020).

Part One

**Accountability—
Listening to the Words of Survivors**

1

Toward Accountability, Trust, and Healing:
It's the System!

Gerard J. McGlone, SJ

Note: *In writing this, emerging and common practices suggest that what is written could be/will be read by many survivors. As a survivor myself, I write this for and to survivors. Some might be of clergy sexual violence as a child or as an adult, survivors of multiple types of traumas in families, in marriages, in dating, in many and varied circumstances and challenges. Please do take care of yourself; if this gets tough, please feel free to stop reading, but, above all, care for yourself.*

Framing Questions and Ecclesial Contexts

Today, we are faced with enormously complex, global, ecclesial, national, and international challenges and issues. One can scarcely remember a time when we were confronted with so many different challenges and traumas—personal, communal, national, global, and existential—all at once. Some of the images of these that one might remember or recall are breathtaking and yet might help begin to set the full context that lies before us. They might provide an essential and important context for this chapter. Context really matters in this area of clergy sexual abuse.[1] In the United States, we have been at this for almost forty years. This abuse reality exists today within the

---

[1] Brian J. Clites, "Breaking Our Silence: A Primer on Research on Clergy Sexual Abuse," *American Catholic Studies Newsletter* 47, no. 2 (Fall 2020): 6–16.

many wars that are raging, seemingly endless natural catastrophes, frightening ecclesial and national divisions, our reckoning with our past and current ecclesial racism, and the seemingly endless reports from across the globe about the extent and depth of the clergy sexual abuse problem within the Roman Catholic Church.

Perhaps we might grasp and understand that we are in a very similar moment to the early Christians who were gathered in the upper room after the crucifixion. This too is an important biblical context for Ignatius of Loyola; it would be creating a "composition of place." If we step back in prayer and imagine, there was confusion; feeling traumatized; having witnessed horrific violence; feeling betrayed by their companions, friends, and religious leaders; a sense of enormous grief and pain; being consumed by a fear of not knowing what the future would entail; feeling utter disgust for their leaders and the abandonment by some of the apostles; and most especially just bearing the confusion and chaos. They bore witness to their trauma, they told their story, and history changed. This historical context is quite like our current reality.

As a faith community, we've been through these realities and these moments before, and we flourished because of them. The example of the early church might give us hope as to how to deal with the current betrayal, how to choose different paths to healing divisions, and even possible forgiveness. Perhaps it might point the way for managing being so utterly tired, exhausted, and overwhelmed with this complex set of realities. It might also welcome us into a new understanding of the realities of being a survivor. This survivor's perspective is what has been missing most in the management of this global, historic, and ongoing atrocity of sexual abuse. Just as the early Christians bore witness to their horror, so too must we bear witness to the horrors suffered by survivors. It also might give us a way, a path, forward.

Our First Duty to Survivors

Paul Tillich's oft-quoted saying is important for our current discussion: "The first duty of love is to listen." It is the essence of a survivor's perspective that demands a new form of justice. It even sounds a "bit synodal." He explains:

> In order to know what is just in a person-to-person encounter,
> love listens. It is its first task to listen. No human relation, espe-
> cially no intimate one, is possible without mutual listening. Re-
> proaches, reactions, defenses may be justified in terms of
> proportional justice. But perhaps they would prove to be unjust
> if there were more mutual listening. All things and all people,
> so to speak, call on us with small or loud voices. They want us
> to listen, they want us to understand their intrinsic claims, their
> justice of being. They want justice from us. But we can give it to
> them only through the love which listens.[2]

The "ever ancient and ever new" sexual abuse reality in many coun-
tries calls for a different response, as described here.[3] It requires a
righteous listening and righteous witnessing. Perhaps it could be
seen in synodal listening sessions, leading to a different understanding and even a different type of analysis or, better, a different
diagnosis of a multifaceted problem.

Treatment providers and researchers attempt to work with one
basic understanding: *you cannot change something unless you know what
is there.* Going forward it is essential to study, analyze, see, and listen
to these atrocities from a survivor's perspective. Survivors—the
voices of children, people of color, descendants of enslaved persons,
and abuse survivors—can and do teach us every day about courage,
grace, resilience, and redemptive suffering in their betrayal and abandonment.[4] Hearing these marginalized victims, all too often ignored
and unseen, would place children and survivors at the center, and
we would be required to understand them at a deeper level than is
currently the case. If we might just be present, accompany, and listen
to their stories, maybe then cultural transformation, change, and
conversion is possible.

---

[2] Paul Tillich, *My Search for Absolutes*, ed. Ruth Nanda Anshen (New York: Simon
and Schuster, 1967).

[3] Brian Clites, "Our Accountability to Survivors," *American Catholic Studies* 130,
no. 2 (2019): 4–7, https://doi.org/10.1353/acs.2019.0031.

[4] Katie Collins, "Catholic Clergy Abuse Survivors Endure Compounded Trauma,"
National Catholic Reporter, September 2023.

Bearing Witness

Just as we have imagined being in the upper room, we might bring to our mind's eye some other recent and important images. We might first recall or remember that incredible moment during the COVID-19 pandemic when Pope Francis was alone in St. Peter's Square. He stood in the dark, in the rain, blessing the world in darkness, the world's fear, and the global chaos in the early stages of the pandemic. In a sense, he blessed the unknown, the fear, the chaos. He bore witness against the darkness. One might also recall or remember current images of bloodied and battered Ukrainian women, Israeli and Palestinian men, women, and children. The world is beginning to become morally outraged by the sheer volume and extent of the violence. Moral outrage in the face of this enduring and current memory is another key path forward for us. This outrage might allow us to become better witnesses.

Being a witness requires a good memory; some final images or memories starting in January 2018 might also help us in this new context. One is of Juan Carlos Ruiz, a Chilean clergy sexual abuse survivor and an incredible witness to the horrors of the Chilean sexual abuse scandal. His now famous confrontation of and a later friendship with Pope Francis is an example of humility, courage, forgiveness, possibility, and determination. Then, in that same year, we remember the former Cardinal McCarrick with many familiar images and news stories about his betrayal and offenses against men and children. One final memory, from August 2018, are the many faces of women and men survivors who were seen in the press conferences upon the release of the Pennsylvania attorney general grand jury report. That horrifying year ignited moral outrage not only at the individual abuses and abusers but also most especially at the abuse, failure, and sheer criminal neglect of bishops and religious leadership in the church. To become a righteous witness, we need that same outrage today to direct a clearer path forward toward healing.

Sadly, since 2018, we have seen a cacophony of reports from around the globe highlighting the same systemic failure we saw here in the United States. Jean Marc Sauvé released the groundbreaking CIASE Report, which went further than most reports but pointed to the systemic issues highlighted in reports from Ireland, England, Australia,

Canada, Belgium, Spain, Portugal, and Germany.[5] Nuala Kenny wrote a wonderful article that was titled: "Enough Is Enough."[6] She points out that what we know now, after all these reports, is enough. It was never simply the bad apple; it was the bad apple in a bad barrel. A barrel that was ruled and controlled by princes, not shepherds, who wanted power and privilege and wanted to protect that power and privilege. We know that it's the system that needs reform and conversion at both a personal and ecclesial level.

What Might Help?

How might the dynamics of a survivor's perspective help? Let's start with the *via negativa:* It is not doing as we have done. One might suggest that the current and past approaches have been centered on a "perpetrator-based approach" from top to bottom. Protecting the church's reputation is and was a criminal act that hid crime! Men in power abusing that power. If it is not a perpetrator-based approach, it is not about protecting that power. It is not about saving reputation; it is not a one-and-done approach. It is not solely about policies and audits. There is no simple solution.

In essence, having a "survivor's perspective" is about being quite traditional; it is simply about regaining, refounding, and reforming our gospel mission. It is, as Nuala Kenny has stated, about an ecclesial and personal conversion. So, what is a survivor's perspective? It is about listening, believing, and listening again, and again. It is about the assurances with clear processes rooted in accountability that no one else will get hurt. It is about compassionate initial and long-term accompaniment. It is accountability with justice! It is about cultural transformation and change. It is developing a new and sustained culture of safeguarding, safety, and trust.

---

[5] Sylvie Corbet, "French Report: 330,000 Children Victims of Church Sexual Abuse," Associated Press (October 3, 2021), https://apnews.com/article/europe-france-child-abuse-sexual-abuse-by-clergy-religion-ab5da1ff10f905b1c338a6f3427a1c66#.

[6] Nuala Kenny, "Enough Is Enough: The Church Does Not Need More Sex Abuse Reports but Personal and Ecclesial Conversion," *La Croix International* (August 13, 2022), https://international.la-croix.com/news/religion/enough-is-enough/15594.

It is a new way of bearing witness. Some key features would be a multidimensional approach in a "new catechesis" of survivors' stories, experiences, and narratives. Survivors' stories seem to heal, seem to lessen a sense of betrayal, while still not threatening one's beliefs and practices.[7] These stories could be placed in every school, in every parish, in every seminary, in every curia, in all leadership trainings, in all dicasteries. It is about "auditing" care and compassionate accompaniment in the long term. It is about having a "trauma-informed" church, pastoral care, and theology. It is about reforming a toxic theological complicity in our beliefs and actions.[8] It is a systemic problem; we need a systemic response.

What Has Been Done or Accomplished?

June 2022 marked twenty years of life with the "Dallas Charter."[9] Let us be very clear: this was the result of enormous outside pressure placed on the bishops in the United States. Many still say that what we have and what was accomplished abandoned the very gospel values of restorative justice and only addressed one aspect of a multidimensional and systemic problem.[10] Zero tolerance was necessary in 2002, but the events of 2018 and thereafter have demonstrated how clearly insufficient this response was because it addressed only one-third of the dilemma, yet again. Zero tolerance removed priests and religious from active ministry, but it never restored healing and justice for victims; it never held bishops accountable. It was an attempt to stop the bleeding, the news stories, and the damaged reputation of the church—which obviously did not work. The Cardinal McCarrick

---

[7] Gerard McGlone, "The Healing Power of Survivors' Stories," Taking Responsibility Research Project, Fordham University (January 2023), https://takingresponsibility.ace.fordham.edu/georgetown-stories-of-survivors/.

[8] Jack Downey, "Colonialism Is Abuse: Reconsidering Triumphalist Narratives in Catholic Studies," *American Catholic Studies* 130, no. 2 (2019): 16–20, https://doi.org/10.1353/acs.2019.0034.

[9] United States Conference of Catholic Bishops (USCCB), Charter for the Protection of Children and Young People (June 2018), https://www.usccb.org/offices/child-and-youth-protection/charter-protection-children-and-young-people.

[10] Brandon Vaidyanathan, Christopher Jacobi, and Chelsea Rae Kelly, "Well-Being, Trust, and Policy in Time of Crisis: Highlights from the National Study of Catholic Priests" (October 2022), https://catholicproject.catholic.edu/wp-content/uploads/2022/10/Catholic-Project-Final.pdf.

scandal in 2018 proved that the system was still in need of deep reform. We need to address these systemic failures that still exist.

Clearly a new infrastructure had been established that was not present prior to 2002. We have some important and new data from three different studies.[11] Policies have been put in place. Audits are done annually. Trainings have been done on a massive scale. The United States Conference of Catholic Bishops (USCCB) has set screening and assessment guidelines for seminarians. Resources seem to be there, generally. In 2018, these efforts worked: McCarrick was caught because of the new internal reporting infrastructure.

The Pennsylvania attorney general grand jury was, however, an example that showed us the fuller dimensions of the horrific atrocity. The McCarrick saga has shown us the real extent of the problem. It's about a feudal system within a feudal formation and promotion scheme that promotes a feudal, systemic clericalism within a feudal system of rewards of position and power seen in what is now called hierarchicalism.[12] Overwhelming national and global examples have exposed several corrupt, grooming, and privileged social classes, the feudal princes—namely, bishops, major superiors, and now regrettably some lay church leaders.

What Is Not Working?

The infrastructure fit the past crisis(es) and clearly is not equipped for the current systemic issues that need different, multidimensional, and more robust approaches. We need more data and research on the short- and long-term effectiveness of this safeguarding programming and this huge investment. There is no audit about the type of care being done for survivors. Especially with so many victim assistance coordinators (VACs), one must ask, "Is this working?" There are too many reports of neglect and indifference. Care for the victims seems to be time limited and inadequate. We know the long-term health effects survivors endure into adulthood, including higher mortality, addictions, impaired interpersonal relationships, depression, anxiety,

---

[11] United States Conference of Catholic Bishops (USCCB), https://www.usccb.org/offices/child-and-youth-protection/research.

[12] James Keenan, "Hierarchicalism," *Theological Studies* 83, no. 1 (2022): 84–108, https://doi.org/10.1177/00405639211070493.

and higher rates of suicide. We support accused priests for their lifetime. Are not the rights of the baptized survivor equally precious?

Where is the research on the survivors now? We do not have data in the USCCB audits about the ethnicity of any survivor. (Ethnicity is crucial to know since we know in the ecclesial and general populations the marginalized communities are victimized sometimes twice as much or more.) How can that be in today's church? Then, that data needs to inform better long-term care and outreach. How do we know if the assessments and screening of candidates are working? Where is the ongoing assessment to determine the health and effectiveness of formation and seminaries? Might Pope Francis assess implementation in a new Vatican Visitation—looking and assessing for clericalism and levels of engagement in discernment, *Amoris Laetitia, Laudato Si'*? We need a total review of the process for selecting, forming, and supervising bishops and major superiors. Hierarchicalism is reinforced when we form seminarians from around the globe by training them in a Roman Clerical School/College of Privilege and Special Status. We need a fuller analysis and more robust solutions derived from this analysis.

Can't Change It till You Know What Is There

The current problem calls for more nuanced pastoral acumen and sensitivity that goes beyond simple conclusions that cause more harm. These simple conclusions also increase mistrust in the church and its leaders and ultimately deny, distract, avoid, and minimize this atrocity all together. These reactions mimic the offenders' reactions. Though the percentage of true pedophiles in the American church was very small, an estimated 1.9 to 2.4 percent, their offending behaviors accounted for over 40 percent of the victims.[13] Pedophiles were just one type of offender, often attracted to a certain age, regardless of sex. These are fixated or "preferential" offenders. By definition, this means that these individuals prefer the company of children and are attracted to children of a certain age. Interestingly, they are often white, heterosexual, married males. Furthermore, one will often see news reports saying that the church has a pedophile problem. It is a myth

---

[13] Gerard J. McGlone and Len Sperry, *The Inner Life of Priests* (Collegeville, MN: Liturgical Press, 2012).

to state that there is a "pedophile problem" in the Catholic Church, as the data simply does not support this statement. Clearly, the church has a major abuse problem, not only with pedophiles, however. Furthermore, since the Dallas Charter and the three John Jay studies, we have identified a second and more prevalent type of offender than the pedophile group.[14] This is known as a "situational offender," or an ephebophile (i.e., those attracted to adolescents). Ephebophiles accounted for the second-greatest number of the offenders in the US church at about 20–30 percent of the offenders. But, there is a third, and the largest, non-diagnosed group that is about 60 percent of the problem that warrants attention and more research.

One of the biggest myths associated with the clergy sexual abuse atrocity is the lack of understanding of assault, rape, or sexual offending. The myth is that this abuse is related to a "bad apple" when the data has overwhelmingly pointed to the "bad apple in a bad barrel." The systemic and individual problems are often misunderstood. It is a classic both/and scenario. Furthermore, these issues demand analyses of their root causes that have not been formulated or executed. These could uncover the complex systemic, cultural, and theological forces that created this perfect storm. We still do not have a precise picture of these dynamics twenty years after the *Boston Globe* investigations highlighted in the Spotlight series. In other words, what we know, and have known since the early 1990s, is that sexual offenses occur within an "interactional event" within certain systems.

There are four elements to this event: the victim, the offender, the situational vortex, and the intercultural system. Simply put, there are factors of victims' vulnerability (e.g., family problems, divorce, previous trauma, physical limitations, neglect, accessibility, and opportunity within her/his world). These vulnerabilities make them more prone to be abused and exploited. Sex offenders tend to exhibit certain characteristics: a lack of sexual integration or knowledge, poor coping skills, immature psychosexual development, poor peer friendships, and a history of trauma. Their attraction to adolescents, whether male or female, is not about the sex but about the ability to dominate and control. Like rape, it is about power. We know that most victims in

---

[14] Karen J. Terry and J. D. Freilich, "Understanding Child Sexual Abuse by Catholic Priests from a Situational Perspective," *Journal of Child Sexual Abuse* 21, no. 4 (2012): 437–55, https://www.tandfonline.com/doi/abs/10.1080/10538712.2012.693579.

the church were adolescent males, and altar girls were not present until the mid- to late 1990s. The aforementioned factors come together to create what the late Benedictine monk and psychotherapist Richard Sipe termed "a secret world"[15]—sexual abuse within an "enabling system" that offers little to no transparency or accountability.[16] This abuse exists within the intercultural system of secrecy, silence, and privilege associated with cultural beliefs about priests and priest-hood, wherein the offender is acting *in persona Christi*. As many have stated,[17] when the priest offends, *it is God who offends*.

This third factor, the interactional event or situational opportunity, is most often addressed by policies and protocols. It fails to address the cultural issues. Since the Dallas Charter, the criminological and legal approaches have focused on one aspect of this event. Though necessary, it has been clearly insufficient, as we see in frequent local and international news reports about this atrocity. These policies and procedures are targeting or attempting to prevent this "opportunity" from occurring. These approaches fail to look at the beliefs of the faithful and the beliefs of/toward the clergy. Privilege, status, and power in a certain culture take on a different diagnosis or disorder.

As stated above, the third most prevalent group, which has no known "diagnosis" that seems situationally/systemically supported or determined, is most prevalent in all the research; this is known as acquired situational narcissism (ASN).[18] Narcissistic features can arise as a response to extreme demands and expectations of one's social environment, even in people who have previously shown no symp-toms of a narcissistic disorder. This is commonly seen in actors and sports figures who suddenly come into fame and riches. What are the features of this disorder? It is a superiority complex wherein one shows different faces to different people, viewing others as superior

---

[15] A. W. Richard Sipe, *A Secret World: Sexuality and the Search for Celibacy* (New York: Brunner/Mazel, 1990).

[16] A. W. Richard Sipe, *Celibacy in Crisis: A Secret World Revisited* (New York: Brunner–Routledge, 2003).

[17] Gerard J. McGlone, "Jesuit Psychologist: Gay Priests Are Not the Cause of the Clergy Sexual Abuse," *Outreach* (2022), https://outreach.faith/2022/11/jesuit-psychologist-gay-priests-are-not-the-cause-of-clergy-sex-abuse/.

[18] Preston Ni, "Five Signs of a Situational Narcissist," *Psychology Today* (January 8, 2017), https://www.psychologytoday.com/us/blog/communication-success/201701/5-signs-of-a-situational-narcissist.

or inferior but rarely equal. This is shown most in a form of entitlement: they expect to be treated as special, which shows itself in condescending verbal and/or nonverbal expressions and bullying. One who was "normal" before achieving this status now appears and acts like a full-blown narcissist.

Until one takes apart the feudal system that supports this form of idolatry, nothing will change. Change cannot occur unless you know what is happening, acknowledge that there even is ASN in the clergy and hierarchy, and attack the roles and system that enable power, privilege, and grooming. This form of clericalism subsists within a system of feudal hierarchicalism. Since we have systemic realities and problems, they need, indeed require, systemic solutions.

Though survivors' experiences have been central to some studies, not one report has detailed the unique long- and short-term effects of physical, medical, psychological, and spiritual woundedness. We are struggling and failing to know the length, breadth, and depth of the spiritual harm. The next twenty years might finally address this gaping hole in the data and in this sacred wound. Perhaps we will have a survivor's perspective rather than a perpetrator's one. Perhaps we will lament and become a more penitent faith community that listens to and lifts up the voices of the survivors, not those of clerical privilege and rank. Perhaps we could become righteous witnesses to their horrors. In clinical research, there is an old saying: "You can't change something unless you know what is there." We know what is there. It's time for change.

A Final Composition of Place

Finally, can we go back to the upper room? Might we go there as a witness and imagine being there when, for the first time after the crucifixion, we see the apostles who betrayed and deserted? We see Thomas, Peter, and Andrew each having to face Mary, who is still wearing her blood-stained mantle that held her bloodied son's body. Can we see them being now held accountable for their betrayal? Being held in that mantle by Mary? You know her. Let us in our fractured wounded body of this church go to her.

What do you know? What do you feel? What do you see? Might we hear the words of Jesus saying to them and to us, "Shalom! Peace!"?

2

Accountability, Healing, and Trust:
Developing a Just Response to Catholic Clergy Sexual Abuse

Jennifer Beste

In his *motu proprio* You Are the Light of the World, Pope Francis writes:

> The crimes of sexual abuse offend Our Lord, cause physical, psychological, and spiritual damage to the victims, and harm the community of the faithful. In order that these phenomena, in all their forms, never happen again, a continuous and profound conversion of hearts is needed, attested by concrete and effective actions that involve everyone in the Church.[1]

In this chapter, I will identify concrete effective actions on four commitments that demonstrate the kind of conversion all Catholics need to undergo if we are to faithfully follow Jesus Christ. I will also name two challenges that threaten to undermine necessary ecclesial reforms. Finally, I will explore how Catholic theology is indispensable for navigating a difficult road ahead.

---

[1] Pope Francis, *motu proprio Vos Estis Lux Mundi* (Vatican City: Libreria Editrice Vaticana, May 7, 2019), https://www.vatican.va/content/francesco/en/motu_proprio/documents/papa-francesco-motu-proprio-20190507_vos-estis-lux-mundi.html.

According to the Catholic tradition, authentic *metanoia* and genuine change occur when a person confesses one's sins, expresses sincere contrition, performs penance, and makes reparation for harm caused. In order to restore fully one's spiritual health and strengthen one's relationship with God and neighbor, the sinner must do "something more than this list" to make amends and make satisfaction for one's sins. Applying this theological logic—and our Catholic penitential rite—to the global clergy sexual abuse crisis translates into prioritizing at least four commitments.

First, all religious leaders need to be transparent about past and present clergy sexual abuse and disclose the truth about how bishops, priests, and laity responded to clergy sexual abusers and victims. Acting on this commitment would involve, for example, making all records and files in archives publicly accessible. Catholic scholars are still being denied access to archives to uncover the truth about the history of clergy sex abuse. Second, the path to conversion requires a commitment to do everything possible to prevent clergy abuse, cover-up, apathy, and other unsupportive responses toward victims. This involves implementing best practices of highly reliable organizations to decrease risk factors for abuse. Third, progress involves a commitment to do whatever is needed to repair all the negative effects of clergy sexual abuse and foster survivors' holistic healing. Fourth, it requires holding priest-perpetrators and leaders accountable by again utilizing best practices like instituting a universal zero-tolerance policy for clergy sex offenders and church officials who engage in cover-up and negligence.

While many challenges threaten our ability to realize these commitments, I wish to focus on two in particular. First, Catholic leaders have not yet acknowledged the scope of clergy sexual abuse and the depth of harm caused by such abuse. For example, Pope Francis has not publicly acknowledged the reality that it is not simply minors, seminarians, and religious sisters who experience clerical abuse of power when sexually abused by priests. According to church officials, the concept of "vulnerable adult" does not include adult women who have use of reason.[2] Adult women have also been sexually and spiri-

---

[2] Ivany Atina Arbi, Evi Mariani, and Dwi Atmanta, "Catholic Church Excludes Adult Women in Talks about Protecting Sexual Abuse Victims," *The Jakarta Post*, July 29, 2020, https://newgelora.thejakartapost.com/news/2020/07/29/catholic-church -excludes-adult-women-in-talks-about-protecting-sexual-abuse-victims.html.

tually abused by clerics due to the nature of the ministerial relationship and power differentials. Such denial in 2024 is not only profoundly ethically concerning but embarrassingly out of step with minimal standards of professional ethics in secular caregiving professions and in other religious denominations. Research overwhelmingly demonstrates the severe harm that results when religious clergy relate sexually to their parishioners. Since the 1990s and early 2000s, mainline Protestant leaders have acknowledged the severe harm of clergy sexual misconduct and have prioritized educating their seminarians about the subtle ways clerics can abuse their power, trust, and authority.[3] They have demonstrated accountability by enacting zero-tolerance policies. These professionals recognize that meaningful consent for sexual activity is not possible in a fiduciary relationship.

Many Catholic leaders have also failed to acknowledge or redress the depth of harm and lifelong debilitating effects of clergy sexual abuse. In the USCCB Charter, for instance, bishops promise to "demonstrate a sincere commitment to victims' spiritual and emotional well-being."[4] Unfortunately, however, the bishops have not published criteria and guidelines specifying what forms of support constitute "a sincere commitment." Nor have they offered a minimal standard of support services for all survivors. Limiting support only to psychological and spiritual domains ignores the severe physiological and somatic harms experienced by survivors that shorten their lifespan. It does not recognize the severe impact the abuse may have

---

[3] Marie Fortune and James Poling, *Sexual Abuse by Clergy: A Crisis for the Church* (Decatur, GA: Journal of Pastoral Care Publications, 1994); John Gonsiorek, *Breach of Trust: A Sexual Exploitation by Health Care Professionals and Clergy* (Thousand Oaks, CA: Sage Publications, 1995). For resources concerning best practices and policies developed in Protestant churches, see https://www.faithtrustinstitute.org; https://socialwork.web.baylor.edu/csa-resources. For an overview of the policies developed by the Episcopal Church and the Evangelical Lutheran Church of America over the past three decades: https://download.elca.org/ELCA%20Resource%20Repository/Clergy_Sexual_Misconduct_Prevention_and_Resources.pdf; https://www.episcopalchurch.org/pastoral-development/title-iv-for-bishops/. See also https://episcopalmn.org/sites/default/files/resource/Safe%20Church%20Policies%20-%20Preventing%20Sexual%20Exploitation.pdf; https://www.episcopalchurch.org/wp-content/uploads/sites/2/2021/02/model_policy_for_the_protection_of_vulnerable_adults_2018.pdf.

[4] United States Conference of Catholic Bishops (USCCB), Charter for the Protection of Children and Young People (June 2018), https://www.usccb.org/resources/Charter-for-the-Protection-of-Children-and-Young-People-2018-final%281%29.pdf.

had on survivors' capacities to form a coherent sense of self, exercise effective agency, and develop healthy interpersonal relationships. Research studies consistently demonstrate that some clergy abuse survivors have been unable to graduate from school or maintain regular employment due to incapacitating physical and mental health issues.[5] Many survivors are homeless.

Failing to provide additional forms of assistance when this is needed for victims' capacity to survive and heal is ethically problematic when we consider that canon law obligates the hierarchy to provide for clergy sex abusers' basic needs (like shelter, food, and health care) for the rest of their lives even though they no longer work. Providing clergy sex offenders with basic needs while denying the same care for their victims violates minimal norms of justice, not to mention our obligations to practice a preferential option for the powerless and marginalized and to prioritize reparation for victims.

A second main challenge is the often-acknowledged negative and toxic clericalist culture and the church's hierarchical organizational structure. Together, these sabotage all four commitments I have named: (1) to disclose the truth, (2) to effectively prevent clergy abuse, (3) to relate justly to victims, and (4) to hold clergy sex offenders and bishops accountable with strict zero-tolerance policies. The USCCB's own appointed John Jay researcher Karen Terry has concluded that the complex hierarchy and structure of the church and "the inherent system of culture and power, and teachings and beliefs" of the church continues to place children at high risk for clergy sexual abuse.[6] Global research findings about the church's hierarchical power structure concur.

---

[5] Scott Easton, Danielle Leone-Sheehan, and Patrick O'Leary, " 'I Will Never Know the Person Who I Could Have Become': Perceived Changes in Self-Identity among Adult Survivors of Clergy-Perpetrated Sexual Abuse," *Journal of Interpersonal Violence* 34, no. 6 (2016): 1148. Rachel Hurcombe et al., "Truth Project Thematic Report: Child Sexual Abuse in the Context of Religious Institutions," *Independent Inquiry Child Sexual Abuse* (2019); D. M. Fergusson, G. F. H. McLeod, and L. J. Horwood, "Childhood Sexual Abuse and Adult Developmental Outcomes: Findings from a 30-Year Longitudinal Study," *New Zealand: Child Abuse and Neglect* 37, no. 9 (2013): 664–74.

[6] Karen Terry and Margaret Smith, "Sexual Abuse of Youth in the Catholic Church and Society: Prevalence, Context, and Future Directions," *Russo Family Lecture: Reckoning and Reform: New Horizons on the Clergy Abuse Crisis*, Fordham University, March 2019. Terry and Smith are researchers and authors of the two John Jay studies commissioned by the National Review Board.

Despite Pope Francis's promise to eradicate clergy sex abuse and pursue justice for survivors, he has not altered the hierarchical structure of the church. Each bishop remains the final arbiter in diocesan decision making. Changes in Francis's 2019 *motu proprio* reinforce and strengthen this clerical privilege. For instance, adherence to the USCCB's Charter for the Protection of Children and Young People is not binding; bishops face no serious consequences, like removal from office or active ministry, if they do not comply with or fully implement charter norms consistently. Due to sovereignty over their dioceses, bishops have also not faced serious disciplinary sanctions if they do not follow recommendations of the National Review Board to implement a more in-depth national audit and require parish audits since this is the only way to assess effective implementation.[7] Instead of being required to use the most effective research-based safe environment program or follow best practices concerning support for survivors' healing, each bishop decides which safe environment program he prefers and what amount of resources and forms of support to offer abuse survivors. Consequently, the quality of safe environment programs and support for survivors varies dramatically throughout dioceses. Survivors have no recourse if their bishop refuses to offer adequate psychological or spiritual support because the bishop is the final arbiter.

In my conversations with survivors over the past fifteen years, I have been deeply troubled as I have listened to them describe the lack of support from many Catholic clergy and laity. Recently one survivor recounted that her diocese limited her therapy to only four sessions, which, she was told, "should be sufficient for her healing." Another survivor shared that the only request she made to her bishop was to create a peer support group for clergy abuse survivors. She had professionally led many support groups and knew how effectively they fostered recovery. Although she met with her bishop annually

---

[7] While Pope Francis has the authority and power to legislate new laws and discipline and remove bishops who do not follow charter recommendations, he has thus far not done so. In their annual report, the National Review Board continued to appeal to bishops to implement parish audits: "Seventy percent of dioceses and eparchies conduct their own parish audits. . . . The data shows a correlation between parish audits and *Charter* compliance. Without monitoring implementation at the parish level, the risk of abuse increases" (Secretariat of Child and Youth Protection, 2023 annual report, vii, https://www.usccb.org/resources/2023%20Annual%20 Report.pdf).

for six years to make this request, the diocese never collaborated or cooperated. In 2021, she gave up: "If the bishop wanted there to be a peer support group, there would be a peer support group. It has been very distressing to me to realize this fact."

Facing significant challenges such as the ones I have briefly considered, how do we move forward, and how can Catholic theology serve as a resource to help us create a genuinely safe, accountable culture? First, theology can help us clearly see what is at stake in whether we undergo serious conversion and radical reform. Theologically, nothing less is at stake than the church's very purpose: to mediate God's love and healing grace to the world. If we take seriously trauma research findings that our capacities to form a constructive sense of self, act freely, and engage in loving relationships can be gravely debilitated by severe interpersonal harm, we recognize our interdependence not only on God but on other persons and creation.[8] Since we are finite, limited beings who experience reality in tangible ways, we need God's grace to be mediated through our embodied experiences. At all times, God is seeking to mediate healing grace to us through creation, the church, and its ministers. Our ability to experience and respond to such grace can, however, be subverted by other persons who perpetrate extreme moral harm or fail to accept responsibility to repair that harm. Pope Francis's framing of clergy perpetrators as "tools of Satan" is not an overreach,[9] for the extent of harm they inflict on victims can and often does result in soul murder,[10] suicide, and so many premature deaths.

Right now, the Body of Christ is broken. Familiar words of Jesus tell us, "Just as you did it to one of the least of these brothers and sisters of mine, you did it to me" (Matt 25:40). It is difficult to think about this, but each time a clergy perpetrator sexually abuses a girl or a boy, a woman or man, he is sexually abusing the body of Jesus

---

[8] For more in-depth analysis, see Jennifer Beste, *God and the Victim: Traumatic Intrusions on Grace and Freedom* (Oxford: Oxford University Press, 2007). See also Jennifer Beste, "Envisioning a Just Response to the Catholic Clergy Abuse Crisis," *Theological Studies* 82, no. 1 (2021): 29–54.

[9] Pope Francis, "Address of His Holiness Pope Francis at the End of the Eucharistic Concelebration," The Protection of Minors in the Church Vatican Meeting (Vatican City: Libreria Editrice Vaticana, February 2019).

[10] Leonard Shengold, *Soul Murder: The Effects of Childhood Abuse and Deprivation* (New Haven, CT: Yale University Press, 1989).

Christ. The Body of Christ is further splintered and fragmented whenever bishops promise publicly to offer adequate support and pastoral care to victims and then fail to do so, whenever clergy and lay Catholics react unsupportively or apathetically to survivors, and whenever church leaders sin by omission by failing to urgently implement best practices to prevent clergy abuse globally and relate to survivors justly. As these sins of commission and omission accumulate, both clergy and laity are complicit in the continued abuse of Christ's and the victims' bodies and spirits.

The good news is that our Catholic faith can provide us the strength and motivation to accompany survivors in solidarity so that evil and traumatization need not be the final word. Exploring the intersection between Catholic theology and trauma research on recovery allows us to recognize that loving support can break the traumatic cycle, enabling survivors' recovery and their ability to relate constructively to themselves, others, and God. Trauma survivors' experiences of recovery strongly suggest that God has ordered creation and redemption in such a way that God relies on our acts of neighbor-love to mediate grace. Is this not deeply embedded in the Catholic affirmation that Christian discipleship involves us working as co-creators—as Pope Francis says, as "co-responsible"—to bring about the kingdom of God?

Moreover, as Catholics, we believe that our communion with Christ and celebration of his resurrection occurs as a result of accompanying him through the events of his passion. Seeing Christ in the least of our brothers and sisters and treating them as Christ would call us all to be in solidarity with survivors. Collectively, Catholics have extraordinarily diverse and abundant gifts and talents to create trauma-informed communities that intentionally provide a safe, supportive space for survivors. When I ask clergy sexual abuse survivors how lay Catholics can best be in solidarity with them, their responses are simple, concrete, and consistent: they want their priests and fellow parishioners to acknowledge their reports of allegation and check in periodically to ask how they are doing, to offer them a ride to Mass and sit with them, to respond supportively when they express feeling triggered or unsafe, and to relate to them in ways that show they are valued members of the community.

It is, of course, incredibly important that we recognize and say a prayer of gratitude to all lay Catholics, clergy, lay ecclesial ministers, teachers, and parish staff who—past and present—have responded to the Holy Spirit's call to protect the safety of all those in their care and support survivors. The challenge before us is to make their lived witness to the gospel the widespread norm for all of us.

Once we understand what is at stake in our response to clergy sexual abuse, a second task of theology is to help us discern what it means to follow Christ and respond as he would to our global crisis of Catholic clergy abuse. Scriptural accounts of Jesus reveal the high priority God places on caring for and protecting children and those who are suffering. Mark, Matthew, and Luke all include the gospel narrative of Jesus rebuking the apostles when they try to prevent children from getting too close. Jesus reacts angrily and responds, "Let the children come to me; do not stop them, for it is to such as these that the kingdom of God belongs. Truly I tell you, whoever does not receive the kingdom of God as a little child will never enter it" (Mark 10:14-16). By affirming that his apostles, their apostolic successors, and his followers must become like children to enter the kingdom of God, Christ subverts the values of the kingdom of the world (with its obsession on status, competition, hierarchy, and power over others) and lauds the opposite values of the kingdom of God.

If space constraints were not an issue, I could engage more deeply with the scriptural and theological narratives of Jesus that clearly demonstrate how Christian discipleship calls us to place support for survivors' healing and the safety of our communities above all other interests and agendas. And yet, perhaps, such lengthy theological exposition is not necessary. Is there anyone among us who finds it hard to imagine that Jesus would *not* immediately prioritize the church's resources to do everything possible to ensure the safety and dignity of Catholics and practice a preferential option for survivors deeply wounded and betrayed by those who are Christ's earthly representatives?

A third task of Catholic theology, indispensable for those who study past and present clergy abuse, is to deconstruct and engage in reforms in the Catholic macrosystem. According to sex abuse prevention specialists, in order to create a safe, transparent, and accountable church, we need to not only reduce risk factors at the individual, interpersonal, and organizational levels of the church, but at the macrosystem level where cultural beliefs, values, norms, the legal system, and ideologies of Catholic culture play out. A crucial job of

Catholic theologians is to identify the theological beliefs, church teachings, values, and norms that increase risk factors for clergy sex abuse, cover-up, and unsupportive responses to victims.

To give one example, I am currently engaged in a historical research project examining priest-perpetrator files in a particular midwestern archdiocese. I am conducting a qualitative analysis to identify the religious beliefs that influenced clergy and lay Catholics to support priest-perpetrators' interests over those of clergy abuse victims. My analysis thus far indicates that theologically problematic and distorted beliefs about God, sin, forgiveness, grace, redemption, the priesthood, and prayer undergirded church officials' and lay Catholics' choices to support and cover up for priest-perpetrators rather than prioritize protection of minors and act in solidarity with victims.

Once we identify the ways in which Catholic beliefs and teachings become subtly distorted and function to enable abuse rather than deter it, our task as Christians is to eradicate these distorted elements of our tradition. As Pope Benedict acknowledged early in his own theological career, "Not everything that exists in the Church must for that reason be also a legitimate tradition; . . . not every tradition that arises in the Church is a true celebration and keeping present of the mystery of Christ. There is a distorting, as well as a legitimate, tradition."[11]

When theologians, clergy, canon lawyers, and Catholic laity have worked together to eradicate these distorted beliefs and traditions, our next creative task is to mine our rich and diverse theological tradition to revise our Catholic beliefs, values, and ecclesial structures to help us create and maintain a genuine culture of safety, transparency, and accountability. Only then—and I emphasize—*only then* will abuse survivors, lay Catholics, and priests be able to trust in the integrity of their leaders and trust that they are part of a church that truly *is* acting as the Body of Christ, mediating divine love and grace in service to humanity and creation.

---

[11] Joseph Ratzinger, "The Transmission of Divine Revelation," *Commentary on the Documents of Vatican II*, vol. 3, ed. Herbert Vorgrimler (New York: Herder & Herder, 1969), 185.

3

Native American Catholic Boarding Schools:
Restorative Justice and the Obligation of the Church[1]

Sarah Gallagher

Introduction

The conference titled "Accountability, Healing, and Trust," from which this chapter comes, was a short exploration of many instances where those serving in various ministries in the church are called to hold themselves to a higher standard as the Body of Christ. This chapter briefly addresses the topics of accountability, healing, and trust between the Catholic Church and Native American communities in the United States. I will be focusing in particular on Native American boarding schools run by the Catholic Church and how we as a church are called to respond to survivors of abuse.

Before I begin, it is important to name the lens through which I approach this topic. I am a non-Native person who has been granted many privileges in life simply based on the color of my white skin. Much of my knowledge and passion for this topic comes from living and working alongside Crow and Northern Cheyenne students and

---

[1] This chapter was taken from an essay for a class assignment in the spring of 2021. I presented that information with a few edits for the Accountability, Healing, and Trust conference in the spring of 2022. There has been little new information added since then. This is a topic that is currently changing and making progress toward healing. Please know that some unanswered questions in this chapter may have answers now that are not included.

elders for two years while I was a guest in Ashland, Montana. Additionally, I work part-time for the American Indian Catholic Schools Network as a part of the Truth and Healing Committee. Though I have conducted a few interviews and completed some research about these communities, I cannot personally know what life was, or is, like for those who attended Native American Catholic boarding schools. What I offer in this chapter is not *the* solution; it is a suggestion that I believe may help bring healing to the Body of Christ. Part of my vocation is to walk alongside Native American communities as a lay minister of the Catholic Church.

History

The history of Native American Catholic boarding schools is a key component to the conversation of healing.[2] This history has been ignored, silenced, and tucked away for too long and needs to be brought to light.[3] Native American communities currently face challenges when seeking accountability and healing in the Catholic Church partially because of the shadowed history. One prevalent challenge is that Native voices have been silenced and ignored by the church for quite some time.[4] This silencing of Native voices started before boarding schools opened, but Native American boarding schools were a systematized way of silencing Native voices even further.

Native American boarding schools were formed with the intention of suppressing the identity and culture of Native children and filling

---

[2] Here is an extended entry from the original *Catholic Encyclopedia* (1907–1912) published by Catholic Answers online. This written history follows the Catholic missionaries; it doesn't give much history on the Native Americans other than when they cross paths with the missionaries or other Europeans. Catholic Answers, "Catholic Indian Missions of the United States: Detailed History of Catholic Missionary Activity to the Native Tribes of America," https://www.catholic.com/encyclopedia/catholic-indian-missions-of-the-united-states.

[3] For information from 2021, please see this webinar from Fordham, "Jesuits and Boarding Schools: Truth, Reconciliation, Responsibility, A Conversation with Tashina Banks Rama, Red Cloud Indian School, Ted Penton, SJ, Jesuit Conference of Canada and the United States, Sarah White, NDN Collective," December 7, 2021, https://takingresponsibility.ace.fordham.edu/jesuits-and-boarding-schools/.

[4] Francis Paul Prucha, *The Churches and the Indian Schools, 1888–1912* (Lincoln, NE: University of Nebraska Press, 1979), xii.

in the void with Western culture and religion.[5] The first boarding school was opened in 1879 by a military man named Richard Henry Pratt; he is famously quoted saying the intention of the school was "that all the Indian there is in the race should be dead. Kill the Indian in him, and save the man."[6] This was the general sentiment of the United States at the time.[7] Instead of continuing to kill and remove Native people from their traditional homelands in order to have more land for European settlers, Pratt founded Carlisle Indian School in order to educate Native children away from their own culture and families. Carlisle Indian School has a notoriously difficult history and was the boarding school on which all other boarding schools were modeled. To attend many boarding schools, Native children were not only forced from their homes but then taken thousands of miles from their families. Catholic boarding schools run by Saint Katharine Drexel were built on or near reservations, which meant children were not taken as far from family in order to attend school.[8] Even though children at Catholic schools were closer to home, they had similar experiences to those attending government-run or Christian-run boarding schools.

Upon their arrival at boarding school, Native children's traditional hairstyles, clothing, and footwear were traded out for European-style hair, clothing, and shoes. Many children were neglected and physically or sexually abused, and sometimes food was used as a tool to gain compliance. Sadly, many Native American children who died at boarding schools were buried in unmarked or mass graves.[9] There has been a surge of requests for ground penetrating radar to be used on the lands that were historically used as boarding schools by the

---

[5] "US Indian Boarding School History," The National Native American Boarding School Healing Coalition, boardingschoolhealing.org/education/us-indian-boarding-school-history/.

[6] "Carlisle Indian School," Carlisle Indian School Project, June 17, 2020, carlisle indianschoolproject.com/.

[7] "US Indian Boarding School History."

[8] Brian S. Collier, "St. Catherine Indian School, Santa Fe, 1887–2006: Catholic Indian Education in New Mexico" (PhD diss., Arizona State University, 2006), 81–82.

[9] Here is a 2022 release from the US Department of the Interior about grave searches and deaths at Native American boarding schools in the United States. There are more articles out there. US Department of the Interior, "Department of the Interior Releases Investigative Report, Outlines Next Steps in Federal Indian Boarding School Initiative," May 11, 2022, https://www.doi.gov/pressreleases/department-interior -releases-investigative-report-outlines-next-steps-federal-indian.

church and government.[10] Native children who attended boarding schools were expected to leave behind their names, languages, religions, and family ties in order to assimilate to the government's preferred culture and the church's preferred religion.

Native American boarding schools were started by the United States government. Very quickly though, Christian churches, including the Catholic Church, dove headfirst into this new system of education and assimilation.[11] Catholic boarding schools existed among other Christian boarding schools and together supported a system of education that silenced Native people through the removal and reeducation of their children. At this time, few people believed in the dignity of the Native American enough to consider their true freedom to potentially choose their own traditional religious practices or traditional cultural practices.[12] Instead of conversing with Native Americans about how best to educate their children and how best to interact between cultures and faiths, the government and the church stepped in and in many cases took children from their homes in order to assimilate them into Western culture and Christian religion.[13]

In 1887, St. Katharine Drexel established her first Native American boarding school.[14] St. Katharine's goal was to open Native American boarding schools located closer to reservations with an eye toward running these schools differently. Although her goal was to situate children closer to home while they attended boarding school, the children were still expected to leave behind their language, culture, and religion as was the expectation of the government, from which boarding schools received funding.[15] Native voices were ignored

---

[10] I do not have much up-to-date research on these requests for ground penetrating radar and what has been found on boarding school grounds other than on Maȟpíya Lúta–Red Cloud Indian School, which I speak about further into the chapter. I hope no unmarked graves of children have been found near Native American boarding schools in the United States. I hope the tribes and families of the children buried at boarding schools are able to have a say in what happens with the remains of their relatives even in the marked graveyards.

[11] Collier, "St. Catherine Indian School," 15; and Prucha, *Churches and the Indian Schools*, x.

[12] Collier, "St. Catherine Indian School," 25.

[13] Prucha, *Churches and the Indian Schools*, xii.

[14] Collier, "St. Catherine Indian School," 81–82.

[15] Collier, "St. Catherine Indian School," 15; and Prucha, *Churches and the Indian Schools*, x.

throughout the boarding-school era and continue to be buried today. In order to find healing between Native communities and the Catholic Church, I suggest that we turn toward the theological lens of restorative justice. Restorative justice is one path that can help heal the Body of Christ.

Restorative Justice

Howard Zehr, one of the founders of the restorative justice movement, believes that restorative justice should be built from the bottom up, by communities, through dialogue and applying the principles of restorative justice to their own situations.[16] Restorative justice focuses on the communities and their needs. In the case of Native Catholic boarding schools, the community we are speaking about includes both those against whom harm has been committed as well as those who enacted the physical, emotional, and mental harm.

It may not be possible to find individuals who enacted crimes against Native children at boarding schools. If this is the case, we as a church, as the Body of Christ, are called to step into this dialogue. We are called to walk with those who were harmed at the hands of ministers of the Catholic Church. The institutional church is built on a "lasting foundation" that has been passed down from St. Peter through his successors to our pope and college of bishops today.[17] It is essential that the pope and bishops who speak for the Catholic Church take steps toward healing the wounds of those harmed at the hands of ministers in the church.

It is fitting here to quote portions of both Saint Pope John Paul II and Pope Francis's addresses or letters to Native people. Though Pope Francis references John Paul II in his apology, I had a difficult time finding an explicit apology to Native people from John Paul II. The closest statement I found reads, "The hour has come to bind up wounds, to heal all divisions. It is a time for forgiveness, for

---

[16] Howard Zehr, *The Little Book of Restorative Justice* (Intercourse, PA: Good Books, 2015), 17.

[17] *Catechism of the Catholic Church* (Vatican City: Libreria Editrice Vaticana, 2019), §§866–69.

reconciliation and for a commitment to building new relationships."[18] I do not see the same explicit sorrow for the wounds inflicted by church ministers here as I do below from Pope Francis. His first apology was issued in Bolivia in 2015. This quote is long and draws inspiration from John Paul II. Pope Francis states,

> I say this to you with regret: many grave sins were committed against the native peoples of America in the name of God. My predecessors acknowledged this. . . . Like Saint John Paul II, I ask that the Church—I repeat what he said—"kneel before God and implore forgiveness for the past and present sins of her sons and daughters."[19] . . . Here I wish to be quite clear, as was Saint John Paul II: I humbly ask forgiveness, not only for the offenses of the Church herself, but also for crimes committed against the native peoples during the so-called conquest of America. . . . There was sin, a great deal of it, for which we did not ask pardon. So for this, we ask forgiveness, I ask forgiveness. But here also, where there was sin, great sin, grace abounded through the men and women who defended the rights of indigenous peoples.[20]

Pope Francis is explicitly clear with his apology: he expresses sorrow for sins committed and asks forgiveness on behalf of the church and himself. In a letter written in 2018, Pope Francis also states,

> Dear brothers and sisters, many of you and your representatives have stated that begging pardon is not the end of the matter. I fully agree: that is only the first step, the starting point. I also recognize that, "looking to the past, no effort to beg pardon and to seek to repair the harm done will ever be sufficient," and that,

---

[18] Pope John Paul II, "Radio and Television Message of Pope John Paul II to Native Peoples of Canada" (Vatican City: Libreria Editrice Vaticana, 1984), 7, https://www.vatican.va/content/john-paul-ii/en/speeches/1984/september/documents/hf_jp-ii_spe_19840918_popolazioni-canada.html.

[19] The quoted section within Pope Francis's statement is from this document written by Pope John Paul II. This quote, however, was not drawn from a statement addressed to, nor does it mention, Native peoples specifically. Pope John Paul II, *Incarnationis Mysterium: Bull of Indiction of the Great Jubilee of the Year of 2000* (Vatican City: Libreria Editrice Vaticana, 1998), 11, http://www.vatican.va/jubilee_2000/docs/documents/hf_jp-ii_doc_30111998_bolla-jubilee_en.html.

[20] Pope Francis, "Participation at the Second World Meeting of Popular Movements Address of the Holy Father," 3.2, https://www.vatican.va/content/francesco/en/speeches/2015/july/documents/papa-francesco_20150709_bolivia-movimenti-popolari.html.

"looking ahead to the future, no effort must be spared to create a culture able to prevent such situations from happening."[21] An important part of this process will be to conduct a serious investigation into the facts of what took place in the past and to assist the survivors of the residential schools to experience healing from the traumas they suffered.[22]

Pope Francis himself states that an apology is not the end. He also calls us to "serious investigation into the facts" in order to assist survivors. Pope Francis has called us to action, and we have so much work to do.

In March 2021, I interviewed Fr. Michael Carson, the assistant director of Native American Affairs at the United States Conference of Catholic Bishops (USCCB).[23] I have also corresponded with him by e-mail both in September 2022 and March 2024. I have found speaking with him and hearing about his work very hopeful. The church is moving, yet has a lot of work still to do. He informed me that one of the first and foremost objectives of the Subcommittee on Native American Affairs is to support listening sessions. This focus toward listening sessions follows the pattern set by the Canadian government when approaching similar traumas experienced at First Nations residential schools in Canada. These listening sessions are a portion of the "serious investigation into the facts" that Pope Francis is calling us to. The other portion of serious investigation must focus on the Catholic Church's involvement in these boarding schools, especially into traumatic experiences. During our interview Fr. Carson

---

[21] The quote within is from Pope Francis, "Letter of His Holiness Pope Francis to the People of God" (2018), intro., https://www.vatican.va/content/francesco/en/letters/2018/documents/papa-francesco_20180820_lettera-popolo-didio.html.

[22] Pope Francis, "Apostolic Journey of His Holiness Pope Francis to Canada: Meeting with Indigenous People; First Nations, Métis and Inuit" (July 25, 2022), https://www.vatican.va/content/francesco/en/speeches/2022/july/documents/20220725-popolazioniindigene-canada.html.

[23] During this interview we spoke about the USCCB's involvement and movements in truth and healing between the Catholic Church and Native American communities. This interview was conducted for the final project of the master of divinity degree of the interviewer and is not accessible to the public. Interview between Sarah Gallagher and Fr. Michael Carson, conducted over Zoom from Notre Dame, IN, March 10, 2021. The paragraphs mentioning Fr. Carson have been reviewed and approved by a media person at the USCCB. This is the USCCB website for the subcommittee for Native American Affairs: https://www.usccb.org/committees/native-american-affairs.

focused primarily on the listening sessions, but he did not speak about opening records or in-depth research into the Catholic Church's involvement in boarding schools. This topic may have been something we didn't have time to cover in our interview, though. There are many documents and videos held in a Native American Collection at the University of Marquette.[24] Even with this collection there are still concerns that individual schools, churches, or religious communities have not made their records public yet.

During our interview, Fr. Carson named five things that he sees as important in these listening sessions. First, the listening sessions need to be culturally appropriate, especially because different Native tribes have different cultural practices. Second, he believes listening sessions need to be run by Native American people from the communities themselves. He sees himself as being present for guidance and to take orders on how to be helpful, and as representing the hierarchy of the Roman Catholic Church. Third, they have to be truthful. Some people had good experiences at boarding schools, and those stories are not told. He recognizes that there were things the boarding schools could have done differently, but there were also some things they had to do because the federal government required them to follow certain rules. For example, they were not allowed to teach in Native Languages. Fourth, these listening sessions must be forward looking. We, the church, must learn what we can do to make sure we don't repeat the problems of the past. Finally, there needs to be an apology. The apology must be the last thing the church does because, if the apology comes first, it could too easily become, "Well, we apologized. What more do you want?" He also said that bishops have a role to play in these conversations. The bishops can also apologize on behalf of the Roman Catholic Church.

These five points gave me hope because I know at least one subcommittee of the USCCB is seriously considering how to create a space for healing and change within Native communities.[25] At the

---

[24] "Native American Collections" held at Marquette University: https://www .marquette.edu/library/archives/indians.php. Their website states, "Post-Columbian collections encompassing Indians/Indigenous peoples of North, South and Central America, the bulk of which pertain to the Catholic Church and Native American people in the United States since 1874."

[25] United States Conference of Catholic Bishops, "Two Rivers: A Report on Catholic Native American Culture and Ministry" (2019), https://www.usccb.org/issues-and -action/cultural-diversity/native-american/resources/upload/Two-Rivers.pdf.

time of the interview in 2021 Fr. Carson said they had yet to hold any listening sessions. Through e-mail correspondence with Fr. Carson and links on the website for the Office of Native American Affairs I have learned that some places have conducted listening sessions or used ground-penetrating radar with support from the USCCB.[26] First, Maȟpíya Lúta–Red Cloud Indian School has conducted ground-penetrating radar and excavation work on their campus with the intention of looking for unmarked graves of children.[27] No remains of children have been found through this process, and they are open to more searches if more information becomes available. Second, the Archdiocese of Oklahoma City began listening sessions in 2022, and people who attended Native American Catholic schools (or their descendants) are able to set up appointments to be interviewed throughout the state.[28] The USCCB is supporting dioceses and arch-dioceses to run their own listening sessions. This is a good starting place, and this work is progressing every year, but I hope the USCCB is able to influence the dioceses and archdioceses to prioritize this work more. Progress has been made in the past three years since my interview with Fr. Carson, but these listening sessions and more concise research for Native American Catholic boarding schools cannot come fast enough. While the listening sessions depend in part on the willingness of Native American Catholic school attendees to step forward, the collecting of records and compiling of research on the Catholic Church's involvement could be something funded by the church at some level. I believe the USCCB needs to continue support-ing research into the Catholic Church's own history.

If we look through the lens of restorative justice, we will see the value of the church's part in listening and dialogue. Restorative justice calls the church to action, calls the church to fulfill her obligation to these practicing and nonpracticing Catholics who exist within the

[26] Fr. Michael Carson, e-mail correspondence with Sarah Gallagher, September 6, 2022. Fr. Carson stated that the USCCB does not conduct the listening sessions them-selves; however, the Office of Native American Affairs is working through dioceses and archdioceses to help them conduct listening sessions.

[27] Maȟpíya Lúta–Red Cloud Indian School, "Ground Penetrating Radar," https://mahpiyaluta.org/ground-penetrating-radar.

[28] Archdiocese of Oklahoma City, "The Oklahoma Catholic Native Schools Project," https://www.archokc.org/oknativeschoolsproject.

Body of Christ. The Catholic Church has an obligation to reveal her own truth and then join together with Native communities to design culturally appropriate, truthful, communal listening sessions.

The USCCB's plans for running listening sessions sounded too one-sided. Their hope was to have Native Catholics request the listening sessions, run the sessions, and come to share their stories. The plan was for this to take place with a representative of the church present but standing to the side, waiting to participate. This model of Native-led listening sessions is intended to allow those harmed to choose the direction for their healing and journey, which can be beautiful and may be what some communities need. This model focuses on those who were harmed, those who need to be heard and believed. This is necessary! Yet, if we look at the restorative justice model it states that, if possible, those who committed the harm should be a part of the conversation too. Catholic bishops, as spiritual descendants of those who ran Catholic boarding schools, are also stakeholders in these conversations and should engage in the dialogue instead of being separate. Also, prior to dialogue the USCCB should continue promoting Pope Francis's call to "serious investigation of facts."

If we look through the lens of restorative justice we can see that the Catholic Church will likely discover two important things when considering listening sessions: First, the listening sessions can be opened up to supportive dialogue, not just listening and recording. Yes, these listening sessions need to first and foremost be a space to listen to those who have had experiences, whether good or bad, at Native American Catholic boarding schools, but they can be conversations too if done well. The church cannot just listen. The church also needs to have an active part in identifying what her own obligations are through this process of healing.[29]

Second, the church has a very important role as a stakeholder in these conversations to tell her own story. Stories are very important in the restorative justice process, not only the stories of those harmed, but also the story of the perpetrator. It is the responsibility of the church to research and open the truth of her own story. If the church

---

[29] See the new document, United States Conference of Catholic Bishops, "Keeping Christ's Sacred Promise: A Pastoral Framework for Indigenous Ministry" (2024), https://www.usccb.org/resources/Indigenous%20Pastoral%20Framework%20 -June%202024-Final%20Text.pdf.

has recognized the importance of hearing the truth from those harmed at boarding schools, then the church cannot stand in the corner and simply listen. The church has an obligation to come to the circle and truthfully tell her story as well. I cannot say this loudly enough: the truth of the church's story cannot be a defensive presentation of what happened at Native American Catholic boarding schools.[30] The church needs to open and research historical records from her boarding schools. The institutional church needs to do her part to reveal the harm done and intentionally covered up at Native American boarding schools. The church needs to present the truth and admit fault for the abuse and harm that was caused at Native Catholic boarding schools.

I find hope that the USCCB has also looked at the example of the Canadian government's response to Catholic-run First Nations boarding schools in Canada. This is hopeful because the Canadian Conference of Catholic Bishops and the Canadian government have done years of work ahead of us and have even met with at least a few First Nations tribes using a restorative justice approach referred to as peacemaking circles.[31] Most of my hope for healing comes from those people who actively care for this topic and are working toward accountability, healing, and trust daily. Hope for the future comes from people like Fr. Michael Carson working within the USCCB to reach out to Native communities. I find hope in those who are a part of the American Indian Catholic Schools Network who educate Native children in their current Catholic (boarding and nonboarding) schools.[32] Hope comes particularly from those who had traumatic experiences at boarding schools who continue to step into these traumatic spaces to ensure that others do not encounter the same

---

[30] I have had far too many conversations with Catholics who have responded to my concerns by saying something similar to "Native Catholic boarding schools couldn't have been that bad" or "They couldn't have been as bad as the other boarding schools." "Not that bad" should never be a goal, especially for a church.

[31] Kay Pranis, *The Little Book of Circle Processes: A New/Old Approach to Peacemaking* (Intercourse, PA: Good Books, 2005), outlines Peacemaking Circles; it is not specific to the Native American Catholic boarding school context.

[32] This is the website for the American Indian Catholic Schools Network (AICSN) that is run through the Alliance for Catholic Education (ACE) at the University of Notre Dame: https://ace.nd.edu/programs/aicsn. AICSN provides a space for current Native American Catholic schools (boarding schools and day schools) to come together and support one another. AICSN also provides opportunities for staff members of these schools to further their education and opportunities for students as well.

experiences they did.[33] I will continue hoping and praying that more Catholics will join together to create a path toward healing from the sins committed at Native American Catholic boarding schools.

If we look back again to the description of Native Catholic boarding school history, we see that the voices of Native Americans were not considered in choosing how their Native religions or culture would interact with Christian religion and European culture. If their voices and narratives are still not listened to now, it can be no wonder that many Native Catholics are leaving the church angry about what was done to them and their ancestors and which continues to be ignored today. If the church does not tell the truth of its own story, including the stories of Native American Catholics who attended boarding schools, then we are missing out on the full extent of our own narrative.[34] We have an obligation as the Body of Christ to remember and tell stories of joy and triumph as well as stories of failure and suffering. Otherwise, the people who experienced this trauma may never be able to see how the church is their home.

Church as Wounded Healer

The image I want to end with is the image of the church as "wounded healer." This is an expansion of Henri Nouwen's image of the minister as "wounded healer." He first says, "A Christian community is therefore a healing community not because wounds are cured and pains are alleviated, but because wounds and pain become openings or occasions for new vision. Mutual confession then becomes a mutual deepening of hope."[35] Next, he goes on to speak

[33] For my final project for my master of divinity degree I conducted an interview with a current teacher at a Catholic Native school who wished to remain anonymous. She was forced to attend a Catholic Native boarding school away from home as a child and experienced trauma. As an adult she chose to work at a Catholic Native school and returned to practicing and loving her faith.

[34] The specific quote I am building on here says that a people only "become a people as they acquire a history through the adventures they share as interpreted through the tradition." Also, "a people are formed by a story that places their history in the texture of the world. Such stories make the world our home." See Stanley Hauerwas, *The Hauerwas Reader*, ed. John Berkman and Michael Cartwright (Durham, NC: Duke University Press, 2001), 173, 175.

[35] Henri J. M. Nouwen, *The Wounded Healer: Ministry in Contemporary Society* (New York: Image Book, 1979), 95.

about the minister as healing his own wounds in preparation to heal the wounds of others. The church, as minister, is called to be the Wounded Healer, "the one who must look after [her] own wounds but at the same time be prepared to heal the wounds of others."[36]

When I have had conversations about healing that involve the Catholic Church, it often sounds like the church is reaching outside to heal those who have been harmed. In expanding Nouwen's image, I see the church not as one reaching out to "the other" who was wounded. The church is called to look within and open the wounds of the Body of Christ in order to find the suffering that is bound there.

The members of the church who are silently suffering from the trauma experienced at Catholic boarding schools must be gently and patiently asked to share their stories while the church herself must commit to telling her own story truthfully. Through interviews I conducted with boarding school survivors who work for Native Catholic schools I was surprised to find Catholics who silently endured their wounds partially out of love of the church! One woman told me she never spoke up about her traumatic experience at Catholic boarding school because she feared harming the image of the church.[37] The church needs to open listening sessions and dialogue around healing with members who attended Native American Catholic boarding schools because these men and women are hidden within the tightly bound wounds of the history of the church. The church must open these tightly bound wounds and speak of the truth buried there. This must be a conversation about a church that reaches within to find those who have been harmed; in the process of opening these wounds the church will bring healing for the entire Body of Christ.

---

[36] Nouwen, *Wounded Healer*, 82.

[37] I find hope in the people who have experienced harm at the hands of ministers for the church but who still follow God. This is a miracle. This woman I interviewed, who wished to remain anonymous, spoke lovingly of the church and the faith she returned to later in adulthood. This is a miracle. That God's love is always infinitely bigger than human sin is a miracle. The fact that we, as the Body of Christ, are called to aid in sharing God's healing love with those harmed by ministers of the church is a miracle.

4

A Survivor-Centered Take on the State of the Catholic Sexual Abuse Crisis Today

Hilary Jerome Scarsella

When I was invited to participate in this conversation about accountability, healing, and trust in light of the Catholic sexual abuse crisis, I was asked to reflect on two particular questions. The first was, "What does the clergy sexual abuse crisis in the Roman Catholic Church look like from the perspective of other Christian denominations?" The second was, "What are the distinctive challenges that have arisen in the Christian churches to address sexual abuse, and how are these communities meeting the challenges?" In what follows, it is my aim to speak to each of these questions briefly, directly, and transparently.

As I do, a word about my context may be useful. I come to this conversation as a person raised in Anabaptist traditions of peace and nonviolence—traditions that are themselves rife with sexual violence.[1] I am the granddaughter, niece, and cousin of devout Italian Catholics, which is to say that Catholic traditions have a home in my

[1] Likely, the most well-known instance of sexual abuse and its cover-up in the North American Mennonite church regards the sexual violence of peace theologian John Howard Yoder. A discussion of this case can be found in Rachel Waltner Goosen's " 'Defanging the Beast': Mennonite Responses to John Howard Yoder's Sexual Abuse," *Mennonite Quarterly Review* 89, no. 1 (2015): 52–81. Information and analysis regarding additional cases are available in the "Blog" and "Reports" sections of Into Account's website (my organization) at https://intoaccount.org/; Into Account's satellite website, Our Stories Untold at http://www.ourstoriesuntold.com/; and in the "Case List"

spirit. I teach theology and ethics at a historically Baptist and functionally ecumenical seminary. I am a survivor of sexual violence myself (though not perpetrated by a religious authority). And I am a professional advocate for survivors of sexual violence across the gamut of Christian contexts—Catholic, Protestant, Anabaptist, Evangelical, conservative, and progressive. One of my more significant experiences of working with survivors in the Roman Catholic Church has been with my advocacy organization, Into Account. In 2021, we published a report on the abuses disclosed to us by over fifty women victimized in Catholic contexts by sacred music composer David Haas, and in our advocacy with and for survivors we have interfaced with a wide range of Roman Catholic authorities and communities.[2] It is from this broad set of vantage points that I have considered the questions posed to me. I am an outsider observing the Catholic United States of America from a bird's-eye view. My remarks represent an impression this wide landscape has made on those, like me, just peeking in for a moment and, most especially, on those of us peeking in while advocating with and for survivors.

What does the clergy sexual abuse crisis in the Catholic Church look like now, in 2022? To be perfectly honest, it does not look good. It has been twenty full years since the beginning of the *Boston Globe*'s reporting.[3] Twenty years since concrete evidence of the systemic problem of clergy sexual abuse in the Roman Catholic Church became widespread knowledge. Twenty years since the church and all of its members have had opportunity to organize for theological, relational, and structural change. A whole generation has grown from infant to adult in this time, and the scale of the problem remains staggering. Clergy abuse of children and adults continues. Cover-ups continue.[4]

---

section of the Mennonite Abuse Prevention (MAP) website at https://www .themaplist.org/the-map-list/.

[2] For survivor stories, supporting documentation, and our formal report on Haas's abuses, see "David Haas Report," Reports, Into Account, August 2021, https://intoaccount.org/reports/.

[3] For the original reports that broke the case in 2002, see the publications available at Spotlight: Clergy Sex Abuse Crisis, *Boston Globe*, https://www3.bostonglobe.com /metro/specials/clergy/.

[4] The organization Bishop Accountability tracks new and historical revelations in sexual abuse allegations and cover-ups. Evidence of ongoing instances of each are apparent. I take such evidence to include reports since 2002 of newly perpetrated sexual abuse, reports of responsible parties failing to appropriately intervene, and

While focus has been on abuses perpetrated and covered up by clergy, sexual violence perpetrated and covered up by lay leaders is also a significant problem, and it ought not be treated as an entirely separate one. Abuses perpetrated by clergy and by lay leaders are interrelated. They each are systemically enabled in the church. While there has been some progress regarding abuses perpetrated by clergy, we must note that the Roman Catholic Church has barely even begun to scratch the surface of its abuse problem among lay leaders.

Of course, change takes time. Crises built over decades (centuries?) tend to take as long to address. It is important that we who address sexual abuse in any church setting commit for the long haul and practice care for our souls along the way. Because change does take time.

What I find concerning, however, is that huge portions of the Catholic Church seem okay with that. Not "okay" as in "accepting of the fact of human limitation," but "okay" as in "resistant to or resentful of the sense of urgency that survivors bring to the table." As I have worked with survivors of David Haas's abuses, I have experienced a distinct lack of urgency and resistance to urgency on the part of many Catholic leaders and structures across the United States. And this resistance, in many cases, is strategic. For example, certain groups choose not to speak about Haas's abuses out of fear that doing so would bring attention to current abuses happening in their own youth programs. This too is a cover-up.

------

reports of previously abusive clerics abusing again (indicating a failure of responsible parties to appropriately intervene). Abuse Tracker, Bishop Accountability, https://www.bishop-accountability.org/category/news-archive/abusetracker/. More organized statistics are available through the annual report(s) on the implementation of the Charter for the Protection of Children and Young People published by United States Conference of Catholic Bishops (USCCB) together with the Secretariat of Child and Youth Protection and the National Review Board. In these reports, however, statistics are gathered based on the year in which abuses are reported, not the year in which reported abuses occurred. Thus, it is difficult (perhaps, not possible) to use the data provided in these reports to interpret the ongoing frequency of the Catholic clerical abuses and cover-ups. The fact that these reports do not systematically attempt to speak to the current frequency of such abuses is a decision that has the effect (if not also the intention) of concealing critical information from the public. These annual reports can be found in the resource library of the USCCB website at https://www.usccb.org/resources/library, or linked through Bishop Accountability's collation of USCCB data at https://www.bishop-accountability.org/AtAGlance/USCCB_Yearly_Data_on_Accused_Priests.htm.

In fact, my colleague, Dr. Stephanie Krehbiel, has helpfully articulated how we should think about cover-ups. As she says,

> Cover-ups are best understood not as nefariously orchestrated plots that are conceived in whole and then executed by a few bad actors, but as a complex series of decisions both influenced by and reflective of shared institutional values and priorities—usually, the priority of institutional self-preservation over the wellbeing of survivors. In Christian settings, self-preservation is easily conflated with preservation of the Church writ large. When this happens, institutional (or community) self-preservation becomes a value infused with divine authority at the expense of victims and survivors.[5]

A community's choice not to openly address Haas's abuses so as to avoid drawing attention to other abuses going on in its midst is a cover-up because it is a choice to prioritize self-preserving silence over speech necessary for solidarity with survivors and prevention of future harm.

While it is true that change takes time, change in the Roman Catholic Church does not need to take *this much* time. The church has all the information, evidence, and resources it needs to pursue and implement needed changes at a pace that is worthy of those who have been harmed. We should not be comfortable with anything less. Until religious and lay leaders and entire Catholic communities are consistently treating the problem of sexual violence with a level of urgency that matches the intensity of survivors' wisdom, perseverance, and gifts of prophetic witness, the state of the Catholic sexual abuse crisis will look to those in positions like mine like an ongoing betrayal of survivors continuing to unfold in real time.

How else does the sexual abuse crisis in the Roman Catholic Church look from the place where I stand?

It looks preventable, though it is still ongoing.

It looks naïve, because sanctioning the most easily identifiable and obviously accountable perpetrators in the church—clergy shown by strict evidentiary standards to have abused multiple children—is not anywhere near enough to dismantle a culture of abuse and enable-

---

[5] Stephanie Krehbiel and Hilary Jerome Scarsella, "Sexual Violence: Christian Theological Legacies and Responsibilities," *Religion Compass* 13, no. 9 (September 2019): 1–13.

ment entrenched throughout the ecclesial, theological, spiritual, and relational system.

It looks underfunded and undervalued. My colleagues who run survivor-centered organizations and projects indispensable to the Catholic Church's progress in addressing sexual abuse—organizations like Bishop Accountability, Awake Milwaukee, and others—are running on strapped budgets wildly unrepresentative of the actual economic power of the Roman Catholic Church to empower survivor-centered initiatives for change if it so chose to value them.

It looks patriarchal and white. Patriarchal (aside from the literal sense) because the church has not found (or, has not decided to find) a way to systematically empower and value survivors as its primary leaders on this issue. Patriarchal because a sophisticated analysis of gender and sexuality and hierarchy—plentifully offered by Catholic feminist theologians and others—has not been made authoritative for understanding or addressing the sexual abuse crisis by decision makers. White because the same can be said—and to a much greater degree—of analyses of race and colonization. White because we know that people of color are at a higher risk of becoming targets of abuse, and yet survivors of color are largely absent (read: systemically excluded) even from spaces created with genuine care by and for survivors in the United States.[6]

And yet, the sexual abuse crisis in the Roman Catholic Church also looks to me like a scapegoat for the rest of the Christian Church in which equally severe problems flourish but benefit from being outside the range of the US "spotlight" focused on the Catholic Church. The only dynamic I have named that is unique to the Roman Catholic Church is the Catholic community's access to concrete, publicly available documentation of the fact and nature of its clergy sexual abuse problem. In the rest of the Christian Church, when abusive leaders are moved from community to community all traces of evidence are

---

[6] For example, while sexual violence statistics are notoriously incomplete, a 2011 survey found that while 20.5 percent of non-Hispanic white women have experienced rape, the number is 32.3 percent for multiracial women. The same survey found that 46.9 percent of non-Hispanic white women have experienced sexual violence other than rape; 64.1 percent of multiracial women have experienced this violence. Matthew J. Breiding et al., "Prevalence and Characteristics of Sexual Violence, Stalking, and Intimate Partner Violence Victimization—National Intimate Partner and Sexual Violence Survey, United States, 2011" (Atlanta: U.S. Department of Health and Human Services), http://www.cdc.gov/mmwr/pdf/ss/ss6308.pdf.

destroyed. Records of survivors' reports are shredded. Files go missing. Hard drives are wiped. Somewhat uniquely, Catholics have a solid foundation of evidence and documentation upon which to organize. That actually puts Catholics, compared to their other Christian siblings, in a more empowered position to strategize for change.

Aside from this distinction, however, the sexual abuse crisis in every Christian denomination—and it exists in all of them—looks preventable, stagnant, naïve. It looks underfunded and undervalued, patriarchal and (in predominately white denominations) white. I work with survivors from all across the Christian Church and interface with Christian leaders and structures in many different denominations. While there are important nuances specific to each context, there is another level on which the basic features of each community's sexual abuse problem look the same.

Sexual abuse is ubiquitous. The enablement and cover-up of sexual abuse in Western Christianities are ubiquitous. The conscious and unconscious dynamics that perpetuate abuse are quite similar from one community to the next, and survivors' experiences likewise share some common features. In this sense, the Catholic sexual abuse crisis, quite honestly, looks mundane. Average. Old hat. Not sensational at all, but a tired story overdue for a plot change.

There is opportunity here. The strategic power of Catholic networks working earnestly to address sexual abuse could be strengthened by joining their efforts together with those of analogous networks in other denominations working toward similar ends. If, as I have suggested, the sexual abuse crises throughout the Christian churches share common characteristics there is no reason these cannot be addressed by common efforts. Those working to stop sexual violence across the Christian landscape could create and accomplish more together if we were able to share wisdom, money, and time. We could make strides toward positive change much more quickly if we were able to divide the work among us and make the fruits of our labor accessible to all. Rather than ten underfunded and under-resourced organizations working to address twenty critical issues each, we could build that set of organizations into a network in which each group specializes in two of those issues and turns to the others in the network for support in the remaining eighteen. At the very least, what the ubiquity of sexual violence throughout the Christian denominations means for Roman Catholics is that Catholics are not alone in addressing the problem, and need not, themselves, build from scratch every wheel necessary for the cart of sexual justice to roll.

I have already begun addressing the second question upon which I was invited to reflect, but I want to turn to it now in earnest: "What are the distinctive challenges that have arisen in the Christian churches to address sexual abuse, and how are these communities meeting the challenges?"

Though I have been emphasizing commonalities, there are, of course, distinct challenges that confront each individual Christian community. For example, leaders in denominations with horizontal polity are not empowered to hold individual congregations accountable for following the recommendations leaders might make regarding sexual violence. Peace churches have the challenge of coming to terms with the role that peace theology has itself played in enabling abuse.[7] The Amish often resist using governmental social support systems, without which appropriate services for survivors are difficult to procure. Conservative Protestant theologies of gender complementarianism actively work against developing analytical tools necessary for preventing and addressing abuse. Progressive Protestants tend to resent survivors who rightfully point out that the community's good intentions frequently fail to translate into right action. Black churches have to contend with the way white supremacy threatens racist ramifications any time black men are identified as abusers in white public spaces. Addressing cultures of sexual violence in any Christian denomination requires thoughtful attention to that context's distinct characteristics.

For the reasons I have previously named, however, I want to talk about strategies for stopping sexual violence and empowering survivors that my organization, Into Account, has found useful across the range of these different contexts. For the sake of brevity, I will focus on two. The first is empowering survivors to lead. And the second is preventing future harm by removing perpetrators' authority, access

---

[7] For analyses of this impact, see Elizabeth G. Yoder, ed., *Peace Theology and Violence against Women* (Elkhart, IN: Institution of Mennonite Studies, 1992); and Ruth Krall, *The Elephants in God's Living Room: Mennonite Church and John Howard Yoder; Collected Essays*, vol. 3: Enduring Space: Transforming Cultures of Violence One Person at a Time, One Moment at a Time (2013), https://ruthkrall.com/books/the-elephants -in-gods-living-room-series/volume-three-the-mennonite-church-and-john-howard -yoder-collected-essays/.

to vulnerable populations, and automatic good regard in communities at risk of enabling their abuse to continue.[8]

Any successful effort to address sexual abuse in the church must prioritize giving survivors resources that empower them to make their own best decisions about how they want to advocate for themselves, advocate for change, and live their lives in ways that build a better future. When I say "give survivors resources" I mean respect, time, money, information, access to knowledge, and access especially to the kinds of knowledge usually protected by gatekeepers. We must provide survivors with resources for navigating day-to-day life amid traumatization, such as high-quality therapy, childcare, medication, and help cleaning the house. We must also offer survivors opportunities to enter and succeed in positions of genuine authority with respect to how our communities engage sexual violence going forward. Survivors' leadership must be empowered to promote forms of change that our communities might not otherwise embrace.

There is a tendency in Christian spaces for survivors to be infantilized. It is common for members of Christian communities to conceive of survivors as broken ones who need to be healed and saved by the church. While it is important for communities to be equipped and willing to extend care to survivors when care is requested, it is equally important to guard against developing a general image of survivors as in need of rescue or an image of the church as the necessary agent of rescue. Rather, what sexual abuses crises across the Christian landscape clearly demonstrate is that it is the church that is in need of radical transformation, and survivors have something to offer the church in its quest to become well. Rather than linking the word "survivor" with a mental image of tormented helplessness, we would do better to conjure an image of prophets anointed by God to show the church the way forward. It is, after all, because of survivors' voices, courage, wisdom, and witness that we know anything today about the sexual abuse crisis in the church at all. Survivors' lived expertise on the nature of the problem is our best hope for constructing effective solutions. To regard survivors as anything less than prophets will keep our progress partial and slow.

---

[8] Credit for developing this framework must be attributed to my organization, Into Account. More specifically, it is a framework developed collaboratively between myself and my Into Account colleagues Jay Yoder, Erin Bergen, and Stephanie Krehbiel. It was Jay who originally put together the language of "authority, access, and good regard" as shorthand for describing our approach.

The priority of resourcing survivors, respecting survivors, empowering survivors, and trusting survivors to lead certainly their own lives and perhaps the life of the church is a necessary foundation for any effort to address sexual abuse in any Christian context. Efforts to address sexual abuse in Christian spaces will not be successful if they do not give survivors what they need to make their own informed decisions with regard to their immediate needs. Such efforts will likewise fail unless they also empower survivors to lead resistance to sexual violence in the church without oversight. Partnership, yes. Solidarity, yes. But not oversight. God does not send prophets so that the messages they carry can be made tame by the very systems of leadership against which they speak.

That's the first strategy. Above all else—above unity, above image, above conflict avoidance, above institutional survival—prioritize giving survivors resources necessary for them to be as empowered as possible to make their own best decisions about how they want to advocate for themselves, to advocate for change, and to live their lives in ways that build a better future.

Now, the second strategy. To stop perpetrators of sexual abuse from causing additional harm, communities have to remove three things: (1) perpetrators' authority, (2) perpetrators' access to vulnerable populations, and (3) perpetrators' automatic good regard in communities at risk of enabling their abuse to continue.

Removing a perpetrator's *authority* is key to stopping abuse because authority is the primary currency perpetrators trade on to abuse and get away with it. Removing a perpetrator's authority means, for example, revoking the clergy status of abusers who are priests and pastors and revoking the licensure of abusers who are mental health workers. It also means using symbolic and social action to restructure the power relationship of that person to the community in which they previously held authority. For example, this is what GIA Publications did when they announced their decision to stop publishing Haas's music and contacted all the Roman Catholic dioceses in the United States to make sure their position was heard.[9] By restructuring the power relationship between themselves and Haas, and by making

---

[9] Erin O'Donnell, "Publisher GIA Contacts All U.S. Dioceses about Catholic Composer David Haas," *Awake Milwaukee*, July 27, 2021, https://www.awake community.org/blog/publisher-gia-contacts-all-us-dioceses-about-catholic -composer-david-haas.

this known to stakeholders who would understand the gravity of this decision, GIA shifted the state of Haas's symbolic authority not only within GIA but throughout the Catholic landscape more broadly.

Removing a perpetrator's *access* to vulnerable populations is necessary for stopping abuse because access is nine-tenths of sexual violence. Limiting access decreases a perpetrator's opportunities to abuse. We can hope that a perpetrator of sexual violence will repent and change their ways, but we cannot count on it.[10] Thus, it is imperative to take measures that ensure a perpetrator who has abused children is not permitted to be around children in the future. A perpetrator who has abused people under their religious care cannot again be permitted to have others under their religious care. A perpetrator who has abused students cannot again be in charge of a classroom. And a perpetrator who has abused their therapy clients cannot again be in a position to have therapy clients. Removal of a perpetrator's access to vulnerable populations is a measure of protection ethically

---

[10] Observed recidivism rates are particularly high for those who perpetrate sexual abuse against persons over whom they hold authority (i.e., perpetrators who are clergy, therapists, teachers, abusers of children, etc.). The US Office of Sex Offender Sentencing, Monitoring, Apprehending, Registering, and Tracking (SMART) reports, "Observed recidivism rates of sex offenders are underestimates of actual reoffending," largely because the majority of abuses are not reported and studies that track recidivism rely on official reports to count reoffences. With the understanding that the numbers are underestimates, SMART notes a study that found the average overall rate of recidivism among all sex offenders in general to be between 27.9 percent and 39.2 percent. With respect to sexual abuse of children, researchers have found that 42 percent of perpetrators convicted for the abuse were subsequently reconvicted for additional abuses. The rate of reconviction for those whose legal records included previous sexual offenses was 77 percent. Two studies of sexually exploitative therapists that relied on self-reporting rather than police reports to collect data found that "between 38% and 80% of therapists who engage in sexual contact with a patient become involved with one more of their patients." References in the order discussed: Roger Przybylski, "Adult Sex Offender Recidivism," in *Sex Offender Management Assessment and Planning Initiative* (Washington, DC: US Department of Justice Office of Sex Offender Sentencing, Monitoring, Apprehending, Registering, and Tracking, 2017), 107, 112. Child Molester Recidivism, Public Safety Canada, last modified August 9, 2022, https://www.publicsafety.gc.ca/cnt/rsrcs/pblctns/chld-mlstr/index-en.aspx. With respect to the 38 percent figure: Glen O. Gabbard, *Sexual Exploitation in Professional Relationships* (Washington DC: American Psychiatric Press, 1989), 18. With respect to the 80 percent figure: N. K. Gartrell et al., "Psychiatrist-Patient Sexual Contact: Results of a National Survey," *The American Journal of Psychiatry* 143, no. 9 (September 1986): 1126–28.

owed to those at risk of becoming future targets of abuse. It is also a measure of accountability that any perpetrator who truly understands and takes responsibility for their violence ought to welcome. Resistance to this form of accountability is a sign that a perpetrator's repentance (i.e., internal transformation and embodied commitment to making amends) is either incomplete or insincere—all the more reason for their access to vulnerable populations to be removed.

While removing authority and access can be controversial, I find that the third recommendation is where Christians tend to struggle most: removing a perpetrator's automatic *good regard* in communities at risk of enabling their abuse to continue. When I say "remove good regard" I do not mean to suggest that a community should announce this person unloved by God or cease treating them with the kind of dignity owed to all God's creation. Rather, a community must cease extending to those who have behaved in sexually abusive ways the benefit of the doubt when it comes to their ethical integrity. Members of such a community must withdraw trust in proportion to the extent the perpetrator has broken it. They must keep the harm a perpetrator has caused and the needs of survivors at the forefront of their minds as they struggle to figure out what treating a perpetrator of sexual abuse with dignity means in the wake of their unacceptably violent and manipulative behavior. This is not only a task for individuals. The removal of a perpetrator's good regard must be cultivated as a collective stance in the communities where it is at all possible that the perpetrator might try to abuse again, because sexual abuse is not only an interpersonal event between two individuals. It takes an entire community to enable abuse. Revelations of abuse impact every member. And it takes an entire community practicing sustained, intentional awareness to prevent abuse from continuing.

While the Catholic Church has made some progress around removing ordained perpetrators' authority and access, it has far to go where lay leaders' abuses are concerned. Across the board, removal of perpetrators' automatic good regard has yet to be adopted as a necessary (or even appropriate) Christian response. While parts of the church have cultivated a degree of sympathy for survivors, attitudes of skepticism and animosity remain common. It remains rare that even a sympathetic community's view of survivors is grounded in respect rather than pity. A comprehensive overhaul of the church's systemic approach to sexual violence is required if survivors are going to be empowered to lead the church's efforts to stop abuse and transform complicit communities into communities of sexual justice, care, and vitality.

5

Walking with Survivors:
What Are We to Do with This Pain?

Marcus Mescher

Early in his pontificate, Pope Francis proposed a vision of the church less like a fortress and more like a "field hospital" after battle, mercifully tending to the wounded.[1] While this offers a compelling vision of being a church that mercifully draws near to those in need, it suggests a model of ministry as a form of triage. Triage, by definition, is only an initial response, sorting the gravity of injuries and prioritizing care. It is not a long-term, sustainable model to heal wounds and falls well short of taking steps to redress or prevent harm. As we continue to learn more about the scope of clergy sexual abuse and its concealment by Catholic Church officials, a church-as-field-hospital model does not provide adequate scale to solve the problems that persist even today. This model also fails to acknowledge the way that abuse and its concealment have broken trust, resulting in a church that does not feel safe to many. How can the church be a source of merciful healing when it is responsible for causing harm and covering it up? If we listen to survivors of clergy sexual abuse, they can help us identify steps toward repairing a wounded church.

---

[1] Pope Francis, interview with Fr. Antonio Spadaro, SJ, "A Big Heart Open to God," *America*, September 30, 2013, http://www.americamagazine.org/pope-interview.

Drawing Near

Gustavo Gutiérrez points out that the word "poor" in Scripture is not just an economic term; it signifies the outcast, the socially insignificant or nonperson, the powerless.[2] As he sees it, to deliver on the "preferential option for the poor" is to follow the example of the Good Samaritan who acts with courage, compassion, and boundary-breaking solidarity in going out of his way and going into the ditch to care for the one beaten, robbed, and left for dead (Luke 10:29-37). It means "leaving the road one is on" and "entering the world" of the vulnerable or excluded person, taking their vantage point, and making it our own.[3] The church must embrace a "preferential option for survivors," that is, following the example of the Samaritan to draw near those who have been abused, to listen and learn from them, and then to work collaboratively as allies and advocates for healing, accountability, and prevention.[4]

For the last several years, I have accompanied survivors of clergy sexual abuse. I started this work with an interest in restorative justice but quickly learned that we cannot heal the wounds unless and until we understand their depth and breadth. Survivors have taught me a great deal—far more than I could articulate in this space—which I summarize with the following five themes.[5]

Betrayal

Clergy sexual abuse is a betrayal of sacred trust. Catholics are raised to respect and trust priests. One survivor reflected, "A priest is higher than a police officer and next to God." Another recounted how he was raised to believe that a priest could never sin, so he

---

[2] Gustavo Gutiérrez, *A Theology of Liberation: History, Politics, and Salvation* (Maryknoll, NY: Orbis Books, 1988), xxi–xxii.

[3] Gustavo Gutiérrez, "The Option for the Poor Arises from Faith in Christ," *Theological Studies* 70 (2009): 317–26, at 318.

[4] I borrow the term "preferential option for survivors" from Jaisy A. Joseph, "Responding to Shame with Solidarity: Sex Abuse Crisis in the Indian Catholic Church," *Horizons* 14, no. 2 (June 2020): 381–92.

[5] For a fuller picture of what survivors shared in a two-year research study funded by Fordham University's Taking Responsibility project, view our public report: https://www.xavier.edu/moral-injury-report/. The following quotes are from survivors interviewed for this research study.

couldn't make sense of why the abuse felt wrong. Whether they were abused as children or as adults, survivors felt like they could not say no to the priest because he represents what is sacred and holy (ordained *in persona Christi*). When a priest is a perpetrator of abuse (whether spiritual or sexual), it implicates God and the church. People go to priests in a spirit of tremendous vulnerability, and when that vulnerability is violated, it makes it very difficult to feel safe again, especially with those in authority. The depth of betrayal is profound; survivors describe their abuse like the "rape" or "murder" of their soul. A few survivors describe feeling angry at God or that their abuse was a form of punishment from God. Even though they recognized the abuse as an injustice, when they would pray for help, "it never came." Because they were abused by priests, numerous survivors reported that their relationship with God, the Catholic Church, and organized religion on the whole was either permanently damaged or completely ruined. The experience of betrayal was compounded when other adults were aware of the abuse and could have intervened but did not.

Shame and Futility

Survivors often blame themselves and are blamed by others for their abuse. Many survivors experience PTSD, although this fear-based trauma does not completely encapsulate the persistent psychological distress, spiritual anguish, moral confusion, social isolation, and distrust for institutions that are more appropriately labeled as "moral injury."[6] Instead, survivors endure a toxic shame that stains their identity and agency. Some survivors shared that they have been left feeling unworthy, bad, empty, or "dead inside." After being abused, several questioned if they ever deserved to feel happy or loved. A few describe feeling they are "nothing," or they are like a "dirty rag that no amount of bleach could clean." Many survivors

---

[6] For more on this topic, see Marcus Mescher, "Clergy Sexual Abuse as Moral Injury: Confronting a Wounded and Wounding Church," in *Doing Theology and Theological Ethics in the Face of the Abuse Crisis*, ed. Daniel J. Fleming, James F. Keenan, and Hans Zollner (Eugene, OR: Wipf and Stock, 2023), 122–39, https://jmt.scholasticahq.com/article/72061-clergy-sexual-abuse-as-moral-injury-confronting-a-wounded-and-wounding-church.

express a sense of hopelessness or powerlessness; as one survivor put it, "I don't feel my actions actually matter." Numerous survivors shared that the reporting process seemed pointless and that neither church leaders nor law enforcement officers were interested in learning the truth or holding anyone accountable. They described feeling insignificant or invisible; in the words of one survivor, "You're left with a broken heart until you die." This sense of futility is poignantly illustrated by the finding that the suicide rate for survivors is fifty times higher than that of the general population.[7]

Weaponization of Faith

Sexual abuse is often paired with spiritual abuse, both by perpetrators and by other members of the church. Children and adults have been coerced by clergy to perform and endure sexual acts as a reenactment of Christ's love or as a purification from sin. One survivor reported that the priest excused his abusive behavior by saying that "he had been sent by God to save my soul because I was an evil child." Survivors are often told to pray for and forgive their perpetrator, often without receiving any acknowledgment or remorse by the perpetrator. One adult survivor was told by the unrepentant priest who abused her: "I went to confession and I completed my penance. I don't owe you anything." In many cases, Jesus's injunction to forgive others is invoked to undermine accountability: forgiveness is imposed on the survivor without any corresponding action from the perpetrator or his superiors to indicate his sincere regret and desire to atone for the harm he caused. Lay Catholics have imparted spiritually harmful recommendations to survivors like "You just need to forgive Father," "Just 'let go and let God,'" "God wouldn't give you anything more than you can handle," or "This is just part of God's mysterious plan." These kinds of phrases ignore, minimize, or reject the pain survivors carry.

---

[7] G. R. Pafumi, "VictimsSpeakDB.org Data Infers Suicide Rates among Victims of Clergy Sex Abuse Exceed 50 Times the General Population," *EIN Presswire*, November 13, 2018, www.einpresswire.com/article/467186245/victimsspeakdb-org -data-infers-suicide-rates-among-victims-of-clergy-sex-abuse-exceed-50-times-the -general-population.

Isolation

Survivors experience intense social displacement and loneliness. Part of this stems from the way survivors were groomed, often set apart from their peers and made to feel special. This is also the result of the stigma, shame, and secrecy typically surrounding human sexuality in the Catholic Church—exacerbated when clergy are responsible for abuse. Many survivors keep their abuse to themselves, which is for a variety of reasons: they fear they will be blamed, they won't be believed, or that it will change how others see them (they will be considered "dirty" or "evil"). A number of survivors kept the abuse hidden from their parents, siblings, and even partners or spouses because they wanted to protect them from the pain they were carrying, or feared it would "break" or "destroy" their loved ones. In some cases, survivors tried to share what they were enduring with family members, but they only received disbelief or disdain or were outright disowned by their parents or siblings. Several survivors described the experience of disclosing to others they thought they could trust as even "more traumatic" than the original abuse. Survivors experience isolation even after suppressing their memories of abuse and report years of feeling lost, alone, and trapped in patterns of self-destructive behavior. Statistically, survivors of sexual abuse are much more likely to engage in sexually promiscuous behavior and turn to alcohol, drugs, and other risk-taking actions to escape or numb the pain. According to the Office of Assistance Ministry to Survivors in the Archdiocese of Chicago, on average, survivors report their abuse twenty-seven years after it occurred. After their abuse—for both the short- and long-term—survivors are rarely believed, understood, or receive genuine concern from lay or ordained members of the church. Today, many survivors report feeling bewildered, sad, angry, and frustrated that many Catholics think survivors just need to "move on" or that it's time to "get past" this issue. Too many nonsurvivors fail to grasp that clergy sexual abuse is not something a person can just leave in the past; it fundamentally alters their identity and their psychological and spiritual well-being, agency, and relationships. The lack of curiosity, compassion, and solidarity on the part of nonsurvivors only perpetuates the isolation experienced by many survivors today. In the words of one survivor, "If the church is one Body, and survivors are part of that body, the rest of the church wants to amputate us. . . . What do I have to do for the church to accept me?"

Institutional Failure

As a global institution, the Catholic Church has been the scene of abuse to millions of victims by thousands of clergy. Many in institutional leadership approach this problem as isolated incidents due to "a few bad apples." The primary focus was on the priest, who broke his vow of celibacy, responsible for the sin of breaking the sixth commandment. In some cases, the perpetrator was temporarily removed from ministry, but this was often more to protect the church's reputation than to protect the laity from future risks of abuse. Church officials are responsible for shielding perpetrators and moving them to socio-economically vulnerable communities: to missionary settings abroad, to impoverished areas, and to neighborhoods with a large number of racial or ethnic minorities, including recent immigrants who could be threatened with deportation.[8] The asymmetry in power between a layperson and a priest is always present, but given the precarity faced by individuals in these communities, they often encountered many social and economic disincentives to report their abuse, whether to ecclesial or to civil authorities. As one survivor put it, "No one knew more and did less than the church authorities." In the United States, church leaders have paid millions to lobbyists to oppose extending the statute of limitations to allow more survivors to report their abuse, and they have shielded billions of dollars in church assets to avoid making financial settlements to survivors.[9] Across the world, at the micro and macro levels of the church, clergy and others in leadership have routinely discouraged survivors from reporting their abuse, discredited survivors who come forward, or tried to handle the abuse as a sin (to be forgiven) rather than a crime (to be investigated, prosecuted, and deliberated). Even when the abuse is recognized by church officials, it often corresponds with a nondisclosure agreement that prevents the survivor from giving voice to their experience. This pattern of obfuscation, intimidation, and secrecy adds another layer of abuse to survivors and hides the truth from all nonsurvivors.

---

[8] See, for example, Susan Bigelow Reynolds, " 'I Will Surely Have You Deported': Undocumenting Clergy Sexual Abuse in an Immigrant Community," *Religion and American Culture* 33, no. 1 (2023): 1–34.

[9] Josh Saul, "Catholic Church Shields $2 Billion in Assets to Limit Abuse Payouts," *Bloomberg*, January 8, 2020, https://www.bloomberg.com/news/features/2020-01-08/the-catholic-church-s-strategy-to-limit-payouts-to-abuse-victims.

Theological Reflection

Grace is present and efficacious in the sacramental life of the church, making possible personal and communal transfiguration. At the same time, the church remains entangled in persistent individual and social sinfulness. The catastrophe of clergy sexual abuse and its concealment reveal how prevalent abuse of power is in the church, especially in the form of clericalism and patriarchalism, sexism and heterosexism, racism, and ableism.[10] For too long, the church has ignored, denied, or minimized clergy abuse in order to prevent scandal.[11] Hiding the truth is yet another abuse of power, since it seeks to maintain control over others by denying them an accurate picture of reality. This runs contrary to Jesus's teaching and healing ministry, where he commanded his disciples not to lord power over others and to embrace a posture of others-centered service (Matt 20:25-27). Crucifixion was an act of sexual violence and public shaming. Victims were stripped naked, tortured, mocked, and killed to showcase the political might of the Roman Empire, making Jesus a survivor of sexual violence who understands the wounds other survivors carry today.[12] Yet Jesus Christ is not embarrassed of his wounds and does not hide them: when Thomas is absent from the disciples' encounter with the Risen Christ and does not believe he appeared to them, Jesus invites Thomas to place his hands in the wounds of his crucified body (John 20:24-29). To do theology in the wake of clergy sexual abuse and its concealment means adopting a *locus theologicus* at the site of the wounds. It is significant that the body of the Risen Christ is still marked by the physical harm of crucifixion: wounds that have not yet begun to heal or scar. Jesus teaches that whatever we do for the least among us, we do for him (Matt 25:40), meaning that he identifies himself with the vulnerable and excluded. The poor—the nonpersons, the powerless—are the innocent victims of history, whom Ignacio

---

[10] We are still learning how widespread clergy and other Catholic leaders preyed upon people with cognitive and physical disabilities.

[11] Angela Senander argues that the clergy sexual abuse crisis is a scandal due in part to church hierarchy aiming to avoid scandal. See *Scandal: The Catholic Church and Public Life* (Collegeville, MN: Liturgical Press, 2012), 26.

[12] For more on this subject, see *When Did We See You Naked? Jesus as a Victim of Sexual Abuse,* ed. Jayme Reaves, David Tombs, and Rocio Figueroa (London: SCM Press, 2021).

Ellacuría describes as the "crucified peoples" of today.[13] Much has been written about the responsibility of Christians to "take the crucified people down from the cross" of economic deprivation, social exclusion, and political corruption. But what does it look like to shoulder our duty to the "crucified peoples" subjected to spiritual and sexual abuse by church leaders?

In the gospels, Jesus is never indifferent to people in pain. He draws near to those who are suffering and listens to them. When Jesus encounters the blind man Bartimaeus, he asks, "What do you want me to do for you?" (Mark 10:51). Jesus listens before acting. Listening is an act of love. Theologically and pastorally, our first priority must be to center survivors and listen to those who have been harmed by clergy sexual abuse. Of course, Jesus does more than listen. He incarnates mercy, offers counsel, consolation, and a healing touch. Jesus encourages others to adopt a habit of loving service. It is also true that he goes beyond the triage model of the field hospital. In the face of violence and oppression, Jesus acted with righteous anger to dismantle unjust systems, as he does in the cleansing of the temple (Matt 21:12-17). This prophetic action provides a moral standard for the courage, compassion, and solidarity necessary to bring about ecclesial reform—locally and globally—today.[14]

Three Principles for Ministry

St. Paul describes the Christian community as the Body of Christ, united such that "[i]f one member suffers, all suffer together with it" (1 Cor 12:26). If survivors feel like "the rest of the church wants to amputate us," it is an indictment of the lack of courage, compassion,

---

[13] This phrase is a generative theme for the work of Jon Sobrino, SJ. See, for example, *The Principle of Mercy: Taking the Crucified People Down from the Cross* (Maryknoll, NY: Orbis Books, 1994).

[14] It is worth noting that in their 1983 pastoral letter, The Challenge of Peace, the US Catholic bishops acknowledge that Jesus's words might "remain an impossible, abstract ideal were it not for" Jesus's actions in the temple, where "Jesus pointed out the injustices of his time and opposed those who laid burdens upon the people" before acting "aggressively and dramatically" to chase from the temple "those who had made God's house into a 'den of robbers.'" The bishops have yet to apply this standard to cleansing the church of sexual predators and their enablers. See paragraph 48: https://www.usccb.org/upload/challenge-peace-gods-promise-our-response-1983.pdf.

and solidarity in parishes, dioceses, and broader experiences of the church. It points to a stubborn failure to acknowledge the truth of what those in power have done and failed to do. Clergy sexual abuse is like a detonated bomb, where survivors carry the most acute pain while the blast radius sends psychological, religious, moral, and social fallout outward to their friends and family members, church employees, and others who feel implicated by the abuse done in their faith community. Entangled with both grace and guilt, promises of repentance and reluctance to cede control, and comprised of members who are ready to roll up their sleeves and others still unable to come to terms with the scope of the wounds, the church is a collection of "clay jars" (2 Cor 4:7) who can never shake free of finitude and sin. Holding fast to the possibilities for *metanoia*, the church must adopt a model of ministry with the following three principles in mind:

1. For many Catholics, the church is not a safe place. In the United States more than 30 million Catholics have left the church (or might say the church has left them), and a sizable number of Catholics express doubt about the authority of the institution and morality of its clergy.[15] If the church cannot take its credibility for granted, lay and ordained leaders must prioritize words and actions marked by integrity, transparency, and accountability. Those in ministry should change the question, "How can we reach them?" and instead ask, "How can we be reached by them?" Here, Pope Francis's "field hospital" may be a fitting model for a church that has no borders, a synodal church that listens, accompanies, and aims to leave no one out or behind.

2. Survivors and their loved ones may not feel safe in church places or participating in parish ministry programs, but to the extent possible, they should be invited to have their voices heard and exercise decision making over pastoral priorities. Trust is rebuilt slowly, over time, and only after a proven track record of modeling genuine concern for their well-being. Ministry as "doing for others" can reinforce a view that those in need are passively waiting for help; it should be replaced by a model of sharing

---

[15] See, for example, Megan Brenan, "US Catholics' Faith in Clergy is Shaken," *Gallup*, January 11, 2019, https://news.gallup.com/poll/245858/catholics-faith -clergy-shaken.aspx.

life together and building relationships rooted in mutual respect, tender mercy, and robust co-responsibility. Gutiérrez reminds us that compassion and solidarity should not lead to some becoming the "voice of the voiceless," as this is another form of paternalism. Rather, in a spirit of friendship, the problems others face become our own. We do not try to fix them but work so that others can be "an agent of one's own history . . . [as] an expression of freedom and dignity."[16]

3. Clergy sexual abuse and its concealment is not a problem that will fade into the past, and it is not something church leaders can "wait out" or otherwise avoid. Time alone will not heal wounds caused by such grave betrayal; neither will healing result from isolated statements of remorse or by episodes of repentance. St. Paul reminds us that discipleship orbits around the gift and task of living as Christ's ambassadors of reconciliation (2 Cor 5:18-20). Reconciliation—through honest truth-telling, authentic expressions of sorrow, and taking steps toward atonement—must be integrated into the lifeblood of every Catholic community. It should be made physically visible through religious art, statues, or tapestries; it ought to inform liturgical ministry through ritual and symbol; it should invite the entire faith community—as a broken Body of Christ—to take part in healing together in and *as* a community. In our hyper-individualistic social context, we often think of healing as a personal commitment, the result of medicine and therapy. But, as those who work with the traumatized know firsthand, "it is the relationship that heals."[17] It is only by re-membering the Body of Christ with tenderness and trustworthiness that wounds can begin to heal and that scars will testify to our courage, compassion, and solidarity.

Building a church to be more like a field hospital is just the first step in attending to the wounds caused by clergy sexual abuse and its concealment. It is the floor, not the ceiling. In the face of so many abuses of power, such widespread shame and secrecy, and ample

---

[16] Gutiérrez, "Option for the Poor Arises from Faith in Christ," 325.

[17] Gregory Boyle, *The Whole Language: The Power of Extravagant Tenderness* (New York: Avid Reader, 2021), 89.

reason for distrust and despair, the church needs a new model of power-sharing to ensure the respect, agency, and right relationships where all members of the church can flourish in the fullness of life Jesus promised (John 10:10). Mending the broken Body of Christ is a responsibility on all our shoulders. When we listen to survivors of clergy sexual abuse and get a fuller picture of the truth, we can pray and reflect, discuss and deliberate, and ultimately "dream together" for a "rebirth" of a church that is a safe and grace-filled place for all.[18]

[18] Pope Francis, *Fratelli Tutti* (Vatican City: Libreria Editrice Vaticana, October 3, 2020), 8.

Part Two

**Healing—
Witnessing to the Lives of Survivors**

6

The Catholic Sexual Abuse Crisis and the Synodal Church:
Insights from the Sixth Commandment

Anselma Dolcich-Ashley

For many contemporary American Catholics, the sexual abuse crisis "began" with the *Boston Globe* Spotlight investigation on January 6, 2002.[1] While we now know that that sexual predators and enablers among clergy have been more widespread than previously understood, a crisis emerged this early day of 2002 because it brought into everyday awareness a severe truth that could no longer be avoided, neither by clergy nor by laity. The US Catholic bishops, as the church's official governors, were, of course, at the center of attention. Episcopal responses in this period showed two features: one, a defense of a kind of ecclesiology—an understanding of the church—either centered on the clergy or symbolized by a top-down triangle with clergy at the top.[2]

---

[1] See The Investigative Staff of *The Boston Globe, Betrayal: The Crisis in the Catholic Church* (New York: Back Bay Books, 2003).

[2] A fuller discussion of bishops' statements can be found in Anselma Dolcich-Ashley, *Precept, Rights and Ecclesial Governance: A Moral-Theological Analysis of the Catholic Sexual Abuse Crisis in the U.S.* (PhD diss., University of Notre Dame, 2011). For a sampling of such statements, see Bernard Cardinal Law, "Action to Address Clergy Sexual Abuse of Minors," *Origins* 31, no. 34 (February 7, 2002); Anthony Cardinal Bevilaqua, "Restoring Trust: Philadelphia Sexual Abuse of Minors Policy," *Origins* 31, no. 39 (March 14, 2002); Bishop Wilton Gregory, "The Renewed Focus on

Indeed, "defensive" is an apt description of the rhetorical posture of many statements, which also invoke inculpable ignorance, highlight the majority of "good priests," emphasize perpetrators as a small minority, and offer exculpatory statements that sound like apologies but sidestep concrete responsibility, including bishops knowingly reassigning—rather than removing—perpetrators. The other characteristic was identifying the actions of abuser-priests according to the strict legal mandates of the Code of Canon Law, rather than the broad moral wisdom of the sixth commandment as a precept of justice. Definition of the problem only as discrete actions of abuse by priests (not betrayal and trauma inflicted horribly on survivors, and indirectly on congregations) frames early attempts at resolving the crisis.

Almost no official responses reflected a comprehensive understanding of the moral theology of the sixth of the Ten Commandments: "You shall not commit adultery" (Exod 20:14). Indeed, laity (survivors, parents) showed a better comprehension of the demands of justice of the sixth commandment in implicitly and explicitly reacting to abuses not only as severely harmful acts but also as violations of justice and gross disturbances of the order of justice in the church. Also, American civil laws and criminal codes that order the civil community—in a country upholding separation of church and state— arguably were more closely aligned to the sixth commandment's demands of justice. Why did the Catholic Church, the enduring community that, of all institutions, ought to have understood and lived by its own moral commandments, fail survivors so spectacularly? How might the abuse crisis, for all its tragedy, lead to recognizable positive changes in the communal life of Catholics and impact the direction of a synodal church?

Clergy Abuse of Minors" and "Margin Notes," *Origins* 31, no. 37 (February 28, 2002). For examples of exculpatory statements, see Bishop William Franklin, "Davenport Diocese Files for Bankruptcy," *Origins* 36, no. 20 (October 26, 2006); and Archbishop Daniel Pilarczyk, "What Were the Bishops Thinking?," *Origins* 33, no. 42 (April 1, 2004). Interestingly, in a gesture that showed potential for healing and reform, the president of the United States Conference of Catholic Bishops (USCCB) modeled his presidential address on the sacrament of reconciliation and penance at the June 2002 bishops' meeting; see Bishop Wilton Gregory, "Presidential Address Opening Dallas Meeting of US Bishops," *Origins* 32, no. 7 (June 27, 2002).

Crime to Crisis

Regarding clergy, canon 1395 of the Code of Canon Law defines a delict against the sixth commandment as a discrete action whereby a priest has broken his vow of celibacy in committing sexual acts outside of marriage. A new addition to this part of the Code of Canon Law would not be enacted until December 8, 2021. The precision of the Catholic Church's legal code, in section 2 of canon 1395, describes a delict (offense) against the sixth commandment (forbidding adultery) by clerics who engage in sexual acts with minors. The canon appropriately focuses on the clerical offender, his action, and his intention (including "force or threats publicly or with a minor"). So prescribed, the canon would have provided a sound starting point for addressing the exploding crisis of 2002, especially given the emergent understanding of how clerics used "force." In revelatory cases, and enormous cause for horror in Catholic communities nationwide, investigators noted how perpetrators often made friendly overtures to potential victims, grooming them for weeks or months so that the eventual, overtly sexual act was perpetrated on victims manipulated to keep quiet and allow the acts to continue.[3] Unfortunately, and arguably because of the canon's focus on the perpetrator's discrete action, authorities began to respond in ways that concentrated on priest-perpetrators (and weeding them out), rather than on survivors and on the order of justice in the church (including bishops who allowed "problem priests" to persist in ministry).

Defining the emerging scandal in terms of canon 1395 §2 glaringly overlooks the direct victims and the original and ongoing trauma sustained by these survivors. It overlooks the horror experienced by their families, loved ones, and communities, shaken by abuse revelations. By itself, the canon does not address the simultaneous crisis of credibility in the ordained now confronting Catholics with eyes open to the problem. It is silent regarding the connection between the overwhelming social-ecclesial power of ordained clergy relative to laity (especially the vulnerable) in the context of the worshiping community. By keeping the crisis defined within the contours of clerical law-breaking, the bishops failed to make use of traditional

---

[3] See Investigative Staff of *The Boston Globe*, *Betrayal*, which uncovered many cases of such strategies.

categories within moral theology that would have contributed to a more comprehensive and accurate understanding of what was going on. It's not that the bishops were unaware of victims; rather, statements focus largely on the act of sexual molesting and the agents (priests) of that act and how to handle them—rather than on helping those who were harmed (either directly or indirectly), or on the gross abuse of power accompanying such actions, enabled by ecclesial governance structures lacking transparency and accountability. What canon law expresses in a bland-sounding statement is a crime causing trauma at the time of the discrete action, throughout the survivor's life, and within the community throughout time.

The crucial point at which the crime of sexual abuse became a crisis can be visualized in those moments of courageous encounter when (mostly) laypeople—survivors and their advocates—fearing condemnation, rejected the orders or pleas from their bishop not to do anything about known clerical abuse and went to their local prosecutor, attorney, police, or investigative journalist. Unable to trust that their own church personnel would take the right steps toward justice, survivors, parents, and advocates essentially claimed their own authority in this matter against the directives or policies of their bishop.

What is the point of governing authority? This somewhat bland philosophical question is decisive at this moment of the crisis. In a basic and preliminary understanding, governing authority exists to promote the flourishing of any group of people to their proper end. In the church, flourishing is the participation of the individual in salvation offered by God through the sacraments and the ecclesial community. Necessarily, the personal safety and protection of the individuals in the church must be maintained so they may seek the fullness of Christian life and expression of baptismal membership. A chief responsibility of anyone in a position of governing authority (whether parents or bishops) is protection of those properly under their care. Likewise, adult survivors who claim personal authority to seek justice for the protection of their own bodies and minds are themselves the chief authority in that matter. Taking a theological turn, we can see governing authority in even richer contours. We can identify parents and adult survivors who themselves have been baptized priest, prophet, and king and who are themselves the proper governing authorities for their own families and their human dignity, exercising their baptismal charisms (cf. *Lumen Gentium* 32, 37, 41) in challenge to the ordained charism of governance on the part of the bishop. Indeed, these survivors and advocates can be considered the true heroes in this enormous tragedy. Only a narrow view would see a zero-sum game here, an unresolvable conflict of baptismal authority of the laity against the ordained authority of the bishop. A key feature of a properly *synodal* church is perceived conflicts leading to greater growth by allowing the full exercise of all charisms, for the purpose of greater depth and fullness of relationship and community. In these early phases of the crisis, the laity calling for justice—however painful that was to official church authorities, whether from embarrassment of the church's failures or from financial losses due to court settlements—were leading by showing the bishops that their exercise of the ordained charism of governance needed to evolve toward an ever-greater expression of justice.

Crisis to Apocalypse

"Apocalypse" often conjures images of catastrophe, but theologically it means a revealing of something unknown or of something we formerly could not understand clearly and now can. In 2002, the crisis became an apocalypse when children and adults revealed themselves to us as survivors of clerical sexual assault and abuse. The words of St. Paul would prove heartrending: "The creation waits with eager longing for the revealing of the children of God" (Rom 8:19).

Let us begin with the revelation of the suffering itself by survivors. Their courage in coming forth was the light shining onto the woefully insufficient church response; in their persons they revealed the sin of priest-perpetrators and massive shortcomings in the exercise of authority by church leaders. When the stories became so numerous, the investigations so far-reaching, when attorneys general from municipalities up to the state level convened grand juries—Catholics could not avoid seeing sin in the church and their pastors and bishops unworthy of trust. The revelations of survivors also shone a light onto the nature of sexual abuse in the church, for example, that it is more terrible and widespread than we think, can happen to anyone, and is a wound that survivors will carry with them their entire lives.

Second, apocalypse also means the revealing of things that *are* known but that we didn't want to think about or deal with or that we thought unimportant. In this regard, the baptism of all Catholics as priest, prophet, and king came to the fore. We already knew that parents and guardians are the first and most important authorities and teachers of the faith to the young, but at a crucial time, parents and survivors recognized their God-given baptismal authority within their own families, which gave them the right to challenge the ordained authority of bishops in the handling of abuse cases. Survivors and parents revealed a much better grasp of the sixth commandment of the Decalogue (against adultery) as a precept of justice. They intuitively and actively understood its moral import, and because of love and a concern for justice—not necessarily expertise in canon law or theology—they accepted responsibility for protecting their children or themselves (in the case of adult survivors).

Third, the crisis revealed that the sixth commandment was poorly understood by church authorities, even though they comprehend the Ten Commandments and its associated canons very well. Indeed, there can exist confusion as to what the crisis really is all about, when a narrow focus on the small minority of priest-abusers obfuscates broader concerns of justice and reconciliation in the church.

The Abuse Crisis and the Sixth Commandment

Exodus 20:14 is straightforward: "You shall not commit adultery." Seen as only these words describing a limited action, disconnected from its broader moral context, the sixth commandment may seem restricted to those who directly broke the rule (the priest-abusers). The complete moral picture, however, must include some account of the effect of sexual abuse on victims, on relationships between clergy and laypeople, and indeed on the common good of church and society. How does the rule stated in Exodus 20:14 address these concerns?

The Catholic moral-theological tradition explores the meaning of the sixth's moral wisdom. According to Thomas Aquinas, all ten commandments are understood as precepts of natural law, as well as moral norms (rules) constituting this divine revelation, as well as "precepts of a particular virtue, namely, justice. . . . The precepts of the second table [of the Decalogue] contain the order of justice to be observed among men, that nothing undue be done to anyone, and that each one be given his due."[4] Like its companion precepts of the

---

[4] Thomas Aquinas, *Summa Theologiae*, I–II, q. 100, a. 8.

second table of the Decalogue, prohibiting adultery expresses a fundamental moral norm of the cardinal virtue of justice for people, who by their very nature live and interact in social contexts. The commandment concerns itself not simply with an individual perpetrator but also with the state of justice within a social context in matters of sexuality, the use of the body, and whether injustices are being perpetrated and victims harmed through the expression of body and sexuality. Aquinas felt that there are specific behaviors, such as refraining from adultery, that express the fundamental precept, because adultery is both a form of harm and a violation of justice in the community. In adultery, the innocent are hurt in actions that also breach sexual boundaries. Because it prohibits harm, the sixth commandment calls attention to stopping potential perpetrators before they do the act that violates the commandment, but, by its own internal logic, prohibiting harm also promotes or upholds the protection of those who would be harmed by prohibited actions.

In this early phase, the sexual abuse crisis resulted in part from an insufficient grasp of the breadth of harms caused by breach of this prohibition. When the crisis is defined as a problem of abuser-priests alone, the remedy becomes a rapid response to allegations and quick removal of these so-called "problem priests." But when the sixth is seen through the lens of its moral grounding in natural and divine law and the cardinal virtue of justice, a far more serious view obtains. The abuse of justice concerns the violation of the humanity and human dignity of thousands of direct victims. Simultaneously—not as a ripple effect, but logically by the abusive action—communally understood sexual boundaries grounded in the sacrament of orders also became unpredictable. Finally, the relational boundaries and governing structures necessary to protect individuals and support a functioning community became unreliable. Vulnerable laity, met with stonewalling or silence or assurances that authorities would fix the matter, began to see that such responses accomplished little to redress harms, heal survivors, and restore a state of justice.

A Sacred Order and Moral Theology

Fundamental moral norms hold deep moral wisdom that provides comprehensive guidance, which can continue to serve us as the sexual abuse crisis unfolds. While I focused here on misunderstandings and mishandlings in 2002 on the part of church authorities, it later became clear that the entire church, the people of God, ought to respond to the crisis and the survivors with a renewed understanding of the demands of the sixth commandment. In grasping this commandment from God both as a rule for personal behavior and as a precept of justice, all the baptized can recognize that the sexual abuse crisis is not over and can undertake action showing that survivors are *not* forgotten, such as welcoming, listening to, and helping to heal survivors—which is their due. All Catholics can help to make necessary changes in structures of church governance.

Pope Francis, in opening the Synod on Synodality in October 2021, identified three synodal themes of communion, participation, and mission, but he highlighted participation because "the words 'communion' and 'mission' can risk remaining somewhat abstract unless we cultivate an ecclesial praxis that expresses the concreteness of synodality at every step . . . encouraging real involvement on the part of each and all."[5] The laity who initially approached and challenged their pastors and bishops regarding the emerging crisis were already demonstrating the kind of participation Francis calls for. But one of the problems contributing to the crisis is that such participation essentially became blocked by appeals to the hierarchical structure of church governance that made it possible for the church's pastors and governors to keep the laity at a distance, hide the full truth, and in some cases rebuff them.

But in the fundamental meaning of hierarchy, we can reimagine how church governance and communities might evolve toward ever greater participation on the part of all the baptized. For the word "hierarchy" does not mean—as it often connotes in English—"higher-archy" (with the laity as "lower-archy"). Rather, "hierarchy" simply translates from the Greek as sacred ("hier") order ("arche"). As a sacred order, the Catholic Church will always have *ordained* governors (the clergy), but it will also always have *baptized* governors serving in their authentic roles, such as those parents and survivors who claimed parental or personal authority in pursuing justice, challenging the "higher-archy."

---

[5] Pope Francis, "Address of His Holiness Pope Francis for the Opening of the Synod," October 9, 2021, https://www.vatican.va/content/francesco/en/speeches/2021/october/documents/20211009-apertura-camminosinodale.html.

To respond to the sexual abuse crisis, a true hierarchy or holy order would look more like a circle than a top-down triangle; it would develop a governance model that enables justice and places itself at the service of those it has wounded. Simultaneously, all the baptized would reflect and act on the comprehensive import of the church's moral tradition, participating actively to promote ever greater communion and mission.

7

Sacramental Clericalism:
Enabler of Abuse, Obstacle to Healing

Bruce T. Morrill, SJ

Introduction

Human processes of healing require astute analysis or diagnosis of the scope, depth, and contributing factors of the affliction. This is true both of individuals and of social bodies and institutions such as communities or churches. Since all manner of sicknesses, individual and collective, have cultural and societal causes as well as physical ones, symbol and ritual (roles, titles, attire, protocols, ceremonies) are integral to understanding and healing any deficit of health. In Roman Catholicism's worldwide disaster of clergy sexual abuse and hierarchical cover-ups, the spiritual and moral authority afforded priests and bishops has figured significantly, if not fundamentally, in the injury, outrage, and demoralization experienced among the faithful and wider population.

The church's sacramental-liturgical life, as both officially and popularly understood and practiced, contains the most powerful symbols melding the spiritual and moral authority of the ordained. The purpose of this chapter is to identify and analyze elements of the church's liturgical doctrine and regulations, particularly those pertaining to the Eucharist and holy orders, to understand how these aided and abetted the mindset and behaviors of the clergy-perpetrators and episcopal enablers as well as the victims and wider membership. My thesis is that a *false sacrality* in sacramental rites significantly contributes to a ruinous clericalism, active among the ordained yet with much lay cooperation. The conclusion will propose principles from the tradition that might help, going forward.

Abusive Sacredness: Individual and Systemic Accounts

The unfolding of the clergy sexual abuse crisis in 2002, activated then chronicled by the *Boston Globe*, shed stark light on the clericalism that has so persistently afflicted Roman Catholicism. Victims' typical explanation for why they concealed the abuse was the absolute, even godlike, power the laity afforded the priesthood ("We were taught the priest is Christ here on earth"). Distressing to read were not a few victims' testimonies to the beating they could expect not only from their fathers but even from their mothers should they have dared describe what the priest had done to them (for altar boys, typically in the sacristy before or after Mass). Even before the crisis broke open, the Boston press had given occasional attention to a handful of protesters (sometimes a single man), victims of clergy assault, standing in front of the cathedral on Sunday mornings. While most of the faithful arriving for Mass skirted the protesters, some would sneer their disapproval, rebuking perceived disrespect for the church or admonishing the sufferers to keep their problems to themselves.

Those behavioral patterns, on the part of clerics and laity, manifest the disastrous dark side to the nearly divine status the hierarchy came to expect from a, to date, largely uncritical-to-indifferent laity. Clericalism not only perpetuates a religious division of labor that cuts off the overwhelming majority of believers from claiming a more active responsibility for the praxis of the faith, including the liturgy. It also reinforces attribution of magical or otherworldly power to the ordained ministers of the gospel that, in the end, distances those in need from the genuine paradoxical power that is the gospel's uniquely divine gift.

The 2018 Pennsylvania grand jury report released fresh evidence of three hundred priests exploiting their sacred status, along with an array of sacramental symbols, in abusing some one thousand victims over the course of seventy years. Individuals provided distressing accounts of priests manipulating victims by explicitly associating various of their sexual actions with elements of sacramental rites, notably the Body and Blood of the eucharistic species, exploiting the official sacramental symbolism of the priest's ordained hands, or giving the child or youth such devotional objects (sacramentals) as rosaries, medals, etc. In this particular version of abusers holding victims to secrecy, some priests would distort the traditional sacramental concept of sacred mystery as rationale for the pastoral incongruence of the immoral violence and enforced silence.

Catholics' images of God and Jesus have widely functioned in mutual reinforcement with their understanding of the priest and the sacraments he dispenses (I use that verb advisedly). We must ask ourselves: What god inspires such dread in people as to incite them to beat their children?[1] What god expects church hierarchs to endanger children and youth in order to defend the reputation of the institution and its clerical caste? What god are people worshiping when they silence and ostracize fellow believers who muster the courage to reveal their personal violation? These questions stand alongside the observation that so many clergy and laity were content to keep on celebrating the Mass and other sacraments, to worship liturgically the God of biblical tradition, even as they worshiped other gods in their practical behavior. This gap between the church's sacramental and ethical actions is, of course, nothing new, let alone unique to the current crisis. The liturgical-ethical gap is a recurrent prophetic concern that has arisen over and again since the earliest generations of the church.[2] Still, particular historical moments require perceptive attention to factors contributing to instances or patterns of incongruity between sacramental ritual symbolism and individual moral or systemic ethical behavior—all the more when that behavior is objectively evil, illegally violent, and inherently scandalous.

The relentless investigative reporting the *Boston Globe* published throughout 2002 effected Catholics' and the wider population's realization of the global scope of the clerical abuse of power, precipitating

---

[1] Here I follow the example of biblical scholar–theologian N. T. Wright by using the lowercase "god" when referring to socio-cultural (including religious) idols. See my *Divine Worship and Human Healing: Liturgical Theology at the Margins of Life and Death* (Collegeville, MN: Liturgical Press, 2009), 34–35.

[2] See, among others, Gordon W. Lathrop, *Holy Ground: A Liturgical Cosmology* (Minneapolis: Fortress Press, 2003), 182–88; and Bruce T. Morrill, *Practical Sacramental Theology: At the Intersection of Liturgy and Ethics* (Eugene, OR: Cascade Books, 2021), 43–44, 97–100, 160–61.

an irreversible crisis.[3] Such potential public exposure was undoubtedly the primary motivation for bishops' decades-long practices of furtively moving pedophile and other abusive priests from one pastoral assignment to another. Reputation is a most fundamental source of power for both individuals (the right to one's "good name") and institutions. In the years shortly before and after 2002, Vatican offices issued a couple of disciplinary documents very much concerned about the status of ordained ministers, notably invoking terminology of abuse. The matters in question, however, were exclusively within the practice of the church's sacramental rites, with the dicasteries expounding how the very nature and function of the priesthood was in peril. Brief analysis of these instructions demonstrates an urgent concern that the sacredness of the ordained receive its proper due, an exaggerated perspective that I argue imbues a false sacrality in the rites and ministerial priesthood that the current crisis exposes.

Contemporary Vatican Instructions on Abuses in the Sacred Liturgy

With pontifical approval in late 1997, eight Vatican offices jointly issued the instruction, "Some Questions Regarding Collaboration of Nonordained Faithful in Priests' Sacred Ministry." The prefects laid out a meticulous distinction between "the nature and mission of sacred ministry and the vocation and secular character of the lay faithful," the blurring of which was causing "true ecclesial communion [to] be damaged."[4] Both the document and an accompanying "Explanatory Note" state that the instruction "is meant to encourage vocations," by which is meant the priesthood or clerical state, which have become less attractive due to ministerial practices misrepresenting the "fundamental equality in difference" between ordained and lay. Great dan-

---

[3] It remains important to note that some fifteen years earlier courageous investigative journalism by Jason Berry and the staff of the *National Catholic Reporter* had exposed horrific clerical sex abuse and diocesan concealment in Louisiana and then elsewhere in the United States. The national news media, however, ignored the issue, with major outlets rejecting Berry's pitches for in-depth articles.

[4] "Some Questions Regarding Collaboration of Nonordained Faithful in Priests' Sacred Ministry," *Origins* 27, no. 24 (November 27, 1997): 398–410; here, 399–400.

ger to the very sacramental nature of the church comes from ignorance of the "ontological configuration" of holy orders, thereby reducing sacred ministry merely to functions. When laity perform extraordinary ministry in the liturgy "it has a different meaning," such that, "viewing things otherwise risks interpreting service in the church as the exercise of power."[5] But therein lies the rub: how can practicing rites and ministries, of any kind, not be exercises of power?

For centuries the church has defined power in the execution of sacramental rites as residing in office (*officium*), not in the particular gifts (*munera*) a person might possess and fittingly offer in service to the life of the church. The 1997 instruction seeks through its precision in ministerial terminology to protect against an implied creeping from *munera* to *officia*, an "undue aspiration to the ordained ministry" comprising an "ambiguous 'advancement of the laity.' "[6] The power of symbol, in the form of ministerial titles, is then delimited: No "nonordained" person—note the negative definition of the vast majority of the baptized people of God—is to have such titles as *"pastor, chaplain, coordinator, moderator,* or other such similar titles" that would "confuse their role" with bishops or priests. Such "disciplinary irregularity in pastoral practice," improper practices that have become "widespread," comprise cases of *abuse*.

The language of abuse (*abusus*) will figure prominently in a subsequent Vatican disciplinary document, issued not long after 2002. For this 1997 instruction, abuse basically amounts to laypeople attempting power grabs. Yet, the document early on extols the "servant nature of the ministerial priesthood,"[7] thereby begging the question of whether or how people aspiring to greater servanthood abuse the church in its *communio*, its people and mission. That, however, admittedly is not the instruction's intent on this point; rather, emphasizing priests and bishops as (uniquely) servants by nature would seem the purpose of countering pervasive attitudes and practices, by clergy and laity alike, that inordinately privilege the ordained. Even such a laudable purpose, however, becomes fraught with dangerous ambiguity when related to the dynamics involved in clergy sexual abuse. The oft repeated "We were taught the priest is Christ here on earth"

---

[5] "Some Questions," 409.

[6] "Some Questions," 402–4.

[7] "Some Questions," 400–401.

clearly amounts to idolatrous exaltation. Still, an emphasis on Christ the servant, instructing his disciples at the Last Supper (which the church identifies as the institution of the priesthood) to be servants among each other, unfortunately also is susceptible to an abusive cleric's manipulations. The traumatized victim might succumb to notions that the priest is rendering an act of service, even privileging the victim by his actions, not least because of the hierarchy's interpretation of the eucharistic mystery predominantly in terms of the material elements changed into Christ's Body and Blood, elevated in the priest's sacred hands.

On Holy Thursday 2003, Pope John Paul II published the encyclical On the Eucharist in Its Relationship to the Church (*Ecclesia de Eucharistia*), enlisting twentieth-century encyclicals, among other sources of Scripture and tradition, to detail how the "Church draws her life from the Eucharist."[8] What immediately becomes evident in the initial article flowing from that straightforward thesis is how tightly the pontiff identifies the Eucharist with the elements on the altar and the action of the priest, with no mention of Christ's presence in the active assembly of the baptized and the proclamation of the Word of God. Rather than develop that multifold presence of Christ in the liturgy, as taught by the Second Vatican Council in *Sacrosanctum Concilium* 7, John Paul quotes from the council's Decree on the Priesthood (*Presbyterorum Ordinis*):

> "For the most holy Eucharist contains the Church's entire spiritual wealth: Christ himself, our passover and living bread. Through his own flesh, now made living and life-giving by the Holy Spirit, he offers life to men." Consequently, the gaze of the Church is constantly turned to her Lord, present in the Sacrament of the Altar, in which she discovers the full manifestation of his boundless love. (EE 1, quoting from PO 5)

The eucharistic piety of the faithful is one of gazing at the consecrated elements, especially the host, as indeed later in the document the pope calls for a global renewal in the adoration of the Blessed Sacrament outside of Mass. While touching on that ritual in the introduc-

---

[8] Pope John Paul II, *Ecclesia de Eucharistia*: Encyclical Letter on the Eucharist in Its Relationship to the Church (Vatican City: Libreria Editrice Vaticana, April 17, 2003), 1.

tion, the pope devotes greater attention to the ministry of the priest "who says [the words of consecration] with the power coming to him from Christ in the Upper Room" (EE 5).

The document continuously exhorts priests and people to "profound amazement and gratitude" for the Blessed Sacrament. Four largely doctrinal chapters lead to a fifth that takes a disciplinary turn toward execution of the liturgy proper to the sacrament's dignity. John Paul laments unauthorized liberties being taken with the Order of Mass, identifying them as "*abuses* which have been a source of suffering to many" (EE 52, italics in original). He concludes the chapter with the promise of "a more specific document, including prescriptions of a juridical nature" to correct misguided ritual adaptations that "undervalue the mystery entrusted to our hands" (EE 52).

Precisely one year later, Holy Thursday 2004, the Congregation for Divine Worship and the Discipline of the Sacraments issued the disciplinary document *Redemptionis Sacramentum*, comprised of 186 articles detailing several dozen *abuses* (abuses, grave matters, irregularities, and *graviora delicta*) to be reprobated or remedied. The language of the document is severe, if not in places alarmist, with terminology of abusing, corrupting, distorting, and danger. With its 295 endnotes it amounts to a veritable compendium of canon and liturgical law for the Mass of the Roman Rite. Protection of the ordained priesthood and the ontology of the Blessed Sacrament are pervasive, interdependent concerns, just as Pope John Paul taught in his encyclical. This document, however, addresses more closely how the laity, through the "common priesthood" bestowed in baptism, "differ in essence and not only in degree" from the "hierarchical Priesthood," thereby substantiating the "danger" in obscuring the lay-cleric distinction (RS 36, 42).

The entire second chapter, having explicated how all the church participate in the one priesthood of Christ, then describing the key lay ministries in service to the liturgy, concludes with a paragraph lauding "the noble custom by which boys and youths, customarily called servers, provide service at the altar" (RS 47).[9] Elaboration ensues on how such service has historically resulted in a multitude of priestly ordinations. Serving the Mass derives from the instituted

---

[9] The paragraph closes by noting that diocesan bishops may allow female altar servers.

ministry of acolyte, as does "the assistance of extraordinary ministers," notably for distribution of Holy Communion, the carefully limited use and execution of which "must not be an occasion for disfiguring the very ministry of Priests" (RS 152). To this reader, the metaphor of disfigurement brings to mind the literal sense, insofar as the admission to seminary formation and eventual ordination of any man with a severe physical debility requires Vatican approval. The regular candidate for ordination should have bodily integrity, that is, not be missing any finger or limb and have full use of all such. In *Redemptionis Sacramentum*, one finds that the suitability of eucharistic hosts depends on the *integrity* of the people who produce them, for introduction of any substances other than pure wheat constitutes "a grave abuse" (RS 48). The integrity, purity, and perfection of the host aligns with those same qualities in the priest who (in addition to the aforementioned physical criteria) must not *corrupt* or *distort* the eucharistic celebration by lack of reverence or modifications in texts or gestures (RS 31). The consecrated host, which the priest elevates with his sacred hands, must have purity of substance and the integrity of perfectly round shape; a priest's breaking the host at consecration constitutes an abuse (RS 55).

Conclusion: Healing through Liturgy Depends on Healing the Rites and Their Ministry

There is altogether an ideology of purity and perfection in the practical Roman theology of sacrament and holy orders that, in light of the pernicious culture of clericalism (Pope Francis's relentless concern), prompts me to counter that the more urgent danger lies in such an excessive equation of sanctity (sacrality) with ritual and corporeal perfection and purity. A counterargument might be that steady emphasis on these mirroring qualities of purity in priest and sacrament may help clerics to maintain lives of strict sexual continence and proper related behaviors. I would counter, however, that the possibility can only be realized if the given man lives a sufficient integration of psychosexual maturity, capacity for both interpersonal and social relationships, and sufficient ability to admit personal lacks in knowledge and wisdom. Integrity thereby entails not static symbolic or physical characteristics but, rather, a dynamic, living process, one that bishops, in fact, have variably been seeking to implement in seminary and ongoing priestly formation programs.

I question, nonetheless, whether the isolated concerns for the status of the priesthood and the handling of ritual objects and gestures in recent Vatican instructions on liturgy and ministry fail in some respects to reflect and nurture the personal-relational characteristics the church itself now recognizes as essential for healthy, nonabusive priests and bishops. When first reading *Redemptionis Sacramentum*, issued at the very time the worldwide clergy sexual abuse crisis was unfolding, I was stunned by the tone-deafness of a major ecclesial document employing the rhetoric of abuse. Yes, the Latin terminology is technically accurate within the isolated realm of ecclesial, juridical ritual discipline, but that only supports my point: The priority in this era, rather, needs to be *pastoral* (SC 11), even to the point of modifying certain priorities and objectives pertaining to priests in the liturgy. Space limitations allow me but one example.

The chapter on Holy Communion instructs: "The Priest celebrant or concelebrant is never to wait until the people's Communion is concluded before receiving Communion himself" (RS 97). Why this clerical priority? It certainly symbolizes the differentiated nature of the ordained priesthood from the common priesthood of the laity, but it does so in a way that asserts privilege and priority of priests over the laity. Is there not a pastoral-liturgical failure, if not internal contradiction, in ritualizing the distinction in this case by means of sequential priority? John Paul's encyclical duly teaches how the Eucharist is both sacrifice (oblation) and meal (sacred banquet). Within the entire sacramental action, Holy Communion functions squarely in the meal dimension, that is, in the sharing (giving and receiving) of food and drink. What sort of host helps himself first to the food and drink in front of an entire table party silently watching him consume his portions before they are served? This human failure in table manners is augmented by a theological contradiction: *Redemptionis Sacramentum*'s first chapter asserts the priest-celebrant's functioning *in persona Christi* while, as we saw earlier, the 1997 disciplinary instruction in doing the same highlighted "the servant nature of the ministerial priesthood."[10] Yet, the rigorously prescribed order for

---

[10] "Some Questions," 400–401.

receiving Holy Communion symbolizes neither theological value but rather, in practice and popular perception, the superiority of clergy over laity.

My observations and analysis of just that one element of the eucharistic liturgy may seem either narrow or excessive,[11] but I would counter that ritual repetition over time has profound symbolic impact on people's beliefs, attitudes, and wider practices. This surely is the rationale driving the 1997 and 2004 Vatican instructions reviewed above. My question is whether the framework and types of abuses over which those documents obsess miss the mark, and fail to align with attention to factors contributing to the clerical sexual abuse and its hierarchical cover-up. With this entire chapter, not least due to its brevity, having been of an exploratory nature, my concluding proposal is likewise only probative, suggestive.

The burden of my argument has been to identify a false sacrality endemic to the clericalism widely practiced among the ordained, supported or at least tolerated by the laity, and sustained by certain theological, symbolic priorities in the church's instructions on the rites and their ministries. The latter, to my reading and observation, widely miss the mark insofar as their proper target, mandated by Vatican II's constitutions on the liturgy and the church, is the restoration and advancement of the sacramental nature of the entire people of God, the Body of Christ.

The theological basis for that restoration and renewal the Constitution on the Sacred Liturgy identifies as the *paschal mystery* (SC 5–10), the divine wisdom (so contrary to that of the world) revealed in Christ Jesus's person, his mission of teaching and healing, his passion and death, and glorification in his resurrection, ascension, and sending of the Holy Spirit into the members and mission of the church. The key to this ancient biblical and traditional notion is that the divine mystery is God's active, ongoing work of salvation for all, placing the church itself, its rites, and its ordered ministries all in proper perspective as means to the ultimate end: God's glorification in the salvation of humanity (indeed, of all creation). As with our savior, so for us who participate in his life by the power of the Spirit, it is our

---

[11] A full argument for and elaboration on an alternative approach, working closely with the laudable elements of the Communion Rite already in the Missal, would require a further essay.

entire lives that comprise the worship of God (see Rom 12:1). Whereas for him this is by his unique nature, for us the sacramental rites generate the graces for salvation we need so as to live the priestly, prophetic, and servant mission that together is ours, his ecclesial body, in and for the world (see 1 Pet 2:4-5, 9-12).

The sacrality genuine and fitting to our celebration of the rites is found in the confluence of the symbols and images proclaimed in the biblical word, the sound characteristics of good human ritualizing (such that grace works through nature) and, yes, the differentiated roles of various ministers and all the assembled baptized in the liturgy. The reformed rites of the church are replete with good words, symbols, gestures, and instructions generative of sacred liturgical experiences worthy of a living tradition, empowering gospel virtues in their participants. The offices of the Vatican are duly concerned that the actual celebrations of rites be executed so as to realize that potential. Not surprisingly, ever since the eruption of the clergy sexual abuse crisis calls for healing have sounded from all quarters, both hierarchical and lay, with liturgical events regularly cited as a crucial means. But in the end, liturgy cannot help heal the ecclesial body, together and in particular members, if it is itself afflicted with pastoral-theological contradictions in symbolism. Amid an ecclesial crisis the council could not foresee, its mandate for promotion and reform of the rites (SC 3) would seem to require revised criteria integrating word, sacrament, and ethics (the lived faith in church and world), in service to the liturgy's fundamental pastoral purpose.

8

Take Away the Stone:
Sacramental Life and the Challenges of Healing Sexual Abuse

Kimberly Hope Belcher

All too often we put off constructing prayer services and rituals responding to the sexual abuse crisis because we are afraid of getting it wrong, but this is akin to not reaching out to people suffering grief because we are afraid of saying the wrong thing.[1] When we are living in something as messy as the ongoing revelation of the Catholic sexual abuse crisis, our liturgies are going to be messy. It is by engaging in the challenging and troubling process of praying together that we will eventually be able to recognize the ways that God is among us even when we experience trauma, crisis, and division.

We can become perfectionists about liturgy if we think it is our job to keep it holy. The good news of Catholic sacramental theology is that God alone has the power to make holy. The sacraments and the liturgies and rituals that are grounded in our baptismal and eucharistic identity bring that holiness right into the mud of our world, but the results are not always immediate and obvious. When the mud is as muddy as our church is in the wake of the revelations of sexual abuse, we will have to begin working together by doing rituals wrong, so that we learn how to do them right.

[1] Outlines for the prayer services that were used at the conference in 2022, as well as another example that also exemplifies the suggestions in this chapter, can be found in the Appendixes.

Recovery from damage as profound as the sexual abuse crisis is a lengthy process of learning and working. To help us think about this process, I'm going to use the narrative of Lazarus in John 11–12. We are perhaps used to thinking of the healing in this narrative as an instantaneous resuscitation of Lazarus, an instance of Jesus's immense divine power, but the story actually reflects an extended process that includes gradual revelation and reversal of damage as well as the healing of the community around Lazarus. Like the story of Lazarus, we might be tempted to imagine recovery from the Catholic sexual abuse crisis as a narrative with one main turning point, to be accomplished by harm reduction, reparation, or simple grace. Instead, the process is bound to be difficult, complex, and confusing. Ritual practice can complement other approaches to that process by tackling the symbolic damage done to the community as a whole and providing a grassroots environment for symbolic renewal.

Healing and Ritual Process

In the grinding reception of the revelations in the *Boston Globe* coverage and elsewhere in the early 2000s, there were some ritualizations of the process of social healing. Unfortunately, even well-intended rites of reconciliation can have mixed effects. For instance, the Boston "Masses of Healing" and "Masses of Reconciliation" addressing the clerical sexual abuse crisis, while generating meaningful experiences for some participants, could seem to reinscribe clerical secrecy and privilege for others.[2] We can learn two things from looking at these early experiments: at a specific level, Mass and sacramental rituals that reproduce clerical privilege and symbolic mystification can be damaging to survivors of church-related abuse.[3] On the other hand, rituals of healing are best when they symbolically invert the system that has inflicted the damage: so if the damage comes from exploiting

---

[2] Bruce T. Morrill, *Divine Worship and Human Healing: Liturgical Theology at the Margins of Life and Death* (Collegeville, MN: Liturgical Press, 2009), 26–30.

[3] David Farina Turnbloom et al., "Liturgy in the Shadow of Trauma," *Religions* 13, no. 7 (July 2022): 583, https://doi.org/10.3390/rel13070583; Annie Selak, "The Power of Memory and Witnessing: A Trauma-Informed Analysis of *Anamnesis* in the Roman Catholic Mass," in *Liturgy + Power*, ed. Brian P. Flanagan and Johann M. Vento (Maryknoll, NY: Orbis Books, 2017), 22–33; see also Bruce Morrill's chapter in this volume.

power differentials, reversing those established hierarchies in the ritual response is very important.

The long process of healing in Lazarus's story reflects the process of healing in traditional societies where it is clear that injury to an individual also causes damage to the social fabric as a whole. Anthropologists Edith and Victor Turner[4] and practical theologian Cas Wepener[5] have described various stages in the process of reconciliation of social groups. Phase 1 rituals focus on uncovering the problem, while phase 2 rituals rebuild the social bonds. No stage is completely accomplished by a ritual, but at the same time, the symbolic and repeated action of ritual can be helpful at each stage.

North Americans have trouble accepting the effectiveness of ritual healing, in part because of the long-term legacy of the Enlightenment, which separated utilitarian material causes and effects from symbolic behaviors like religion and ritual.[6] At the same time, medical research increasingly confirms traditional societies' convictions about the interconnection of biophysical, mental and emotional, and social well-being.[7] Ritual intervention is especially helpful at a personal

---

[4] See, for instance, Edith L. B. Turner, "The Healing of the Soul: Anthropological Insights from Four Different Traditions," *Pastoral Sciences/Sciences Pastorales* 24, no. 1 (2005): 35–57; Edith L. B. Turner, *Among the Healers: Stories of Spiritual and Ritual Healing Around the World* (New York: Praeger Publishers, 2006); Victor Turner, *From Ritual to Theatre: The Human Seriousness of Play*, Performance Studies Series 1 (New York: Performing Arts Journal Publications, 2008); Victor Turner, "Social Dramas and Stories about Them," *Critical Inquiry* 7, no. 1 (1980): 141–68.

[5] See, for example, Hilton Scott and Cas Wepener, "Healing as Transformation and Restoration: A Ritual-Liturgical Exploration," *Hervormde Teologiese Studies* 73, no. 4 (2017): 1–9, https://doi.org/10.4102/hts.v73i4.4064; Cas Wepener, "Ritual Route-Markers for Reconciliation: Insights from a South African Exploration," *Studia Liturgica* 36, no. 2 (2006): 173–84; Cas Wepener, *From Fast to Feast: A Ritual-Liturgical Exploration of Reconciliation in South African Cultural Contexts*, Liturgia Condenda 19 (Leuven: Peeters, 2009).

[6] See Talal Asad, *Genealogies of Religion: Discipline and Reasons of Power in Christianity and Islam* (Baltimore: Johns Hopkins University Press, 1993), chap. 1.

[7] See, for instance, Helen Herrman and Eva Jané-Llopis, "The Status of Mental Health Promotion," *Public Health Reviews* 34, no. 2 (2012): 1–21, https://doi.org/10.1007/BF03391674; for the overlap with health outcomes in societies with ritual healing, see Paul Farmer and Gustavo Gutiérrez, *In the Company of the Poor: Conversations with Dr. Paul Farmer and Fr. Gustavo Gutiérrez*, ed. Michael Griffin and Jennie Weiss Block (Maryknoll, NY: Orbis Books, 2013); Frédérique Apffel-Marglin, *Subversive Spiritualities: How Rituals Enact the World*, Oxford Ritual Studies (New York: Oxford University Press, 2012). For a compelling introduction to the ideas of ritual

level for systemic issues, including depression, trauma, abuse, and chronic pain.[8] It is even more evident that healing from the sexual abuse crisis involves physical, mental, emotional, and social levels.

The table below lays out my understanding of the ritual involved in the social healing process of a crisis as large and unwieldy as the Catholic sexual abuse crisis in the last three rows, shown compared to the work of Edith and Victor Turner and Cas Wepener in the first two rows. For each phase, I will explain the ritual stages involved, use comparisons to the Lazarus narrative to explain their impact, and suggest specific techniques that might be helpful in ritual responses to the sexual abuse crisis.

Phase 1: Diagnosis, Exposure, and Redress

The first section of the Lazarus pericope (11:1-16) implies that the narrative as a whole is about revelation: the glory of God, the glory of the Son of Man, and the light. Jesus has information about damage that has been done to the community that the disciples do not have. They all know that Lazarus has been sick, but only Jesus knows that he has died. The act of telling the truth extends the damage from Lazarus himself and those who are in on the secret to the disciples. The disciples resist, because knowing the truth is damaging. Victor Turner

---

and healing in traditional societies, see Malidoma Patrice Some, *Ritual: Power, Healing and Community* (New York: Penguin Books, 1997).

[8] Thomas J. Csordas, "Elements of Charismatic Persuasion and Healing," *Medical Anthropology Quarterly* 2, no. 2 (1988): 121–42, https://doi.org/10.1525/maq.1988.2.2.02a00030; Thomas J. Csordas and Elizabeth Lewton, "Practice, Performance, and Experience in Ritual Healing," *Transcultural Psychiatry* 35, no. 4 (1998): 435–512, https://doi.org/10.1177/136346159803500401; Jill Dubisch, "Healing 'The Wounds That Are Not Visible': A Vietnam Veterans' Motorcycle Pilgrimage," in *Pilgrimage and Healing*, ed. Jill Dubisch and Michael Winkelman (Tucson: University of Arizona Press, 2014), 135–54; Elizabeth Fisher, "Ritual as a Treatment for Domestic Violence," *Journal of Ritual Studies* 32, no. 1 (2018): 41–63; Jean Jackson, "Chronic Pain and the Tension between the Body as Subject and Object," in *Embodiment and Experience: The Existential Ground of Culture and Self*, ed. Thomas J. Csordas (Cambridge: Cambridge University Press, 1994), 201–28; Dirk G. Lange, "Trauma Theory and Liturgy: A Disruption of Ritual," *Liturgical Ministry* 17, no. 3 (2008): 127–32; Danielle Wozniak and Karen Allen, "Ritual and Performance in Domestic Violence Healing: From Survivor to Thriver through Rites of Passage," *Culture, Medicine, and Psychiatry* 36, no. 1 (2012): 80–101, https://doi.org/10.1007/s11013-011-9236-9.

STAGES OF THE RITUAL PROCESS OF AFFLICTION, AS ADAPTED TO THE SEXUAL ABUSE CRISIS

Turner: stages of ritual process	Breach	Crisis	Redress		Reintegration or schism	
Wepener's ritual typology	Protest	Confession	Therapeutic/ healing	Acceptance/ forgiveness	Reintegration/ binding	Reparation
		Phase 1			Phase 2	
New proposed stages	Breach	Crisis and diagnostics	Redress/ therapeutic	Acceptance and forgiveness	Binding or schism	Joint mission
Lazarus	Damage: "Lazarus has fallen asleep"	Exposure, diagnosis: "Lazarus is dead," "Your brother will rise," "Take away the stone"	Redress: "Take away the stone," "Unbind him"	Acceptance: "Let him go"	Binding: "Lazarus was one of those at table"	Mission: "The chief priests planned to put Lazarus to death as well"

says that social crisis results when a breach of the accepted social relationships brings to light simmering social tensions and cannot be contained by the usual authority figures.[9]

Similarly, the first phase of ritual recovery is a process of coming to know, as a community, the extent, causes, and best treatments of the damage. Sexual abuse survivors enter the scene not only recovering from personal crisis but also with privileged knowledge about the damage that has been done to the church. The process of disseminating that knowledge throughout the church, like Jesus's disclosure, is often resisted, because the dissemination of knowledge does a secondary, symbolic damage. Hearing about terrible sins committed by priests, bishops, and other religious leaders introduces a fracture into the symbolic ways God is known and experienced. This knowledge imperils the whole symbolic system that reassures Christians that God, the church, and other people can be trusted. The resistance to this knowledge unfairly burdens survivors, who already bear the brunt of the damage, with the symbolic crisis as well. Both the overall study of the sexual abuse crisis and the personal disclosure of particular survivors are often stymied by hearers who are unprepared to hear and thus experience the damage that has been done.

---

[9] Turner, *From Ritual to Theatre*, 70.

In the Lazarus narrative, as in the sexual abuse crisis, this leads to a recurring pattern of repeated disclosures. The ongoing *exposure* of damage comes together with constant effort at *diagnosing* the cause of the problem. Jesus's pronouncements and responses ("Lazarus has fallen asleep," "Lazarus is dead," "Your brother will rise," "Take away the stone") represent an ongoing exposure of the damage, to which his well-meaning interlocutors continually respond in a way that reveals their misunderstanding. When Jesus tells Martha, "Your brother will rise," she accepts this in a general way but is unprepared for its fulfillment in this moment. Thus, when Jesus tells those standing around to remove the stone, she is expecting the stench of decay, a problem with an individual body. Instead, the problem is that Lazarus is bound up in the burial cloths his friends have tried to use to help him, and he needs a social process ("unbind him") to solve this problem.

In the wake of the sexual abuse crisis, every survivor's narrative and every historical treatment is also data that points to the cause of the problem. Ritualizing these narratives, for example, by means of vigils and lament liturgies, as well as telling these stories in news media and other outlets has already revealed that what was originally understood as a Catholic clergy sexual abuse crisis is actually not just clergy, not just Catholic, and not just sex: it is the exploitation of hierarchies of power, willful ignorance, and silence.

It might be useful to think of ritual responses to sexual abuse as rites of affliction rather than rites of healing.[10] The language of "rituals of healing" encourages participants to believe that each ritual action should make participants feel better. But protest or exposure rituals may need to make many individuals feel worse—to spread out and ameliorate the damage done to survivors by disseminating knowledge and allowing the community at large to begin to accept and evaluate the symbolic damage to their social world. Ritual responses to affliction, like those after a natural disaster or a genocide, may be primarily expressive of pain and marked by lament.

The ritual process attends to multiple groups of people in different ways. For traumatized survivors, healing means being permitted to

---

[10] Catherine Bell defines this category: "Rituals of affliction attempt to rectify a state of affairs that has been disturbed or disordered: they heal, exorcise, protect, and purify." Note that "protect" and "purify" do not necessarily produce immediately evident therapeutic results. *Ritual: Perspectives and Dimensions* (New York: Oxford University, 1997), 115.

experience, organize, and narrate their traumatic memories within a supportive and safe environment. This heals trauma over time; each intervention does not necessarily make the survivor feel immediately better. Other community members, especially leaders and those with some authority, need to attend to these narratives, not only to care for traumatized members, but also to expose the truth about the community's history. This work of exposure is unlikely to make members feel better, but it is still part of the process of healing. The needs of survivors and the needs of the community as a whole are therefore linked: the process of exposure and early stage healing requires building a safe place for the transmission of narratives. Some of this work can be done ritually: for instance, the words and stories of survivors can be presented by survivor advocates or in ritual form to put a safe mediator between the survivors who tell the stories and community members who might resist or lash out against this knowledge.

In the healing process, rituals of exposure are often closely linked to rituals of redress. For instance, in the African ritual healing studied by Edith and Victor Turner, the healing rite often isolates a potential cause or partial cause and then exercises some kind of socio-medical *redress* to lessen the damage. Then the rite again evaluates or diagnoses the issue; if the damage continues to be evident, then the redress is not finished. Another partial or potential cause must be exposed and redressed. Ritual redress often takes the form of a *symbolic reversal of the damage or its cause*; a complex matter with a number of causes and various types of damage will require a variety of kinds of redress.

The Catholic sex abuse crisis has been a long exercise in which attempts at redress often expose other types of damage. To take just two examples, the exposure of the scale of abuse and the cover-up of that abuse exposed a secondary crisis about the trustworthiness of Catholic bishops in hearing and evaluating testimony about abusive priests. Symbolically, bishops who participated in a cover-up chose abusive priests over their victims, jeopardizing their identity as pastors and representatives of Christ.

Another example comes from the first identification of pedophilia by priests as the entire scope of the abuse crisis. Even as the church began some ways of addressing this, for instance, by publishing lists of credibly accused priests and implementing safe environment policies for ministry with children, the scope of sexual activity in a church context that was abusive expanded. Once Catholics were looking for sexual abuse and had become familiar with its manifestations, abuse of vulnerable adults (especially disabled and Indigenous persons) and those who were recruited for sexual activity in a spiritual context became visible. Lay ministers' abusive behavior came to light. Parallels between the Catholic context and those of other churches and schools also expanded the scope of the crisis.

As the scope of the crisis broadens, of course the modes of redress would have to broaden. At the same time, the ritual gestures assist in uncovering the shape of the damage. For example, in the early 2000s ritual responses,

> Baltimore Cardinal William Keeler's pastoral response . . . was a liturgical one: a "healing Mass" with some one hundred people, wherein he performed "an act of public atonement to victims" by kneeling before them and reciting the Confiteor. That symbolic gesture of "healing and reconciliation" drew this reaction from one woman: "You have no idea of the healing that came out of that for me."[11]

In the light of the revelation of the cover-up, public and voluntary self-humbling was experienced as a symbolic reversal of the secrecy by which bishops failed to disclose or act on abuse and thus served as a kind of redress for at least one participant.

Phase 1 liturgies for the sex abuse crisis are likely to include expressions of raw pain. They should center the narratives of survivors, and at the same time survivors should be shielded from the inevitable resistance of church members who are encountering the damage for the first time. They should include symbolic reversals of known or suspected causes of damage. These might take the form of the reversal of performed hierarchical power, for instance, by spotlighting lay ministers, or of public enactment of humility by exalted church leaders. Symbolic reversals that are experienced as effective may need to be repeated as more damage comes to light. Survivors should be recruited to assist in planning these liturgies, simultaneously involving them in the production of their narrative and giving them agency in a church where many have felt alienated and set aside.

Physical memorials or shrines might be an underappreciated ritual resource for Catholics in the wake of the sex abuse crisis. They natu-

---

[11] Morrill, *Divine Worship and Human Healing*, 30.

rally shift over time, allow for a variety of types of engagement, and can be entirely lay-created. Rites of redress for individual survivors might include offering the anointing of the sick to those who have been harmed. Survivors who have been away from the church for a time should not be pressured to return. If they wish to return, I recommend a pastoral visit from a survivor advocate paired with a priest in street clothes. Bishops should consider giving a priest in this ministry permission to use Rite C for reconciliation ("Rite for Reconciliation of Penitents with General Confession and Absolution") with the survivor before offering communion, as requiring private confession may be stigmatizing and for some survivors may renew the pastoral privilege that was exploited in the original abuse.[12]

Phase 1 liturgies are unlikely to feel satisfactory—certainly not to everyone but perhaps not to anyone. The rituals are a set of diagnostic tests. They are useful not only for suggesting possible causes and treatments but also as a way of identifying authorities, narratives, and terminologies that can be received by the community as adequate (or at least less inadequate) to address the crisis. Phase 1 rituals will be tentative, will need to be repeated over and over, and will need to be changed as new narratives and understandings of the crisis emerge.

Phase 2:
Acceptance, Rebinding, and Common Mission

The second phase can begin when the community has a commonly agreed-upon sense of the scope of the crisis, damage, and its causes and has symbolic representatives to mediate solutions. At this point, redress that is met with acceptance and forgiveness will gradually provoke less pointing to new damage and backlash. The two groups might split instead of entering phase 2, if sufficient grounds are not

---

[12] For some survivors, confession privately to a priest may be a "moral impossibility" and "a serious need" as defined in paragraph 31 of the Introduction to the Rite of Penance (2010), which would make it possible to use Rite C ("Rite for Reconciliation of Penitents with General Confession and Absolution"). This discernment of moral impossibility and serious need belongs to the bishop. A priest deputed with this responsibility could (if permitted by his bishop) discern with the survivor whether individual confession or general confession (perhaps made by survivor, survivor advocate, and priest together) is a better path to reconciliation for the survivor in that moment.

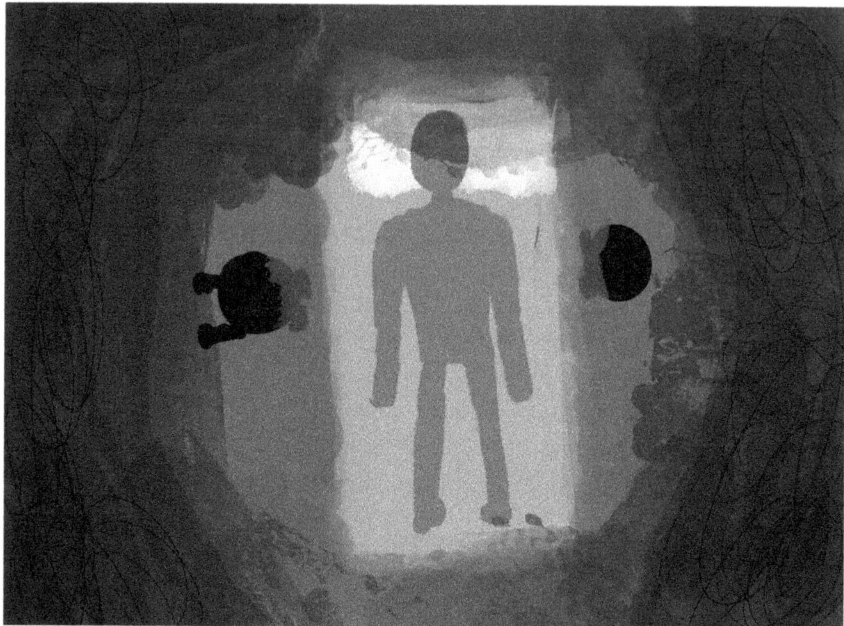

Figure 1. *"Lazarus Is Dead": Damage*, by B. Belcher.
Used with permission.

identified for restoring relationship. The Catholic sexual abuse crisis has not yet reached phase 2; nor is it in schism.

In the Lazarus narrative, phase 2 begins when Jesus says, "Unbind him and let him go." The damage done by Lazarus's death is reversed, and the community participates in redressing the remaining issues, some of which have been caused by their own misguided attempts to help. *Acceptance and forgiveness* rites release the harmed party from the expectations of the community as a whole, transforming as much as possible the harms that have been done into the community's shared lament. In complex cases of social reconciliation, however, someone needs to be able to speak convincingly on behalf of those who have been hurt. Perhaps this person, who emerges as a leader in phase 1, is one of the injured (but one who is not only among the injured but who can bear the weight of symbolic representation of all those who have been injured). The party may be a mediator or, in the case of intergenerational repair, a descendant of the primary injured party.

Figure 2. *"Lazarus, Come Out!" Exposure*, by B. Belcher.
Used with permission.

It is hard to predict who the representative or representatives will prove to be in the Catholic sexual abuse crisis, but there are already some small-scale examples of this phenomenon. For instance, Erin O'Donnell writes about Maka Black Elk as one who "holds a complex set of identities. He is a member of the Oglala-Sioux Tribe, the son and grandson of people who attended an Indian boarding school, and a survivor of childhood sexual abuse. He is also Catholic and employed by a former Indian boarding school, a Catholic institution that has been run by the Jesuits for its entire history."[13] Black Elk's various roles grant him credibility as well as expert knowledge, but his ability to offer redress on behalf of the perpetrator institution is sometimes (not always) in question: "I've been in spaces where the feeling has been 'You're not the person that we want to hear from,'"

[13] Erin O'Donnell, "Grappling with the Church's History as a 'Perpetrator Institution,'" *Awake* (blog), February 7, 2023, https://www.awakecommunity.org/blog/grappling-with-the-churchs-history-as-a-perpetrator-institution.

Figure 3. *"Unbind him": Redress*, by B. Belcher.
Used with permission.

Black Elk recounts. " 'We want to hear from the Jesuits, we want to hear from the provincial. We want to hear from the president. We don't want them to put the person of color who's from here in front of us.' "[14] As redress progresses, Black Elk and others like him should be more easily recognized as legitimate mediators for this crisis.

In phase 1, the redress offered might be tentative, an attempt to discern a way forward; in phase 2, however, it is critical that the rituals of redress are symbols of real redress that are taking place in nonritual environments. Rituals of redress alone are likely to be seen as meaningless substitutes for real change. Only if they can be recognized as manifestations of changes that are taking place will they be accepted and forgiveness for the initial damage be offered.

One way of enacting forgiveness and acceptance is for participants from both parties or symbolic representatives of both parties to begin

---

[14] O'Donnell, "Grappling with the Church's History."

Figure 4. *"Let Him Go": Acceptance and Forgiveness*, by B. Belcher. Used with permission.

the rite spatially separated or wearing distinct types of clothing or visually distinct in some other way. Then, during the rite, the boundaries between the estranged communities can be transgressed (one group crosses over to join the other or the visual distinction is eliminated in some other way).

It is important to recognize that merely enacting rituals of acceptance and forgiveness will not in itself advance the process of acceptance and forgiveness. It will only be received by a community that is prepared to be reconciled: that is, that has come to a consensus about the causes of damage and recognized representatives that are authorized by both parties to grant forgiveness. Of course, in the complications of real social crisis, there are many groups. It may be possible and even healing to ritually do some acceptance and forgiveness during phase 1, for example, with an individual survivor who has done some healing, desires reconciliation, and trusts a particular representative of the church (their parish, a lay minister, or a priest) to offer redress on behalf of the institution. The crisis as a whole is

Figure 5. *"Lazarus Was One of Those at the Table": Rebinding,*
by B. Belcher. Used with permission.

not solved by such a rite, but it may be very healing to an individual. Such redress and acceptance can help the process of diagnosis in phase 1.

The conclusion of phase 2 is (re)binding and common mission. John 12 shows Lazarus restored to his family, at table with Jesus and his sisters, when Mary anoints Jesus's feet in gratitude. Rather than crossing from the realm of the dead to the realm of the living as we saw in John 11, here Lazarus is one among the group. The following verses show that Lazarus has now become so closely identified with Jesus's mission that "the chief priests planned to put Lazarus to death as well" (John 12:10). Rebinding and common mission rituals emphasize the mutuality and common belonging of the previously estranged groups to one another, both as internally perceived (rebinding) and as they act in the world outside (common mission).

Ritually, rebinding is often demonstrated, as in John 12, with a common meal or by symmetrical relationships that replace the symbolic reversals of phase 1. Boundaries that were previously main-

Figure 6. *"The Chief Priests Planned to Put Lazarus to Death": Common Mission,* by B. Belcher. Used with permission.

tained, whether spatial or visual, will be eradicated in these rites. Rebinding and common mission may also be demonstrated by symbols or narratives that outline the common history or ancestry of the groups that have been at odds with one another. Phase 2 rituals, however, often depend on symbols of the future. The Catholic context is challenging because the Eucharist provides our most powerful symbol of unity and of the future, but in it clerical privilege is made very visible. Ministers will need to evaluate carefully at what point in phase 2 particular communities are ready to celebrate Mass, and this decision should be made in consultation with survivors or representatives who are trusted by survivors or their descendants. The difficulty could be lessened by having a baptismal renewal of vows, conducted in a nonhierarchical fashion such as by a communal procession to the font, as a vivid part of the liturgy. For communities where many members may still be reckoning with diagnosis and exposure, a renewal of baptismal vows and service of lament or communal penance service might be an appropriate liturgy.

If phase 1 liturgies are likely to be painful and wounding, phase 2 liturgies will be best experienced if they are expected to mix contrition, sorrow, and lament with recommitment to one another as a community (rebinding) and a willingness to be taken up into the transformative mission of Jesus Christ (common mission). The community offers its painful history—both the sorrow of knowing the community has failed some of its members and the witness and strength of survivors and their stories—to Christ to become part of his work, changing sin into reconciliation, death into resurrection, sorrow into joy.

Conclusion

The repentance and reconciliation required after the Catholic sexual abuse crisis cannot be accomplished by a few healing masses or a papal visit, but that does not mean that ritual cannot play a helpful role in this process. Each community, as well as the Catholic Church as a whole, needs to be able to discern what kinds of ritual are appropriate to the community's and the church's place in the process of healing. Phase 1 will be marked by truth-telling rituals that reveal the damage that has been done and reflect ongoing realizations about the depth and scope of that damage. It will center the narratives of survivors, but they should be protected from the inevitable raw pain of those who are coming to know the truth and who may lash out. Bishops and priests who are normally leaders will need to consent to ritually exercising humility, and lay leaders and survivors and their advocates will need to be ritual leaders. The dignity of baptism may be an important sacramental motif that will promote lay leadership and healing. If survivors desire sacramental healing, the sacraments of healing can be offered in a way that promotes psychological and social as well as spiritual healing.

Individual survivors may enter phase 2 with their communities, but the church as a whole cannot enter phase 2 until there is widespread acceptance of and consensus on the causes of the history of sexual abuse in the church. Sexual abuse cannot be separated from issues of the church's cooperation with the colonial enterprise, racism, sexism, and exploitation of children and people with disabilities. Survivors and descendants of survivors will need to speak about the damage that has been done to these communities, experience redress, and identify those who they trust to speak on their behalf. At that point, phase 2 liturgies at a larger level may begin by proclaiming in a symbolic way the narratives of injury, performing symbolic redress that represents the ways the church as a perpetrator institution has begun to remedy the damage outside the ritual environment, performing symbolic acceptance of this redress, and symbolically rebinding representative survivors or descendants with trusted representatives of a chastened institution.

9

Lessons from Litigation for Ministry in the Church

Patrick J. Wall

Clerical sexual assault of minors is a crime in the tradition going back to the *Didache* of the first century.[1] Listen to the entire tradition. One ironic twist of this chronic two-millennia pattern of conduct is that lawyers became the voice crying out from the desert on behalf of those who had no voice. The lesson from forty years of litigation is quite simply to make survivors your focus.

I offer two core lessons from forty years of litigation. The first lesson is to know that many came before us who studied fallen clerics. That wisdom should be part of our tradition and memory. A second lesson is that the civil, criminal, bankruptcy, and grand jury systems have attempted to change the bishops' behavior, placing the safety of minor children above the reputations of clerics and religious. Always make survivors your focus and be ready to intervene early and often.[2]

---

[1] Thomas P. Doyle, A. W. Richard Sipe, and Patrick J. Wall, *Sex, Priests, and Secret Codes: The Catholic Church's 2,000-Year Paper Trail of Sexual Abuse*, 2nd ed. (Lanham, MD: Taylor Trade Publishing, 2006).

[2] Thank you to the survivors who have shared their secrets as victims of crime, to Saint John's Abbey for all the training and experience inside, and to my family and friends for their loyal support.

Wisdom Sources

Where do we start and what principles do we follow? Begin with humility (Rule of Benedict 7) and the natural law. The clerical sexual assault of minors is not a new or English-speaking phenomenon. I suggest reading the greats for your *lectio divina* to inform what is already known of clerical perpetrators and the damage done to survivors. One such example is the early work of Reverend Thomas Verner Moore, OSB, MD, at The Catholic University of America on the detection of prepsychotics who apply for admission to priesthood or religious communities. Additionally, the correspondence and lessons learned by Gerald Fitzgerald, sP, treating fallen priests in the deserts of New Mexico and Leo Bartemeier, MD, et al., at the Seton Institute in Baltimore frame the mid-twentieth-century knowledge of bad actors. The research of John Money, PhD, at Johns Hopkins and a thirty-year ethnographic study of celibacy by Aquinas Walter Richard Sipe paint a new language geography of the secret world of clerical offenders that only bishops know. Finally, the source that cracked the episcopal armor was an internal report (The Manual) from Thomas Patrick Doyle, JCD, Michael Peterson, MD, and F. Ray Mouton, JD.[3]

Putting survivors first is a paradigm shift and means you have permission to feel the survivors' damage done by the clerical offenders. Going beyond empathy, you will process communication and hear with your heart the subtlety of survivors. A source to start with is *The Body Keeps the Score* by Bessel van der Kolk, MD, at Harvard.[4] The trauma, though decades old, reverberates through the body and affects future health outcomes. A second foundational data source is the "Adverse Childhood Experiences" (ACEs) study that was conducted at Kaiser Permanente.[5] The ACE study for many is the aha dataset that opens their minds to the depth and deprivation a survivor will go through in order to never again be vulnerable to sexual assault.

Now that we have read, reflected, and developed a new understanding for service to survivors and their families, where to start?

[3] "The Problem of Sexual Molestation by Roman Catholic Clergy: Meeting the Problem in a Comprehensive and Responsible Manner," https://www.bishop-accountability.org/reports/1985_06_09_Doyle_Manual/.

[4] Bessel A. van der Kolk, *The Body Keeps the Score: Brain, Mind, and Body in the Healing of Trauma* (New York: Viking, 2014).

[5] "About the CDC-Kaiser ACE Study," U.S. Centers for Disease Control and Prevention, https://www.cdc.gov/violenceprevention/aces/about.html.

First Principle: When Working with Survivors,
Do No Further Harm

1. Listen with the attitude of "We believe you." None of us can change the past; it is what it is.

2. Acknowledge. The pope knew; the bishops knew. They created the Servants of the Paraclete, Saint John Vianney Institute, Southdown, and the Saint Luke Institute.[6]

3. Offer to help the families of survivors, including spouses, partners, parents, siblings, and all those affected in the survivor's family system.

4. Let survivors decide when and where they are ready to come forward.

5. If a survivor declines your offer, let them know you will be here when they are ready.

Second Principle: The Body Keeps the Score

Here, in short, is my thesis. Because survivors experienced trauma from clerical sexual assault at such a vulnerable point in their human development, by a person they believed represented God, the criminal conduct reverberates inside every cell of their body throughout their shortened lives. What matters is intervention, early and often.

When you intervene and serve the survivor in need, remember to ask, what is your ecclesiology? You need to understand your own worldview. What are the models you hold as your core, among those outlined by Cardinal Avery Dulles, SJ?[7] Are all the models in balance or is one dominating your thoughts and deeds? Herald: how much energy do you give to outreach for the widow, orphan, and alien? Institution: how much time do you spend on administrative upkeep of bricks, mortar, and Excel spreadsheets? Mystical communion: how many spiritual traditions have you studied or experienced and integrated into your prayer and work? Sacrament: what percentage of the time is your life visible to the local community and not just

---

[6] For one example of these organizations' function, see Thomas P. Doyle, "Paraclete Report," January 11, 2011, http://www.awrsipe.com/doyle/2011/2011-01-11--paraclete_report.htm.

[7] Avery Cardinal Dulles, *Models of the Church* (Garden City, NY: Doubleday, 1974).

contributing parishioners? Servant: does the larger society even know you exist? People of God as disciples: are you integrating daily customs of prayer and work?

Third Principle: Become Elijahs; Intervention Starts Healing

Intervention means listening and believing a survivor and their families without judgment. At this stage in history the bishops have admitted to over seven thousand clerics having sexually assaulted minors in the United States since 1950.[8] Intervention means asking, "What do you need to heal?" Sometimes just the simple but profound act of listening is life-changing for a survivor.

Fourth Principle: The Past Is Prologue to Future Conduct unless the Bishops Choose to Humble Themselves and Dismantle the Clerical Culture[9]

Litigation is what we do in society when we have a conflict that is unresolved. Make no mistake, litigation is adversarial and resembles verbal hand-to-hand combat. When conflict reaches the point of litigation, it is historically a long-unresolved problem, as the average citizen does not seek out litigation. Clerical sexual assault of minors is no different and the reason why survivors make a police report, file a civil complaint, or file a bankruptcy claim is simple: no one can change the past, but they want to keep children safe in the future.

One of the earliest known criminal cases against a Roman Catholic cleric for lewd and lascivious acts with a minor is the 1980 matter of Donald Patrick Roemer in the Archdiocese of Los Angeles.[10] Most of the criminal complaints against a cleric were erased quietly, as brilliantly told in film in *Spotlight* (2015), *The Keepers* (2017), and *Sins of the Father* (2022).

---

[8] See Bishop Accountability, "Lists of Accused Priests Released by Dioceses and Religious Institutes," https://www.bishop-accountability.org/AtAGlance/diocesan_and_order_lists.htm.

[9] Francis J. Weber, *Past Is Prologue: Some Historical Recollections, 1961–1991* (Los Angeles: Saint Francis Historical Society, 1992).

[10] Archdiocese of Los Angeles, "Clergy Files Produced by Archdiocese of Los Angeles," https://clergyfiles.la-archdiocese.org/listing.html.

There were two primary defense strategies before 2002: the "geographic solution," or "cure," as Father Gerald Fitzgerald, sP, named it, and asserting a statute of limitations defense. The "geographic solution" is my term for the administrative ecosystem of reassigning a cleric after he has previously offended to another domicile where he is not known to avoid public scandal.[11] The solution to the scandal, changing the perpetrators' geography, became a business practice employed by every bishop and religious superior around the world.

The second defense strategy is aggressively asserting a "statute of limitations" defense even when knowing the cleric had sexually assaulted minors. Hundreds of civil lawsuits cases were brought beginning in the early 1980s up to 2002, but only a handful prevailed: against Father Thomas Adamson of the Diocese of Winona, Father Oliver O'Grady of the Diocese of Stockton, Father Rudy Kos of the Diocese of Dallas, Father Michael Harris of the Diocese of Orange, and Archbishop Robert Sanchez of the Archdiocese of Santa Fe.[12] On the whole, twentieth-century criminal and civil courts did not reform the bishops' conduct in handling clerics and religious who sexually assaulted minors. The law proved only a minor existential threat to exposing the chronic scandal. The scandal, from the bishops' vantage point, appeared successfully contained.

Civil and Criminal Litigation

California's first reform of the statutes of limitations went into effect in 2003, reviving over three thousand previously time-barred cases. Civil discovery unearthed that Cardinal Roger Mahony was actively thwarting criminal investigations on dozens of priests, most notably Michael Baker and Peter Garcia. The US Supreme Court astutely ruled in *Stogner v. California* that the *ex post facto* doctrine made it unconstitutional to retroactively change or revive an expired

---

[11] Code of Canon Law, https://www.vatican.va/archive/cod-iuris-canonici/eng/documents/cic_lib6-cann1364-1399_en.html.

[12] See, for instance, Dennis Hevesi, "Archbishop Robert F. Sanchez, Who Fought Discrimination, Dies at 77," *New York Times*, January 24, 2012, sec. US, https://www.nytimes.com/2012/01/24/us/archbishop-robert-f-sanchez-who-fought-discrimination-dies-at-77.html.

criminal statute, and most clerics were set free. A statute of limitations is a core value of the Constitution where a legislature cannot go back in time and change the rule on crimes.

Boston brought a radically different result. Judge Constance Sweeney ordered the deposition of Cardinal Bernard Law on Boston priest Reverend Paul R. Shanley into the open.[13] The public outcry was so great and the public pressure of the *Boston Globe* reporting so effective that Cardinal Law departed for Rome never to return to the United States.

Scandal again was contained, not having reached critical mass.

"Expect the unexpected" is a common adage. Few foresaw Archbishop John Vlazny (and the Holy See's approval, since it exceeded the archbishop's spending limits) opening the institution to the federal courts in 2004 by putting the Archdiocese of Portland, Oregon, in chapter 11 bankruptcy. This established a new diocesan custom of filing bankruptcy to stop clerical sexual assault trials: there have now been thirty-seven such filings.[14] The legal tactic achieved in the short term a stay of all state court civil actions. Federal law trumps state law, so the jury never heard the case. In average state court litigation, a diocese is not mandated to turn over large amounts of financial documents, but in bankruptcy court, since they are essentially pleading poverty and the inability to pay the bills, they have to show the financial machine. One of the many consequences are the first ever financial disclosures, literally looking under the hood of the church's economic engine, for what many observers describe as a byzantine accounting system.

Bankruptcy has caused at least four unforeseen results. First, the court may dismiss the filing as fraudulent and essentially force a diocese to settle (e.g., San Diego). Second, the filing may trigger an additional bankruptcy, as when the Diocese of Fairbanks filing provoked the Jesuit Oregon Province filing. Third, the filing exposed financial records of abuse, such as Cardinal Timothy Dolan's transfer of millions of dollars from one church corporation to a cemetery fund in Milwaukee. Fourth is substantive consolidation: a judge can view the various dioceses' simultaneous bankruptcies as related entities

---

[13] Deposition of Cardinal Bernard Law, October 11, 2002, offices of Greenberg Traurig.

[14] "Catholic Dioceses in Bankruptcy," PennState Law, https://elibrary.law.psu.edu/bankruptcy/.

and combine all their property to resolve the claims. Only time will tell if the bishops have walked themselves into substantive consolidation by filing ten plus reorganizations in proximity.[15]

The Pennsylvania grand jury report changed the threat quotient for the personal criminal liability of a bishop. One direct result is the quick production of credibly accused lists increasing the number of known perpetrators from less than 3,500 to over 7,400.[16]

The new lists, compounded by hundreds of simultaneous filed cases in California, New York, and New Jersey, brought such a scale of actual knowledge to the bishops' doorsteps that the average jury went from questioning if a celibate priest could possibly sexually assault a minor to believing that it likely happened and that the bishops knew enough and most likely covered it up. After listening to Father Oliver O'Grady in *Deliver Us from Evil* (2006), how could his multiple bishops not have known?

The scale of knowledge is mind-bending. Clerical perpetrators are now known to have operated at every level of church leadership, from Father Angus McDonald, the pastor in tiny Barrow, Alaska, to Cardinal Theodore McCarrick ("Uncle Ted"), archbishop of Washington, DC, who rubbed elbows with national leadership, to Marcial Maciel, LC, who governed a worldwide religious institute. The Vatican Apostolic Archive in Rome and many dioceses' chancery offices contain notice on Maciel as far back as 1958.[17]

The massive scale of data unearthed the fruit of the poisonous tree. The cases revealed three common crimes being perpetrated on minors: criminal sexual assault, creating and distributing child imagery, and trafficking minors for the purpose of other clerics sexually assaulting minors. The most infamous case of child imagery is the priest secretary to the papal nuncio in Washington, Monsignor Carlo Alberto Capella.[18]

---

[15] "Substantive Consolidation and Nondebtor Entities: The Fight Continues," Jones Day, May/June 2011, https://www.jonesday.com/en/insights/2011/06/substantive-consolidation-and-nondebtor-entities-the-fight-continues.

[16] Bishop Accountability, "Lists of Accused Priests."

[17] "La Voluntad de no Saber," Fernando M. Gonzalez, March 2012, http://www.lavoluntaddenosaber.com/index.php?%20option=com_content&view=article&id=2&Itemid=58.

[18] Gerard O'Connell, "Vatican Diplomat Sentenced to Five Years in Prison for Child Pornography Crimes," *America*, June 23, 2018, https://www.americamagazine.org/faith/2018/06/23/vatican-diplomat-sentenced-five-years-prison-child-pornography-crimes.

If the examined life is to be part of maturation and a value in service to others, one must ask: What is the policy of ordained leadership over the past forty years on the chronic problem of clerics sexually assaulting minors? My thesis is the bishops have adopted *patient ambiguity* as their legal coat of arms. The bishops overestimated their own raw power in society. Survivors continue to haul them into common law courts to answer for knowing enough but not doing enough to protect kids.

Ultimately, the bishops have also underestimated the Me Too movement. The gravity of the Michael Jackson, Prince Andrew, Harvey Weinstein, Bill Cosby, and Jeffrey Epstein cases affects judges and juries. As revolutionary as the printing press, the internet now connects survivors worldwide and gives advocates the ability to analyze the bishops' business practices, exponentially enhanced by artificial intelligence tools. These combined factors sharpen the common awareness that bishops protected clerics instead of children.

Put survivors first. That is the tough lesson from forty years of litigation.

10

Wounded Healers Who Proclaim the Word:
Ministry and Preaching amid Unresolved Trauma

Kenneth W. Schmidt

The Problem

Let's stop calling the issue "clergy sexual abuse in the church," which *is* a significant problem. But the real issue is so much bigger: it's more than abuse; it's more than clergy; and it's not confined to the Catholic Church.

The issue is *trauma,* which is *a significant event (or series of events) coupled with vulnerability that, when untreated, interrupts and creates obstacles to normal human development.* Traumatic events include any kind of *abuse* (physical, emotional, verbal, and sexual) as well as *neglect* (which has the same effects as abuse). Traumatic events include *abandonment* (by physical absence or departure, divorce, death, emotional distancing, separation due to physical or mental health, and suicide). Traumatic events include *natural disasters* (floods, hurricanes, and fires) and *tragedies* (accidents and intentional violence). Trauma can result from a *sense of not belonging* (exclusion, bullying, oppression, disability, sexual orientation and identity, and minority status within a majority culture). Traumatic events are profound experiences of *powerlessness.* About two-thirds of American adults have at least one traumatic experience during their childhood.[1]

---

[1] Elizabeth A. Swedo et al., "Prevalence of Adverse Childhood Experiences Among U.S. Adults—Behavioral Risk Factor Surveillance System, 2011–2020," *Morbidity and Mortality Weekly Report* 72 (2023), https://doi.org/10.15585/mmwr.mm7226a2.

When those traumatic events occur in childhood, or in situations where resources are lacking to support and care for the victim, or when the traumatized person already has experienced other trauma or for any other reason lacks resilience, then the impact will be *trauma*. Trauma survivors are not *them*; they are *us*!

What Does Trauma Do?

Traumatic events are profound experiences of vulnerability and powerlessness. When those events are experienced but do not heal, they become trauma. The initial experiences and the absence of treatment and recovery have deep and long-lasting impact, which does not simply disappear with the passage of time or distance. That impact can even be passed from generation to generation, as we have learned, for example, after the Holocaust and the genocide in Rwanda.

Unresolved trauma affects the entire person—body, mind, and spirit; emotions, thinking and behavior; individually and communally; personally, interpersonally, and one's relationship with the Divine. Very briefly, what flows from trauma includes victim-survivors'

a. lack of skill at managing feelings and attempting to avoid emotions in order to feel safe;

b. distorted understanding of the world, relationships, and God related to the traumatic experience(s);

c. adoption of survival skills in order to live with and manage one's suffering (e.g., bad habits, addictions, self-harm, violence, extreme emotions [or none], depression, rage, suicidality);

d. belief that trauma is their fault, that they are bad and therefore loaded with shame, which in turn leads to hiding their trauma (so other people won't know how bad they are);

e. difficulty in relationships because their experience of love and trust is so skewed or damaged or destroyed.

The Response

In the last twenty years, as we became more aware of the extent of clergy sex abuse, how has the Catholic Church responded? There have been pockets of compassion and assistance; there is more acknowledgment of the reality; there are more prevention programs for child safety; there is some more accountability.

In general, however, the church is known much more for *other responses*—avoidance, repeated denial, suspicion, blaming others, and revictimizing the victims. In general, the responses have been more legal than pastoral. The responses are often rooted in *fear*: What will happen if the truth comes out about what happened? What will happen if there's a lawsuit? What will happen if we admit our own mistakes? We could very well be accused of having suffered a serious gunshot wound and then shooting ourselves in the other foot (with the crazy idea that it makes the situation better)!

In some dioceses, there has been provision for individual therapy for some of the victims. Programs such as the Trauma Recovery Program in the Diocese of Kalamazoo have been created. But overall, the response does not seem to coincide with the charter that the US bishops approved in 2002:

> We commit ourselves to do all we can to heal the trauma that victims/survivors and their families are suffering and the wound that the whole church is experiencing.[2]

Granted, the charter didn't promise healing for everyone, and in that document they were only addressing the issue of clergy sexual abuse. But now that the church is aware of the extent of trauma in our midst, can we ignore it and only focus on clergy sexual abuse?

Another Response

While the church can be a source and a place of trauma, imaginative faith recognizes that the church also can be a source and place of our healing. As the Body of Christ, when one member is wounded, all are wounded; when one member suffers, all suffer; and as one heals, the whole Body moves toward healing (1 Cor 12:26). Jesus showed us that healing is a sign of the reign of God, which is here

---

[2] United States Conference of Catholic Bishops (USCCB), Charter for the Protection of Children and Young People (June 2018), Preamble, https://www.usccb.org/offices/child-and-youth-protection/charter-protection-children-and-young-people.

and now. God's desire is for our healing, especially because we cannot heal ourselves. Therefore, the church should be known for its commitment and dedication of personnel and resources to healing.

The memories and the consequences of traumatic events don't "go away"; trauma survivors don't "grow out of it" simply because their bodies get bigger. Traumatic events can have a deep and long-lasting impact. The good news is that we know how to help people recover, although the victims have to do the hard work; others cannot do it for them (which is unfair, but true).

We humans try to make sense of and find meaning in events. But traumatic events cause great confusion about things like personal safety, how to be in healthy relationships, God's protection and alleged punishment, rights and values that are prized but not upheld (such as equality and human dignity), and expressions of love and care that come from people also causing harm. The desire for understanding amid confusion can lead to false, childlike conclusions about oneself, other people, how the world works, and what God does and doesn't do. When we understand trauma and its effects, we can respond compassionately and be effective listeners, supporters, and referral agents, rather than getting angry and walking away.[3]

Trauma Is Everywhere

Trauma is not limited to individuals who have suffered a personal injury. Trauma can be caused by corporate behavior and by not taking action. In the church, trauma can be caused by clericalism, sexism, racism, and other ecclesial divisions of the Body of Christ; the abuse crisis; the conquest of aboriginal peoples; the Crusades, the Reformation, and Counter-Reformation; and on it goes. (This history may seem a stretch, except we have evidence that the impact of trauma can be passed genetically from generation to generation.)

The widespread existence of trauma requires us to attend to the congregations we serve, because well over half of their members have been traumatized. In addition, trauma affects presbyterates, parishes, congregations of consecrated life, dioceses, and national conferences

---

[3] Appended to this chapter are "Signs of Unresolved Trauma" and also "Core Concepts and Skills" for healing trauma.

of bishops. The profound experiences of danger, harm, loss, vulnerability, and powerlessness have left scars and open wounds in the lives of millions of people in our country alone.

Beyond the church, our nation and the world are affected by trauma, and not just as individuals. Communally, trauma can result from racism, sexism, violence, war, genocide, social injustice, poverty, food insecurity, homelessness, emigration and refugee status, medical inequity, and most recently a worldwide pandemic.

All of these experiences stir up the debilitating experiences of vulnerability and powerlessness. The past has not passed; it is very much present and often continues to wreak havoc.

Wounded Healers in Ministry and Preaching

After twenty years, more eyes are open and more people are *trauma-aware*—they know that trauma is all around them and perhaps within themselves. The Body of Christ is deeply wounded, and much needs to be done. The disciples of Jesus, who himself devoted so much of his ministry to healing, ought to be at the forefront of healing the world.

Sustained efforts are necessary to become *trauma-informed*—to understand its impact and provide the assistance that victims deserve. The church and its members must understand and assume their mission and proper roles as *trauma-healers in persona Christi*.

We are called to bring healing to a wounded community. As preachers we are well-situated for this ministry because of our public position and our access to large numbers of people through the pulpit. We can inform others about the impact of trauma; we can stir up empathy and compassion for the victim-survivors of trauma; we can teach about how to recover from trauma; we can provide hope for healing and support during the journey of recovery; we can set good examples of healthy behavior for victim-survivors to see.

The gospel shows us two major objectives of Jesus's public ministry: he came to make it known that the reign of God is here and now and that God's desire is for our healing. God's church should be known for healing (not for the horror stories of clerical sexual abuse experienced by those who should have been safe, or for terrible experiences during confession when they should have encountered the Lord in the Seat of Mercy). The church is one of God's instruments for healing, which is so needed in the world because, as the wisdom of the Twelve Step programs teach us, we cannot heal ourselves!

To bring healing to others, preachers must be in touch with their own experiences of woundedness, vulnerability, and powerlessness. They don't have to proclaim the awful details, but they should draw on their memories of their experiences, the impact, and the outcomes, when they read the Scriptures and help their listeners connect the Word to their lives. They will be able to express compassion and understanding rather than frustration and blaming.

Preachers must also be healthy themselves. They must be able to manage their own emotions and behavior in order to receive and handle the anger, fear, and pain entrusted to them by others (not shut it down). People watch to see if their helpers can handle the intense emotions; they are deciding whether to place their trust in what preachers say.

If preachers are not in touch with their own traumatic experiences, and if they are not able to manage their own emotional lives, then they need to seek help so they don't cause more harm to the Body of Christ.

How Can We Preach about Trauma?

First, and perhaps most important at this time, we must talk about trauma. Pretending it does not exist, avoiding the subject, or treating it as if it is shameful simply keeps the wounds open. It sends an implicit message to the victims to "keep quiet." Yet traumatic events are a common part of our human experience.

As preachers, one of our tasks is to help people to recall events, to interpret what is happening, to understand, and to find meaning. When traumatic events have occurred, often coupled with a sense of injustice, people try to make sense of what doesn't make sense. Preachers are in a great position to help them!

Even if we don't know people's particular traumatic events, we know they may be living in shame. It's more likely that people are keeping their trauma hidden. We do well not to promote more pain and suffering with preaching that manifests shaming, blaming, moralizing, condemning, and (perhaps unwittingly) revictimizing victims.

Rather, to paraphrase, "the wounded must have the Good News preached to them."

Our preaching helps people to encounter the Lord by conveying that we understand their behavior, which is often borne of pain, sorrow, and old wounds, not evil intentions. We can show them a path out of their suffering by modelling healthy behaviors ourselves. As preachers we can offer good examples of healthy behavior from the Scriptures and from the world around us.

We can avoid speaking as if the world is easily divided and explained in black-and-white terms. We can allow for many shades of gray to exist. We can avoid childlike and rigid thinking and instead model complexity, multiplicity, nuance, and the power of the word "and" (rather than "either/or," "but").

Preachers are also in a great position to preach about healing that we call "grief" and "forgiveness." They can make sure that these paths are properly understood and provide resources and support for those who are thus engaged. Grief and forgiveness are not signs of weakness or failure, nor are they "gifts" or signs of victory of a perpetrator. Nor are they burdens or duties. Rather, preachers can help victim-survivors escape inappropriate and debilitating guilt and shame.

Preachers may well have their own trauma that needs healing. They are well-positioned to receive the grace of healing and then be wounded healers for those to whom they proclaim the Word.

Signs of Unresolved Trauma

A pattern of out-of-control and self-injurious behavior

- Addictive behaviors (over-/undereating, gambling, drinking, OCD, smoking, etc.)

- Patterns of repeated behavior to avoid feelings (promiscuity, internet use, sleeping, etc.)

- Chaos in life (problems with relationships, employment, finances, etc.)

- Self-harmful behavior (often "alluded to" but not obvious) such as scratching and cutting, burning oneself, hair pulling, etc.

Staying stuck in the victim, perpetrator, or rescuer roles

- Seeking out relationships with abusive people

- Inducing abuse from others rather than waiting for it to happen

- Perceiving abuse, which confirms the belief that they are unworthy and unlovable

- Hurting others (different from appropriate self-protection)

- Acting aggressively toward others who are weak and vulnerable

- Helping others compulsively, often to their own detriment

- Acting generously in ways not in accord with the relationship

Inability to tolerate feelings or conflicts

- Bluntness or numbness, withdrawal, no obvious affect in appropriate situations

- Movement to intense or overwhelming feelings (e.g., rage) suddenly and rapidly

- Depression (problems sleeping or eating, poor energy, low motivation, poor self-esteem, poor memory, or anxiety)

- Panic feelings (trouble breathing, feeling as if having a heart attack, fearfulness, anxiety, etc.)

Intense self-blame and feelings of unworthiness
or belief their life is "ruined"

- Belief that they were responsible for original traumatic event

- Irrational/illogical beliefs about responsibility for events in the present

- Belief that they are bad, a failure, unlovable, a loser, damaged, insignificant, worthless

- May induce others to treat them badly

Disorganized attachment patterns

- Inability to tolerate their ambivalence toward the perpetrator even after the trauma ceases

- Inability to tolerate their ambivalence toward other trusted figures, such as failed rescuers or those who denied the traumatic event

- Inability to tolerate their ambivalence toward significant persons currently in their lives

Difficulty maintaining healthy relationships

- Avoid relationships altogether

- Avoid close relationships because of inherent risk

- Avoid situations that might lead to closeness

- Protect themselves, e.g., act unfriendly to others before others are unfriendly to them

- Have intense but brief relationships

- Remain attached even when the relationship is unhealthy

- Perceive the relationship in a distorted manner

Black-and-white thinking and other cognitive distortions

- Childlike, concrete, and magical thinking

- What they think is normal and real does not coincide with "real life"

- "Life rules" and "automatic thoughts" derive from childhood distortions

- Cling to the distortions despite challenge or contrary evidence

- Provoke a nonexistent reality into being in order to verify a distortion

- Collect evidence to support the distortion while ignoring evidence to the contrary

- Patterns of distorted thinking (such as generalizations, all or nothing, discounting, jumping to conclusions, assuming, labeling, and emotional reasoning)

Suicidal ideation

- Talk about suicide

- Wish they were dead

- Have a plan to end their life

Pathological dissociation

- Loss of (long) spaces of time (can't remember what they said or did)

- Appear to "switch" personalities, or be different people, even in speech and behavior

- Trances or sleepwalking

- Childhood companions, "voices," "too much noise in my head"

- Inability to recall important information, usually of a stressful or traumatic nature

- Confusion about personal identity or assumption of a new identity

Intrusive thoughts, including images, feelings, memories, and nightmares.

Extensive comorbidity, i.e., multiple diagnoses, which may include addictions, mood disorders, and personality disorders.

Core Concepts and Skills

The good news is that we also know how to help traumatized people heal. Here are some core concepts and skills that can help people move beyond the confusion, distress, and maladaptive practices that are common in trauma.

Grounding

Some people become experts at keeping their bodies in the present while their thoughts and emotions are somewhere else. Survivors utilize their five senses to keep their thoughts and emotions in the present, in order to perceive and respond appropriately to the situation at hand rather than perceiving and responding through the lens of traumatic events and the aftermath in their past.

Attachment Ambivalence

Humans have a biological need to be connected in relationships. For young children, life itself depends on these connections. When an individual experiences a traumatic event, there is also a biological urge to recoil from the source of the injury. This contradiction in biological urges, to connect and to recoil, creates ambivalent feelings about attachment. The more that the individual's real or experienced survival depended on a perpetrator, the more dramatic the internal conflict.

Avoiding, Feeling, and Integrating Feelings

In order to survive deep pain, some people learn to disconnect from their feelings. They become "phobic about their feelings," developing extreme strategies to avoid their feelings. Our programs encourage people to experience their feelings while learning strategies to manage them effectively.[4] They must learn how to integrate their emotions with their thinking and their behavior in order to live a healthy life. The ultimate goal is to experience their deep sadness and grieve the losses they have experienced due to their painful past.

Correcting Cognitive Distortions

People exposed to traumatic experiences are prone to cognitive distortions. Their understandings of the world and people are influenced by their painful experiences. Those may be generalized into

---

[4] Trauma Recovery Associates (www.TraumaRecoveryAssociates.org) offers healing programs for community members, and also on behalf of the Diocese of Kalamazoo, and provides training for mental health professionals and spiritual caregivers.

"survival rules" that then interfere with examining each new situation and judging it for itself. They become so used to thinking in certain ways that when something new comes along, they do not see the event or person for itself but instead move into their automatic thought patterns. It is very hard to correct cognitive distortions because "they seem true." In reality, they are at least partially distorted, if not entirely inaccurate. Cognitive distortions tend to "fan the flames" of survivors' feelings, which then lead to more extreme behaviors. As survivors correct their cognitive distortions, the intensity of their feelings diminish and behavior will become less extreme.

Calming the Body's Stress Response

People tend to carry stress in their bodies; this is especially true for people with painful pasts. This is because they react to negative triggers in the present as if the triggers are as threatening as painful events in their past. These physical changes induce a sense of urgency that escalates negative emotions and activates behavioral responses. Therefore, it is imperative that people learn skills to interrupt their physical stress responses. Prayer, meditation, yoga, guided imagery, and exercise are a few of the techniques known to be effective. Just as the body can learn to respond to a negative trigger with a stress response, it can learn to respond to a negative trigger with a relaxation response.

Gradual Exposure to Triggers

When survivors of trauma encounter a situation that reminds them of their painful history, they are likely to experience intense emotions. These emotions can be so uncomfortable that survivors take extreme measures to avoid triggering situations. Recovery requires that they willfully resist this pattern and embrace opportunities to expose themselves gradually to triggers while they practice techniques to regulate their feelings.

Locus of Control Shift

People who have been harmed or neglected may place the locus of control for the ill-treatment within themselves; this is especially true for children who have been traumatized. Often, a perpetrator also promoted this mindset. Additionally, the mindset helped the children avoid feeling helpless, vulnerable, and powerless in the face of the mistreatment. In their young minds, the maltreatment is happening because "I am bad." They can hope that, if they change, the harm or neglect will stop. In its original context this is a protective illusion. That illusion continues as a presumption of responsibility for events not under their control, and the long-term effect is deep shame. These beliefs keep victims locked in a cycle of bad feelings, self-abuse, and destructive relationships. When a survivor contradicts the locus of control shift, it eventually leads to self-acceptance, grieving, and healing.

Victim/Rescuer/Perpetrator Triangle

In the original situation of ill-treatment, there was a victim, a perpetrator, and a failed-rescuer. Adult survivors reenact this triangle in other relationships, assigning themselves and finding others who behave according to prescribed thought patterns and behaviors on the triangle. Healing consists of "getting off the triangle," by moving away from those extremes and adopting skills for self-care and mutually respectful relationships.

Forgiveness

Forgiveness is a process of healing by a person who has been deeply and personally injured or harmed. Forgiveness is not something given to the perpetrator but rather a gift to the self-survivor. Forgiveness is a series of conscious thoughts and actions, an inner response, which includes letting go of a desire for vengeance or harm toward the offender and letting go of negative emotions such as resentment. Letting go creates a positive change in the injured person's physical, mental, and emotional well-being. Forgiveness restores a sense of personal power and can lead to improved interpersonal relationships. Forgiveness is often confused with other things. It does not require an apology or even contact with the person who caused the harm. It does not mean to forget the injury, to condone what happened, or even to tolerate injuries. Forgiveness does not require reconciliation with the offender, because that person may be dangerous, unavailable, or dead.

Grief

Grief is one of the primary feelings that many people try to avoid. The grief stage comes late in recovery because survivors set up defenses against the deep pain they will experience during grieving. The content during early stages of therapy usually focuses on the bad things that happened to them. The content of the grief stage focuses on the good things that should have happened but didn't. As people mourn a childhood they didn't have, the extreme behaviors and defenses become quiet, and the benefits of recovery work begin to emerge externally as well as internally.

Part Three

Trust—Re-forming the Body of Christ

11

Accountability, Healing, and Trust:
Formation for Ministry

Stacey Noem

Seminaries and graduate programs in ministry are implicitly structured to prioritize intellectual formation, too often to the detriment of the human, spiritual, pastoral, and communal formation necessary to support a life of ministry.[1]

We see this priority evident in the weekly schedule of a ministry student. We see this priority in the disposition among both students and faculty when they distinguish pastoral courses from "academic" coursework, as though there was a tiered system of value in which "academic" courses rise definitively to the top. We see this priority in the resources allotted for intellectual pursuits over and above (and often to the exclusion of) resources for human, spiritual, pastoral, and communal formation. We see this priority in the disproportionately low amount of attention given to explicit formation humanly and communally. We see this priority in the sizes of faculty versus formation staff, spiritual directors, and support staff. We see this priority in the level of expertise and credentialing insisted upon to lead intellectual formation versus the virtually nonexistent preparatory training offered for those leading human, spiritual, and pastoral

---

[1] For details on how this is currently the case, see James Keating, "Beyond Schooling," in *Configured to Christ: On Spiritual Direction and Clergy Formation* (Steubenville, OH: Emmaus Road, 2021).

formation. As Deacon Edward McCormack writes in his new *Guide to Formation Advising*, "Most people who are asked to participate in formation work lack the specialized training and skill development that are needed for this important and complex ministry."[2]

These are just a few examples of how we see a structured primacy of place for intellectual formation. I have seen this implicit primacy of intellectual formation play out firsthand in our classrooms just this last semester. At one point, a professor was offering to cancel class and rearrange the syllabus slightly so that the more than twenty-five ministry students (lay and religious) could attend the opening keynote for a conference being held on campus regarding the church's ongoing response to the clergy sexual abuse crisis. More than one student voiced that they valued their classes as a primary responsibility and thought that other opportunities should fit around them in priority.

In the moment, this was a beautifully articulated statement of investment and commitment. The conference in question, however, might have been one of the most important opportunities in formation on accountability, healing, and trust that our US church has seen in two decades. The fact that it was offered right in their backyard made it all the more compelling as an opportunity for formation, which the professor of the class, to his credit, recognized. I will return to this classroom experience below.

Why is it a danger if we allow seminaries and formation programs to maintain primacy of place for intellectual formation? Let's turn to recent data to begin to answer this question.

The Center for Applied Research in the Apostolate (CARA) gathered data in 2018 to quantify the number of alleged offenses of sexual abuse in the church in five-year increments. Offenses were reported as far back as prior to 1954. We already know that 80 percent of cases that came to light in the abuse crisis of 2002 happened before 1985.[3]

---

[2] Edward McCormack, *Guide to Formation Advising for Seminary Faculty: Accompaniment, Participation, and Evaluation* (Washington, DC: The Catholic University of America Press, 2020), 3.

[3] See John Jay College Research Team, *The Causes and Context of Sexual Abuse of Minors by Catholic Priests in the United States, 1950–2010* (Washington, DC: USCCB, May 2011), https://www.usccb.org/sites/default/files/issues-and-action/child-and-youth-protection/upload/The-Causes-and-Context-of-Sexual-Abuse-of-Minors-by-Catholic-Priests-in-the-United-States-1950-2010.pdf.

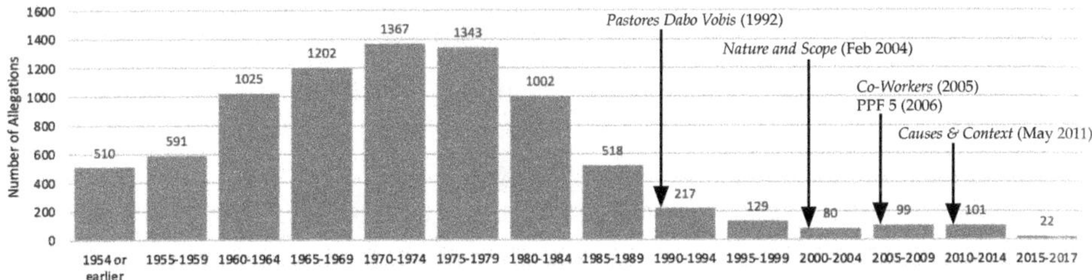

Source: CARA Report: vol. 24, no. 2 (Fall 2018)

Layering on a few additional historical markers assists us in absorbing what the graph has to offer. Namely, in 1992 Pope Saint John Paul II released the apostolic exhortation *Pastores Dabo Vobis*. Monsignor Michael Heintz wrote of this document:

> *Pastores Dabo Vobis* was truly a game-changer in ministerial formation. John Paul II, typically attentive to anthropological concerns, introduced, among other things, the category of human formation to seminary work. The humanity of the man to be ordained is critically important, as it is the instrument through which his priesthood is mediated. The work of grace, building on nature, is thus better served when a healthy, integrated humanity is the context of substratum *in* which, *from* which, and *through* which such grace operates.[4]

The data depicted in this chart reflects the impact this exhortation began to have. Then in December 2001 the USCCB began the first phase of the revision of the *Program of Priestly Formation* (PPF). This edition (PPF 5) was greatly influenced by *Pastores Dabo Vobis*.[5] Then in 2005 and 2006, *Co-Workers in the Vineyard of the Lord* and the fifth edition of the Program for Priestly Formation were promulgated. Each document carefully articulated methods and elements of human formation in their respective constituencies. In 2011, the second John Jay report was released, which described the historical, sociological,

---

[4] Foreword to Keating, "Beyond Schooling," 6–7; emphasis mine.
[5] Not recorded on the chart, the US bishops first passed their Charter, *Promise to Protect and Call to Heal*, in 2002 (updated in 2011 and 2018).

seminary, and organizational contexts that led to abuse.[6] One of its many essential insights is the finding that while priest abusers did not differ from healthy priests significantly in intelligence or psychology tests, they did have intimacy deficits and absence of close personal relationships before and during seminary. Additionally, most had no human formation. For clarity: human formation addresses exactly these types of intimacy deficits in candidates for ecclesial ministry.

Let us return to our question: Why is it a danger to allow seminaries and formation programs to maintain primacy of place for intellectual formation? It is dangerous because human formation—not intellectual formation—is a significant, documented, determining element in the health of our ecclesial ministers and their subsequent behaviors personally and professionally.

Put bluntly, ministers do not abuse because they were not adequately formed intellectually. Bishops, priests, deacons, and other ministers do not violate boundaries and make unhealthy, damaging choices because they do not have all the answers theologically, or because they do not know how to formulate an analytical argument, or because they cannot perform an adequate close textual reading. They burn out, and subsequently make increasingly unhealthy decisions—as documented in a plurality of Lilly-funded studies through their Flourishing in Ministry grant initiative[7]—because they do not adequately attend to their ongoing human, spiritual, and communal needs.

And why would they? Why would they adequately attend to human, spiritual, and communal formation if they were trained to evaluate those needs as of a lesser importance in seminary? Or worse, why would they attend to them if formation around those needs were dismissed disparagingly and a snide or cynical culture was permitted to develop around them?

It is human nature to perform the way we train. My mother graduated from the School (now College) of Architecture at the University of Notre Dame. Growing up, she would tell me stories of spending entire nights in the architecture building at her drafting table in order

---

[6] John Jay College Research Team, *Causes and Context of Sexual Abuse.*

[7] One seminal multiphase grant was led by Matt Bloom, https://workwellresearch.org/research-projects/flourishing-in-ministry. Other additional findings are available directly through the Lilly Endowment, https://lillyendowment.org/stories/circles-of-friends/.

to complete projects. In her more than forty years of professional practice, she continues to pull all-nighters to finish a project. She performs as she trained. We know this pattern to be true in sports as well. Why do athletes try to get so many repetitions in on the court, field, rink? They do it because, as one former football coach at Notre Dame said, "You don't rise to the occasion. You sink to the level of your preparation."[8] Throughout the waves of the abuse crises our church has faced, we have sunk to our level of preparation. I will even go so far as to say that we have sunk to our level of formation.

In the midst of the most recent wave of the abuse crisis, the greatest challenge to the formation of ordained and lay ecclesial ministers was choosing to address the crisis head-on and to carefully craft ways for the formation community to hold the unfolding experience, and their commensurate reactions, in common.

In subsequent years, the challenge in formation remains naming the reality of the ministerial context in which we find ourselves. We need to educate young students about the actual facts of the abuse, timelines, handling of it, contributing factors, etc. We must help them prepare to enter a ministerial environment where the dynamics of this history are still active, which means developing their awareness of risk factors that could lead to dangerous situations[9] in their own ministerial lives, and strategies[10] for how to avoid them.

Let's turn from primarily diagnostic insights to the meaningful, effective practices that could build or restore accountability, healing, and trust in seminary and university contexts. I will name three of the most prominent practices from my vantage point as a ministerial formator for lay and religious at an academically rigorous institution.

The first practice is utter transparency—or, said differently, "No silence; no hidden information." In our shared formation program (lay and religious), we communicate a clear message: this is a formation program where we all seek to build the kingdom of God and serve the church; for that reason, we have the duty and ability to speak into one another's lives personally and professionally. If a

---

[8] Brian Kelly, proving self-knowledge is not the sole contributing factor to accomplishing successful outcomes.

[9] Burnout, boundary violations, isolation, lack of resiliency, and intimacy deficits to name a few.

[10] Consistent spiritual direction, a nonnegotiable prayer life, maintaining and cultivating essential relationships, and habits of wellness attending to such things as sleep, nutrition, restorative activities, and physical activity.

classmate notices a behavior, experiences a situation, or becomes aware of a concern in a peer—no matter how large or small—we ask them to name it to a member of the formation staff. Staff can then competently decide how best to handle it.

Undoubtedly, this type of transparency gives formators helpful information to see a more complete picture of individual candidates for ministry. We explicitly take silence and hiding off the table during orientation and in ongoing, opportune conversations. This shared and intentional practice is a way to build a culture in our institution and formation community. For this practice to function as it should, we have to cultivate and maintain good, trusting relationships among the formation staff, faculty, administration, and candidates for ecclesial ministry.

Interestingly, we have evidence that this practice bears fruit beyond our immediate formation community. Recently, when two of our students were serving in a summer immersion program in the South, they had the opportunity to work alongside other diocesan and religious seminarians from a different community. Over the course of their time together, our students noticed problematic behaviors in one of the diocesan seminarians. Deeply formed in the practice of not remaining silent when noticing concerning behavior, they recognized the responsibility that fell to them to name it. First, they checked in with their own formator about how to have a conversation with the seminarian directly. After having that conversation, the behaviors went unchanged and, in fact, worsened, so they began to consider sharing their observations with the seminarian's formator (in this case, the diocesan director of vocations). They scheduled a meeting with him and consulted their own formator to prepare. They carefully formulated their simple informational observations without personal commentary or invective and offered them humbly and respectfully. Happily, they were received with a spirit of gratitude. What a beautiful example of co-responsibility and accountability.

Next, to build accountability in seminaries and universities, we need diversity in the formation community in gender, ordination status, and age. We need to train seminarians and lay candidates for ecclesial ministry together. As I have written elsewhere,[11] there is a

---

[11] Stacey Noem, "We Need to Stop Separating Seminarians and Lay Ministers in Formation," *America,* November 20, 2019, https://www.americamagazine.org/faith/2019/11/20/we-need-stop-separating-seminarians-lay-ministers-formation.

difference between "together" and "alongside one another." I do not mean ministry candidates should simply share a campus, facilities, or instructors. I mean they should be in class, in ministry, in conversation, in prayer, in community—together. We cannot form graduate ministry candidates to serve the people of God in isolation from the people of God (i.e., the laity). Seminarians and candidates for religious life are not breaking the formation community bubble when they go to a ministry placement for only six to eight hours a week.

Formation in an integrated, communal context produces precisely the type of ecclesial ministers we need in order to move forward as a church. Community relationships form leaders who are authentic, resilient, and empathetic. They comfortably share power rather than gathering it to themselves. In the shared formation context, they learn to be accountable in every aspect of church ministry—from administration to pastoral care, from preaching to stewardship, and from professional integrity to affective maturity. This makes them stronger, healthier, more balanced future servants of the church because it exponentially magnifies opportunities for human formation while simultaneously breaking down any potential isolation from the people of God.

Back to my earlier classroom anecdote to illustrate this point. As I mentioned, some students initially responded to potentially canceling class to attend the opening conference keynote with a beautifully articulated ideology that valued classes as a primary responsibility and placed other elements in a lower priority. Before the professor even responded to this initial statement, another student (of different ordination status) raised their hand and stated that they valued all aspects of their formation equally, of which class was but one. When they are formed together, candidates for ecclesial ministry can organically act as checks and balances to one another.

Point of information: Shared formation does not happen in the vast majority of seminaries in the United States or in any that train diocesan seminarians.

Third, we need well-trained, diverse formators. Formation is a complex, intricate, multifaceted, tender, highly specialized, still-evolving art *and* science. It is challenging, taxing, and vulnerable work for the formator. Why? Because anyone working in formation is subject to ongoing formation themselves.

In *Christifideles Laici,* John Paul II writes, "There is the conviction that one cannot offer a true and effective formation to others if the individual has not taken on or developed a personal responsibility for [their own] formation."[12] As formators, we cannot be hypocritical. We have to be willing to do and live what we ask our students to do and live. A lot of folks are not comfortable with or interested in signing up for that level of radical integration and personal challenge. Among the ordained, "formation work is not often a person's first choice of ministry."[13] For all these reasons, it is essential to form formators intentionally and well.

I conclude with a thought on co-responsibility, which describes how the university and the local church might work together to form future ministers for the church. In a speech given in August 2012, Pope Benedict XVI stated:

> Co-responsibility demands a change in mindset especially concerning the role of lay people in the Church. They should not be regarded as "collaborators" of the clergy, but, rather, as people who are really "co-responsible" for the Church's being and acting. It is therefore important that a mature and committed laity . . . make its own specific contribution to the ecclesial mission with respect for the ministries and tasks that each one has in the life of the Church and always in cordial communion with the bishops.[14]

Here Pope Benedict XVI makes the distinction between "collaboration" and "co-responsibility." This is an important theological distinction to which I will add a third category. Collaboration implies that, as a layperson, authority may or may not rest with me, and I therefore have room to distance myself from responsibility when the going gets rough. Co-working (even as it appears in the title, *Co-workers in the Vineyard of the Lord*) has clearly been described as subordinates participating in the power and authority of ordained superiors such as bishops. But *co-responsibility* holds up my own proper role and authority.

---

[12] Pope Saint John Paul II, postsynodal apostolic exhortation *Christifideles Laici* (Vatican City: Libreria Editrice Vaticana, December 30, 1988), 63.

[13] McCormack, *Guide to Formation Advising*, 1.

[14] Pope Benedict XVI, Message on the Occasion of the Sixth Ordinary Assembly of the International Forum of Catholic Action, August 10, 2012.

Thus, to provide a personal illustration as an example: as a professor and formator, co-responsibility acknowledges that I do not participate in the authority of my (beloved) bishop when I am forming seminary students. Rather, this work is an exercise of my *personal* power and authority afforded me through full initiation into the Body of Christ through the sacraments of baptism, Eucharist, and confirmation. My work as a formator is an exercise of my *expert* power and authority earned through my education, formation, credentialing, and decades of experience in ministry, teaching, community formation, and spiritual direction. And this role is an exercise of my *referent* power and authority developed, again, through ministerial experience and also through the relationships I cultivate and continue to foster.

From the perspective of co-responsibility, I need not participate in the power and authority of the bishop to serve the church's ecclesial mission. Nevertheless, all of our work is infused with the Holy Spirit by our shared choice (the bishop's and ours in the MDiv program) to openly cooperate. Theologically, we model co-responsibility when we participate in the perichoretic nature of our triune God—when we work toward mutual in-dwelling instead of compartmentalizing. Practically, this means mutual invitation and creating space for the free flow of communication, as well as sharing resources, expertise, and best practices.

Co-responsibility—as both a concept and lived reality—is only newly being articulated and explored. The current synod process is one example of how we, as a church, are trying to figure it out. It may not go smoothly at first, but none of us can abdicate our obligation to, and investment in, the Body of Christ. Beautifully, this shared responsibility focuses on abundance, magnifies our gifts, and augments our freedom to conform ourselves—individually and communally—ever more closely to God.

12

On Ministry:
Professionalization, Authority, and the Whole Christ

Kevin G. Grove, CSC

Introduction

The following reflections concern the abuse crisis and the training of ministers. The purpose of these considerations of ministry is not to ascertain the causes of the crisis or to evaluate the ministerial formation programs and structures that might have contributed to those causes or the crisis in itself. Rather, the humbler scope of this chapter is to begin considering ministerial training from the vantage of those who have only known a church in crisis. Thus, I am particularly concerned with those who have begun in ministry since 2001 and 2002. There are references to the University of Notre Dame's formation programs through the Department of Theology, since this is the place of my work. I recognize that fine formation programs exist throughout the country but have limited these reflections to the one that I know best.

After considering the vantage point of ministers who have worked in the Catholic Church only after the 2002 public revelations of the US abuse crisis, I look at three aspects of ministry in the church today: the professionalization of ministry; new chapters concerning authority; and reasons for hope, or theological paradigms for the wholeness of Christ.

Continuing Crisis:
New Ministers in the Church after 2002

Ordained in 2010, I am no longer a new priest. But, as an adult and certainly as a minister, the Catholic Church as shattered by the abuse crisis is the only church that I have known. This vantage distinguishes those we might call "young adults" and "young people" from prior generations of Catholics. For those who have come into adulthood around the turn of the millennium, a Catholic Church before the abuse crisis is only a matter for history or speculation, but not lived experience.

I can provide by means of my own story two insights into this vantage. I was a sophomore in college when the abuse crisis broke in Boston's newspapers. Upon graduation from college I entered formation in the Congregation of Holy Cross—the religious order at Notre Dame and in which I continue as a vowed religious and priest. In terms of vantage: First, I had to grapple with this Catholic Church— in an abuse crisis—as a place to do ministry at the same time I was discerning religious life and priesthood as an undergraduate. Second, the way in which one can observe ministerial priesthood depicted in mid-twentieth-century culture (Rossellini movies, etc.) and how some of my friends—both lay colleagues and confreres in religious life— describe the way in which Catholics equated the church with a vener- ated ordained priesthood has always been alarming but also never my experience. I was a transitional deacon when I first as a minister heard the story of a parent and churchgoer whose child had been abused by a Catholic priest. I had been a priest less than a year before I was asked by a stranger on the street if I were a child molester. I am in no way speaking against the righteous anger of those who rightly stand up for the abused, the marginalized, and those whose voices have been taken away. But when that anger by extension or associa- tion is cast at oneself, it is arresting in such a powerful way that it can make one miss a step.

The church in which I minister and teach is one that has for the entirety of that time been coming to terms with its ongoing broken- ness. My experience of that has been in three ministerial contexts. I worked in two Midwestern US parishes and then as an assistant chaplain for the students and faculty of the University of Cambridge while a graduate student. Since that time, I have been at Notre Dame, teaching students in the theology department and serving as a priest in residence, or pastoral minister, in a residential community. I offer all of that by way of introducing the heart of my comments on ministry—for we have been living in the church of the abuse crisis for long enough that we now have more than one generational vantage upon it. Moreover, for those with a middle-aged and younger perspective, a church in crisis is the only one they have known.

Professionalization of Ministry

One of the very good things that has emerged—beginning in earnest after the Dallas Charter (2002), but now continuing in lay and seminary ministerial formation programs—is what I am calling as a shorthand the "professionalization" of ministry. This has not been a fearful thing at all. People wondered at the time the abuse scandal broke if meaningful interactions between ministers and those whom they were serving would be possible without mediating or supervising entities. The last twenty years have proven that more professional development of our ministers is good all the way around. This is observable in four ways.

The first gain of the professionalization of ministry is the development of healthy ministerial boundaries. At the University of Notre Dame, for example, our master of divinity degree, in partnership with Moreau Seminary, provides formation for both lay and ordained ministers. Since the abuse crisis, that formation has included extensive and ongoing reflection about boundaries that are healthy. Some of these were obvious correctives for times in which vulnerable people were taken advantage of in times past. Ministers are no longer alone with minors in cars, in places of residence, and the like. That was the easy and the obvious. But this has brought about consideration of boundaries that help ministers to think about their own identities and what it means for them to serve in ways that are healthy for themselves and those around them. I am the dedicated chaplain to our lay formation program and have been truly impressed to see our lay ministers establish boundaries in terms of the difference between their ministries and their families, their life of work and what sustains them spiritually and emotionally. Similarly, our priests and religious in formation now look at the way their commitment to their communal life of faith sharing, spiritual direction, and support allow them to minister in healthy ways. In short, the broad-field development and establishment by professional ministers of boundaries does not keep them from doing good ministry but supports them in it.

The second is professionalization of volunteer service and clergy activity. On the ground, the church responded impressively in terms of basic formation for parishes and schools in terms of safeguarding. I mentioned above that I live in an undergraduate dormitory. The students in my dorm are planning this academic year to do tutoring at a local Catholic primary school. They have taken into account the fact that their background checks and safeguarding training all have to be processed before they can begin. This is actually good formation for them—an awareness of what a local Catholic primary school should demand of them or any other volunteer. This is also true now of clergy (at least in the United States and some parts of the world). Gone are the days when a priest could go roving around presiding at weddings, baptizing, or saying Masses with just the card that in the old days was called a "celebret" (Latin for "let him celebrate"). Rather, paperwork for priests in good standing must be processed and approved anywhere in this country. Chanceries and religious orders have grown remarkably efficient in getting this work done. And in this regard, having lived elsewhere in the world, what the US Catholic Church has accomplished—in terms of professionalization of identity checks for both volunteers and clergy—is impressive. That students, coaches, afterschool carers, and others should de facto be trained in abuse prevention and reporting is noble and impressive.

The third good aspect of the professionalization of ministry concerns the structure of reporting abuses. Mandatory reporting for all situations outside of the seal of confession allows for competent authorities to determine whether or not action needs to be taken in a particular situation. Even for the sacramental spaces that demand confidence—many of these have been adjusted for transparency. At Notre Dame, confessions are on offer three times per day. This continues, but the confessional space has been subtly modified to have a panel of frosted glass behind the priest. The penitent retains his or her privacy. The priest can be seen to be sitting in a confessional chair. It is subtle in architectural appearance, but a good way to ensure ecclesial transparency.

The fourth point of professionalization has to do with formation in both lay and seminary contexts. In both lay and seminary formation in our program, formation for integrated human sexuality is part and parcel of formation for ministry. Prior generations frequently speak about how integrated human formation inclusive of issues surrounding healthy sexuality were not a part of their training and may have even been taboo. That is no longer the case, and sessions on right relationship for ministry in the Catholic Church are part of both our lay and seminarian students' experience before they even set foot in the classroom. They continue, in an ongoing way, throughout their time in formation.

These four aspects of professionalization of our ministry formation programs (boundaries, safeguarding, reporting, and formation for integrated human sexuality) are a multipronged approach that is working and should be encouraged. None of these professionalization practices can be considered a guarantor against abuse, but together they do form a bedrock on which good ministry might take place.

Authority

If the first point about the professionalization of ministry was optimistic, this next one, unfortunately, is not. In the summer of 2018, then American Cardinal Theodore McCarrick resigned from the College of Cardinals and was eventually laicized on account of abuse of minors. In terms of power and authority, there is no doubt that McCarrick had it. The news has already well covered the way in which he was embedded in ecclesial and national life with access to funding, personages, and clout. Without recounting all of the details, I recall thinking this was even worse than the news breaking of the scandal in 2002, for one of the very authorities committed to reform had in fact himself been a serial offender. At the university level, honorary degrees were rescinded; McCarrick at that time went into a life of seclusion in a religious house, and he was eventually removed from the clerical state. But something broke open anew in that terrible moment: a realization that the good professionalization that had happened on the ground in the Catholic Church was not matched by the same thing at the level of authority. And while this is no knock against the many truly wonderful leaders who currently continue to work in the church, we have only begun to start to think as a church about what shared responsibility for the Body of Christ means at the level of ecclesial shepherding. This is going to take time.

At the University of Notre Dame, in light of the McCarrick scandal, for the first time in my ministry, we, the Holy Cross community together, addressed the abuse crisis in a concerted effort in our preaching at Masses across campus beginning with the opening of the school year Mass in 2018. These book chapters are part of the university's effort in that regard. The conversations are still ongoing. And I must add that the 2019 *motu proprio Vos Estis* published by Pope Francis is yet another step, though a new enough one that we are still seeing how it might function.[1] Nevertheless, it is an attempt to fill a gap— that authorities have to be appropriately responsible for abuse, just as coaches of Catholic Youth Organization teams and local pastors are. Francis's move is a "professionalization" of ecclesial leaders in this regard.

Paradigms for Hope: The Whole Christ

My final point is one that I borrow from St. Augustine, who thought deeply about a fractured and wounded church in his own time and on whom I draw extensively for my own academic work. I also am drawing on an academic publication concerning Augustine's sermons by the Jesuit theologian Michael McCarthy, who wrote a splendid article in *Theological Studies* in 2005 called "An Ecclesiology of Groaning."[2] Without going too far into the weeds, Augustine's insight as he preached was of an ever increasing understanding of what it means to be the "whole Christ," that is, of Christ the head of a body in which we are the members.

This realization, for Augustine, emerged out of the psalms of lament. One drew closest to Christ when groaning. In his cry of dereliction, Jesus cried out, "My God, my God, why have you forsaken me?"

---

[1] Pope Francis, *motu proprio Vos Estis Lux Mundi* (Vatican City: Libreria Editrice Vaticana, May 7, 2019), https://www.vatican.va/content/francesco/en/motu_proprio /documents/papa-francesco-motu-proprio-20190507_vos-estis-lux-mundi.html.

[2] Michael McCarthy, "An Ecclesiology of Groaning: Augustine, the Psalms, and the Making of Church," *Theological Studies* 66, no. 1 (2005): 23–48.

In that extraordinary moment from the cross, he did not choose to speak a new line but to quote Psalm 22. If we think about it, that is an odd line to choose. For if he were truly God, then he was not forsaken. But if he were not truly forsaken, then divinity could be using humanity like a puppet, as if God were some sort of divine ventriloquist. Augustine's great insight was that in that moment Christ took up human experience at the farthest point from God: abandoned, utterly alone, and unto death. And there he spoke in our words so that we might speak in his. He did not take away our pain but joined us in it such that we might not be alone. And thus when we lament, when we groan, we might do so in Christ. That lowest point became a locus of the most marvelous christological exchange that helped Augustine and the people in his North African church to discover the wholeness of Christ in a way that really challenged them.

If one understands that Christ really was speaking in the Scriptures in the voices of broken humans, then Augustine beautifully claims that Christ was speaking in the experience of those in their own time. This obligated them in a new way to recognize Christ's voice in their midst in the widow, the poor, the orphan. They were to find themselves shifting, like Saul did in becoming Paul (Acts 9), to hear the voice of the Lord in their midst and start to serve the members of his body right around them.

Augustine's theological paradigm can bring us hope because we may well need to be—in an ongoing way, it seems—a church that laments and groans. Not only do we do so in acknowledgment of our sins, but in order that here at the seemingly farthest point from Christ we might find him speaking in us once more. The courage to lament this brokenness together has the potential in humble prayer to unite us once more in the whole Christ.

Conclusions

At the end of the day, I still love this church because it is Christ's. I explained this to a secular colleague who could not seem to comprehend that point by offering the following explanation. There are parts of all of our identities that we have to grieve. I can offer a non-ecclesial example. I am an American. While I can be and am proud of that identity, that does not insulate me from occasions of shame and even grieving for the brokenness within my own nation. That example is helpful for, though not symmetrical to, thinking about the church. The difference is, of course, the method of engagement. My citizenship and my vote make me an American. After baptism, my membership in the Body of Christ is a grace that is given from above. And ways in which we engage as the Body of Christ now—even if by lamenting and groaning—are central parts of the work of growing together as we follow Christ our head. For though the issues I mentioned in the first sections—professionalization of ministry and responsible authority—are essential, they are structural elements. Alone they cannot bring about the healing that we will ultimately need—together—to find in Christ. For that, we as his Body may need to lament and to groan, in the hope that in our shattered landscape Christ's voice might emerge to guide the work ahead.

13

Shifting the Overton Window on Spiritual Care for Sexual Violence

Peter Capretto

Introduction

Theologians who teach around sexual violence face a peculiar challenge when training future faith leaders: while they are neither the therapists nor pastors of their students, they also have little choice but to interrogate the personal and spiritual formation of their students. This frequently puts theological educators in an awkward position that is difficult to explain to ministers in training. Particularly in chaplaincy and spiritual care contexts, the most established method for addressing this is through assignments requiring ministers in training to "work through" their emotional pasts. And yet, students are more than justified in critiquing such requirements as a form of interpersonal educational violence, where would-be pastors are coerced into disclosing their own traumatic histories before their professional superiors for academic credit. Particularly given the fact that trauma theorists have reached a near consensus that sexual violence derives primarily from abuses and weaponizations of power,[1]

---

[1] This principle in trauma studies is now widely shared, but it was strengthened considerably by Judith Herman in *Trauma and Recovery: The Aftermath of Violence—from Domestic Abuse to Political Terror* (New York: Basic Books, 1992). More recently, Herman expanded this analysis considerably in *Truth and Repair: How Trauma Survivors Envision Justice* (New York: Basic Books, 2023). See also the important contribution of womanist pastoral theologian Stephanie Crumpton in *A Womanist Pastoral Theology against*

it becomes difficult to support the claim that pedagogical practices rooted in emotional coercion might culminate in a spiritual formation that contests that same practice. As a result, attempts to contextualize such work—as important as it may be—can easily come across as conflictual or self-defeating:

> "Yes, your long-term success as an ethical spiritual caregiver requires that you take an inventory of your personal history. No, doing this work is not a therapeutic exercise, though it has therapeutic effects that are crucial for your ability to mitigate harm in the future care work you do—particularly around sexual abuse and trauma. Yes, your personal inventory will be graded, but not on the content of your life. No, I am not emotionally invested in the particularities of the history you disclose; yes, I do care for you as a person. No, you do not have to disclose details that you do not feel comfortable sharing; yes, you will miss vital opportunities for self-awareness if you withhold too much. No, I am not just doing this to you because it was done to me; yes, there is purpose in the process. All of this is awkward for me too, though probably not as much as it is for you."

For this reason, as faith leaders continue to reckon with the ongoing effects and proliferation of sexual violence in churches and communities of faith, I'm convinced that the common mantra that theological educators must be "pastor to the pastors" is fundamentally misguided—particularly in contexts of training faith leaders around sexual violence and survivor-centered care.[2] This is because practices of accountability in theological educational settings are

---

Intimate and Cultural Violence (New York: Palgrave MacMillan, 2014). Crumpton expands upon this principle considerably in her analysis of intimate partner and cultural violence in relation to race.

[2] While the trope of the "pastor to the pastors" has gained traction within some informal ministry contexts, it has also found increasing and positive attention within theological education research in recent decades. See, for instance, Judy Rois, Daphne Rixon, Alex Faseruk, "Organizational Perspectives on Stained Glass Ceilings for Female Bishops in the Anglican Communion: A Case Study of the Church of England," *Journal of Business Diversity* 13 (2013): 29; James L. Tegelhutter, "A Phenomenological Study of Pastoral Accountability in Covenant Community" (PhD diss., Southeastern University, 2022); Dondi Enos Costin, "Essential Leadership Competencies for U.S. Air Force Wing Chaplains" (PhD diss., Southern Baptist Theological Seminary, 2008). The paradigm is used to describe both faith leaders with higher-level ecclesial standings, such as bishops, and theological educators themselves.

constantly in tension with professional and emotional boundaries, which means that it would require a highly proprietary and illegible definition of "pastor" to successfully negotiate this tension.[3] While pastors may at times need their own pastors, a crucial complication is their position of greater power and potential to inflict harm upon persons in vulnerable positions than others hold. Sometimes what a would-be pastor needs more than anything is a theologian to tell them to find another career—or, even, demand it. Despite popular derisions of the concept, gatekeeping is not simply an insider's game of discriminately excluding persons from positions of power; gatekeeping is a mechanism for ensuring that those positioned to help others are actually trained toward that end, which includes the necessary formation to do no harm. Pastors regularly defend their profession as equally if not more significant societally as any other skilled field such as law or medicine, yet cries of "gatekeeping" against vigilante surgeons is notably absent from such discourse.

With these tensions around the training of future faith leaders in view, the following chapter interrogates the tendency of spiritual care training around sexual violence in theological education and how it often fails survivors of sexual violence. More specifically, it argues that much of the most ostensibly "responsible" spiritual care training is deemed as such precisely because it focuses primarily on liability management in the form of boundaries training and harm mitigation. While I remain fully supportive of such measures, my contention is that making liability mitigation the focal point of spiritual care training around sexual violence has unwittingly shifted our Overton Windows—the default scope of acceptable behavior—away from practices that might actually begin to establish trust with survivors of sexual violence. As counterintuitive as it may seem, the most effective method for establishing trust with survivors will be letting go of any fixation on whether or not spiritual caregivers are trustworthy and instead embracing the question, "What ugly fights must we fight, sacrifices must we make, and visions of purity must we grieve so that our faith institutions might make unrepentant abusers afraid to enter them?"

---

[3] For a foundational and systematic definition of the pastor in pastoral care contexts, see Seward Hiltner, *Preface to Pastoral Theology: The Ministry and Theory of Shepherding* (Nashville: Abingdon Press, 1958).

Negotiating Lived Experience in Spiritual Care Training

One of the grounding principles of training of anyone moving into the work of spiritual care emerges from the founder of the modern clinical pastoral education movement, Anton Boisen, who insisted that any chance for theology to live up to its name requires that we treat those we serve as what he called "living human documents."[4] Whenever I share this principle with my pastoral care students, it is almost always met with immediate appreciation. Students typically understand the principle to be saying, "We need to take lived experience seriously." This is, of course, true. As fraught as the concept of lived experience or *Erlebnis* is in the history of philosophy,[5] psychology,[6] phenomenology,[7] and trauma theory,[8] much of the harm enacted by ecclesial and cultural institutions is indeed a function of a lack of respect for the lived experiences of others.

Reducing Boisen's insight merely to a comment about lived experience, however, also misses something crucial about what it means to approach one another as "documents." Namely, we do not pay arbitrary deference to documents; rather, we pay closer attention to them. Often this is to understand what these documents are saying, but just as commonly it is to discern what those documents do not speak to. Strangely, this sort of attention is more demanding than deference. Anyone who has had to put in the personal work to refrain

---

[4] Anton Boisen, *The Exploration of the Inner World* (New York: Willett, Clark, 1936), 185. For subsequent historical uses of Boisen's important concept for pastoral care, see Bonnie Miller-McLemore, "The Human Web: Reflections on the State of Pastoral Theology," *The Christian Century*, April 7, 1993; Richard Coble, "From Web to Cyborg: Tracing Power in Care," *Journal of Pastoral Theology* 26 (2016).

[5] See Wilhelm Dilthey, *Selected Works: Hermeneutics and the Study of History*, vol. 4, ed. Rudolf A. Makkreel and Frithjof Rodi (Princeton: Princeton University Press, 1996); Wilhelm Dilthey, "The Rise of Hermeneutics," trans. Frederic Jameson, *New Literary History* 3 (1972): 229–44.

[6] See Max van Manen, *Researching Lived Experience: Human Science for an Action Sensitive Pedagogy*, 2nd ed. (New York: Routledge, 2015).

[7] Hans-Georg Gadamer, *Truth and Method*, 2nd ed., trans. Joel Weinsheimer and Donald G. Marshall (New York: Continuum, [1960] 1975), 54–55.

[8] For a fuller treatment of lived experience's uses and abuses in trauma theory and the philosophy of religion, see Peter Capretto, "The Psychic Economy and Fetishization of Traumatic Lived Experience," *Trauma and Transcendence: Suffering and the Limits of Theory*, ed. Eric Boynton and Peter Capretto (New York: Fordham University Press, 2018), 195–219.

from oversharing with others—so as not to co-opt a pastoral or therapeutic space to work out one's own emotional baggage—will understand that treating ourselves and those around us as living human documents just as frequently involves a negative or apophatic process. In the context of my work training future pastoral caregivers, I find myself more regularly emphasizing a claim I hadn't anticipated needing to communicate: "Your story is both more important and less important than you may realize." Much of the labor of spiritual formation is this process of discerning where epistemic deference[9] ends and where countertransference[10] begins.

One of the biggest pedagogical obstacles I face in working with progressive seminarians is overcoming their self-assurance that they and their liberal congregations are impervious to the patterns of abuse that have been more strongly associated with Catholic and evangelical churches. Not only have faith leaders in progressive, open and affirming, and liberal Protestant congregations enacted many of the same sexual violences against their congregants, and not only have they frequently failed to advocate for the survivors of sexual violence under their auspices, but their veneer of sexual inclusivity and allyship has also very often made them more resistant to holding themselves accountable for these failures. While I would not go so far as to argue that this means progressive Protestants face a more difficult task than Catholics in building trust in relation to abuse, there is no question in my mind that very few things are more damaging to the prospect of long-term trust building than an unwavering commitment to the idea that one's faith community is beyond reproach and trustworthy when it comes to spiritual care for abuse.

Defensiveness, Identification, and Trustworthiness

This matter of trustworthiness is often where I encounter spiritual caregivers beginning to become defensive as they interrogate themselves and their identities as advocates for trauma survivors. There is

---

[9] For a representative and thorough treatment of the concept of epistemic deference within the literature of deference epistemology, see Sofia Ellinor Bokros, "A Deference Model of Epistemic Authority," *Synthese* 198 (2021): 12041–69.

[10] For the most sustained treatment of countertransference in pastoral theological training, see Pamela Cooper-White, *Shared Wisdom: Use of the Self in Pastoral Care and Counseling* (Minneapolis: Fortress Press, 2004).

nothing inherently wrong with being defensive, insofar as defensiveness is very often what makes surviving trauma possible.[11] All too often, pastoral caregivers misunderstand the importance of "bringing one's full self" as somehow implying that trauma responses like dissociation and compartmentalization are somehow not "authentic," which is nothing more than an overconfident form of victim blaming cloaked in pop psychology. The pejorative connotation that we tend to associate with defensiveness derives more precisely from defensiveness that follows identification. That is, we become defensive about identities that are important to us yet that we feel uncertain about. Defensiveness then becomes a proxy for an overzealous insecurity, which often does warrant some critique.

Of course, it's all too easy to point out the defensive insecurities of our social and political rivals, some of whom identify so intensely with masculine bravado or grotesque fantasies of white power that merely drawing attention to these traits sends them racing to Twitter to protest just a bit too much. Yet no one is without identification, and each of us has things we want to believe about ourselves. "I'm not racist." "I haven't internalized misogyny." "I may not be perfect, but deep down I'm a good person."

This is not to suggest that all identifications and their ensuing defenses are equal. While overidentifying as a "good preacher" may breed some homiletical stagnancy in the long-term, overidentifying as "good white person who is not a racist" will rather quickly make oneself immune to opportunities for growth as an accomplice against white supremacy. These patterns are not on the same playing field, and we should all have low levels of tolerance for bad-faith false equivalences, which only ever tip the power back toward those who relish everyone except them engaging in ever-escalating practices of self-flagellation. It does, however, help us to identify what I'm convinced is the most crucial trap that threatens any answer to the question of how it is that the church can restore trust in the years ahead around sexual violence and trauma.

That trap, quite simply yet deceptively, is the desire of the faith leaders and the church to be viewed by others as trustworthy. This, I recognize, is a peculiar identification to take aim at. Trust is, of course, a noble and crucial aim. While there is tremendous disagree-

---

[11] Anna Freud, *The Ego and the Mechanisms of Defense,* trans. Cecil Baines (New York: International Universities Press, 1966).

ment in developmental theories of identity and attachment among pastoral theologians and psychologists,[12] there is general consensus on the importance of creating environments of trust for those around us. From cultivating secure attachments in children to fostering strong therapeutic alliances to journeying with survivors in recovery processes, trust is a durable constant.

There is, however, a subtle yet profoundly consequential difference between, on the one hand, a desire to restore one's sense of trustworthiness and, on the other, the intention to create a space that vulnerable persons feel that they can trust. What is this difference? I would insist that this is more than a matter of mere rhetorical chicanery. The difference is that the desire to restore one's sense of trustworthiness will forever be beholden to the identification with a reputation, whereas the goal of creating a space that vulnerable persons can trust will readily forfeit that reputation if it means increasing that sense of safety.

Boundaries Training and Liability Management in Spiritual Care Training

Perhaps this apparent trap of identification around trustworthiness feels too abstract or impractical. Or perhaps some would be skeptical of the distinction between the desire to be seen as trustworthy and the desire to create safety, because, after all, one may contest, "How can one ever be able to create spaces of trust for others unless one has successfully communicated to them that one is trustworthy?"

What does avoiding this trap look like practically as a rubric for restoring trustworthy spaces for survivors of abuse and for creating a truth-telling community? An immediate obstacle is that many of the most important answers to this question are so obvious that they risk being insulting to name among those already reflecting on sexual violence in theological contexts: churches must be willing to make not merely convenient but costly investments in the safety of survivors, centering their experiences and making it obvious to anyone looking on that our ecclesial bodies—Catholic, Protestant, or otherwise—

---

[12] For a representative sample of the diverse perspectives in this area, see the contributions found in Felicity Kelcourse, ed., *Human Development and Faith: Life-Cycle Stages of Body, Mind, and Soul*, 2nd ed. (St. Louis, MO: Chalice Press, 2015).

genuinely care about the well-being of survivors more than even their own survival. Note that I describe these as obvious not because they are not difficult to follow through on but rather precisely because it is so easy for someone like me to score cheap points by championing them among those who are already sold on the need to do better. As the youths once said in a tone of derision, "So stunning; so brave." Allow me to put a bit more skin in the game and talk practically about what it might look like to negotiate this in the area where I spend the overwhelming majority of my professional life: educating future faith leaders in spiritual and pastoral care.

Like many who train future pastors, priests, and lay ministers, I find that the prospect that keeps me up at night is the thought that one of my students will one day become someone who sexually abuses a congregant, someone under their care, or anyone at all. It is not that I take personal responsibility or ownership for the actions of my students; they are their own persons with their own motivations and inner lives. But I'm also keenly aware that it would be a cowardly disavowal of my own institutional power to act as if I do not wield influence over my students on their paths to ordination—even if only through one measly required course in a seminary curriculum.

In dwelling on this prospect, my temptation, I'll confess, is to give in to the gravity of this fear and allow it to take center stage in the pedagogical tone I take with my students. What would this look like? Surprisingly, it looks quite responsible. It looks like making the focal point of spiritual care training around sexual abuse about boundaries training, liability management, and neoliberal compliance to legal structures that hopefully keep faith leaders out of the spotlight of crisis.[13] Particularly for those committed to a harm mitigation approach to sexual assault advocacy—which I myself endorse—these tactics should not be understated in their significance for meeting some of the most pressing crises facing faith institutions on this issue: healing and restoring trust is a nice idea, but that is not possible until one at least stops inflicting more violence. It is for this reason that, in many contexts, this is what much of the training in pastoral care for

---

[13] For further details on the history and methodology of boundaries training, see Marie Fortune, *Love Does No Harm: Sexual Ethics for the Rest of Us* (New York: Continuum, 1995).

sexual abuse and trauma looks like: a very responsible program that hopefully helps alumni stay out of the headlines, helps universities and theological institutions limit their legal liabilities, and helps professors like me ease our anxiety about advisees coming back to haunt them.

Shifting the Overton Window on Spiritual Care for Sexual Violence

There is, of course, nothing wrong with boundary training and compliance. The problem, rather, is how such focal points in the spiritual formation of future clergy frame what we understand as a trustworthy response to abuse.

In their studies of behavioral discourse in electoral politics, political scientists have coined what I believe is a very helpful heuristic for tracking this pattern and problem, which is known as the Overton Window.[14] The Overton Window describes the spectrum of behavior each of us deems acceptable along a certain continuum. In the world of electoral politics, this is most often used to explain how public opinion's sense of what counts as moderate shifts according to the mores of a particular moment; when the Republican Party declares a white supremacist insurrection on the Capitol that resulted in several deaths "legitimate political discourse," everyday voter disenfranchisement efforts and assaults on health care that mitigates transgender youth suicide seem more normal. When you feel a melancholic numbness upon witnessing institutional or cultural norms erode before your eyes, you are experiencing the Overton Window shifting away from the moral arc of the universe, which you hoped would be bending a bit more toward justice by now.

Yet, one of the counterintuitive takeaways from this research is that, contrary to conventional thinking that a hearts-and-minds approach is best achieved through moderate incrementalism, the most effective way for political actors to shift someone's Overton Window of acceptable behavior is not to target the moderate margins of that window. Rather, if one wants to shift a large group of people's behavior and

---

[14] Herbert H. Haines, "Radical Flank Effects," in *The Wiley-Blackwell Encyclopedia of Social and Political Movements*, ed. David A. Snow et al. (Oxford: Blackwell, 2013).

thought in a particular direction, one needs to take aim at the radical flanks of an issue—far beyond the scope of what they previously viewed as acceptable behavior. The reason for this is that public consensuses on what passes as "normal" are slow to change. Offering someone a gentle nudge to recalibrate their ethical attention is almost never enough to overcome the inertia of entrenched windows of normativity. Instead, if one wants to move others an inch on an issue, one must aim a mile past it.

One thing both Catholics and Protestants seem to understand on a deep, intuitive level is that their Overton Windows of acceptable and expected pastoral intervention on sexual abuse have not merely been inadequate but have stagnated prematurely. The problem with boundaries training and fixation on neoliberal compliance is precisely because everyone committed to sexual assault advocacy recognizes that these measures aren't even coming close to earning the trust of survivors of abuse and of younger generations for whom trust in the church has never been a default position. Even if such compliance measures are necessary, they prime future clergy with the lukewarm sensibility, "The way to build trust among survivors is to not abuse anyone." Stated baldly like this, one can already feel viscerally how anemic and, frankly, gross, this sensibility is. This attitude toward trust ultimately undergirds men's rights activists in the conviction that being nice to women entitles them to sex, that kindness is a currency put into a machine until intimacy falls out, that abstaining from abuse is a token that makes the church deserving of trust.

Fostering trust in the church is going to require shifting our Overton Window on acceptable spiritual care drastically beyond boundaries and compliance and into the territory of riskier work as spiritual accomplices who center the experience of survivors. And here, I must be crystal clear: the risk must be for the church, not the survivors it aspires to serve. One of the most counterintuitive features of this imperative is that it is going to mean an escalation in liability, not a mitigation. One of the most painful conversations I have with my pastoral care students through clinical assignments is inviting them to reflect in advance on how becoming a pastoral accomplice with survivors of sexual abuse is going to make them important enemies and that they need to prepare themselves for not backing down.

Conclusion: Fighting Ugly Fights

> "Do you think that I have come to bring peace to the earth?
> No, I tell you, but rather division!" (Luke 12:51)

So as not to mislead others, I must clarify that my fears around this issue remain very real. It is terrifying for me not to dwell at length with students on the question, "How do I keep myself from crossing boundaries with my congregants?" There is a part of me that wants to believe that, surely, clergy sexual abuse is already such a taboo that we have already moved our Overton Window beyond this long ago. And yet, the patterns of churches tell a different story of failure, which overshadows that fear. It is a fear that makes me embarrassed for any church that even aspires to be seen as trustworthy until it starts asking, "What ugly fights must we fight, sacrifices must we make, and visions of purity must we grieve so that this church might make unrepentant abusers afraid to enter it?"

It pains me knowing that many of us are not ready to ask this question of ourselves and those we serve and that a certain amount of theological training enables so many of us to obviate its claim on us. Yet, if you find yourself resistant to this question and continue wrestling with why so few survivors trust the church today, I would invite you to consider, as nondefensively as possible, that these two things might be connected.

14

Speaking and Enacting the Truth:
Language and Virtue in Ecclesial Formation[1]

Melanie Susan Barrett

In 2018, following the demise of Theodore McCarrick and the release of the Pennsylvania grand jury report, my seminary rector (Fr. John Kartje) asked our faculty to discuss what *we* could do to prevent such horrific abuse from occurring in the future. To develop effective solutions, however, we first needed to assess the problem correctly. This proved somewhat of a challenge, because even though the abuse itself can be explained doctrinally by original sin and the mystery of evil, such theological concepts (though entirely accurate) seem insufficient to explain the *institutional permissiveness* that enabled such abuse not only to occur but to reoccur—repeatedly. For if the Catholic Church is the "Body of Christ," as St. Paul famously taught, then should we not expect of it higher standards of conduct than those found in other human institutions—like Hollywood, the media, and corporate America—in which #MeToo cases were rampant? My colleagues and I were especially puzzled, dismayed, and disheartened by the bad behavior of many Catholic bishops who neither held the perpetrators accountable nor actively sought to facilitate healing for the victims.

---

[1] Portions of this chapter were published in Melanie Susan Barrett, "Virtuous Obedience Amidst Competing Loyalties: Navigating the Ecclesial Landscape," in *A True and Mature Obedience: Seminary Formation and Freedom*, ed. James Keating (Omaha: IPF Publications, 2021).

A keen insight was proposed by one of our church historians, Fr. Marty Zielinski. He surmised that diocesan bishops (and their staff members) who had engaged in a cover-up—rather than justice, reconciliation, and healing—probably were motivated by *love* for the *church*, but that they thought of "the church" primarily as "the institution" rather than as "the people of God." My colleagues thus concurred that in a seminary context, forming men for the priesthood, we ought to present *sacrificial love for the people of God* as the priest's principal mission. But such a mission is not exclusive to the priest. Because all of us—clergy, lay ecclesial ministers, catechetical volunteers, and parishioners—comprise the people of God, all of us bear responsibility (albeit to differing degrees) for building up the people of God through sacrificial love.

What type of moral formation do we need to concretize this shared mission, to make it a lived reality? I will focus on two aspects: (1) utilizing language that corresponds truthfully to reality and (2) developing key virtues that empower people to promote justice and healing in response to sexual abuse.

Beginning with the first: if we fail to use language to correspond truthfully to reality, then we risk "euphemizing" the scandal away so as to encourage complicity. Two examples: one from World War II, and one specific to the recent abuse crisis. In Germany in the 1940s, a government official by the name of Adolf Eichmann coordinated the mass deportation of Jews to concentration camps. After the war, Eichmann was sentenced to death by a court in Jerusalem for war crimes, crimes against the Jewish people, and crimes against humanity. In her book chronicling Eichmann's trial, the philosopher Hannah Arendt seeks to explain *how* Eichmann deceived himself that his evil acts were good acts.[2] One piece of the puzzle that she illuminates concerns the use of neutral or sanitized language, by those in authority, to downplay harm to victims. Arendt refers to various "language rules" that were "carefully contrived to deceive and to camouflage": not only the term "Final Solution" (to designate mass killing of the Jews and other innocent human beings), but also the phrase "to grant a mercy death" in place of the more accurate word—"murder"—in Hitler's first war decree.[3] This veiled language successfully helped

---

[2] Hannah Arendt, *Eichmann in Jerusalem: A Report on the Banality of Evil*, rev. ed. (New York: Penguin, 1963).

[3] Arendt, *Eichmann in Jerusalem*, 108.

to blur consciences, including that of Eichmann, who expressed "sincere outrage" at the SS men who had committed various "cruelties and atrocities" and took extreme offense only when accused of beating a Jewish boy to death.[4] In Eichmann's mind, Arendt reasons, the Jews were destined to certain death anyway, so "the unforgiveable sin was not to kill people but to cause unnecessary pain."[5]

Notwithstanding substantial differences between the two contexts, actions taken by Pennsylvania clergy who covered up sexual abuse illuminate language rules that similarly served to blur consciences. Although the institutional church neither authorized nor approved of the immoral acts that occurred—many of them "horrific instances of abuse" such as "a priest who raped a young girl in the hospital after she had her tonsils taken out; a victim tied up and whipped with leather straps by a priest; and another priest who was allowed to stay in ministry after impregnating a young girl and arranging for her to have an abortion"—in the words of Attorney General Josh Shapiro, its leaders "showed a complete disdain for victims [and] protected the institution at all costs."[6] For example, Pennsylvania church officials chose not to report many cases of child sexual abuse to the police and reassigned known abusers to new locations.[7] According to the Pennsylvania grand jury, such actions comprised "a playbook for concealing the truth" that was undergirded by specific language rules: using "euphemisms rather than real words . . . in diocesan documents . . . to describe sexual assaults," such as "inappropriate contact" or "boundary issues" rather than "rape."[8] Such sanitized language facilitated the blurring of consciences that was necessary for church leaders to defer to the recommendations of well-intentioned but misguided therapists and lawyers at the moral expense of the children and adults who were victimized by those in positions of ecclesial power.

---

[4] Arendt, 109.

[5] Arendt, 108–9.

[6] Laurie Goodstein and Sharon Otterman, "Catholic Priests Abused 1,000 Children in Pennsylvania, Report Says," *New York Times*, August 14, 2018, https://www .nytimes.com/2018/08/14/us/catholic-church-sex-abuse-pennsylvania.html.

[7] Commonwealth of Pennsylvania Office of Attorney General, "A Report of the Fortieth Statewide Investigating Grand Jury," redacted version, July 27, 2018, https://www.attorneygeneral.gov/report/.

[8] Commonwealth of Pennsylvania, "A Report."

Both Eichmann and the Pennsylvania report illustrate the need to use language that corresponds truthfully to reality, so that we can perceive evil clearly, in the fullness of its depravity. Only then will our emotions be properly inflamed to seek justice for the perpetrators and healing for the victims, rather than to turn a blind eye to the corruption or shroud it under a false veil of normalcy, of business as usual.

Turning now to my second solution: developing key virtues that empower people to respond to sexual abuse by promoting justice and healing, rather than ignoring the problem or engaging in a cover-up. I will delineate this by utilizing resources from Thomistic virtue ethics, especially the virtues of prudence, charity, temperance, fortitude, perseverance, and patience.

All of these virtues are important, because if any of them are absent, then the church leader cannot be relied on to act rightly when encountering injustice. Thomas Aquinas defines prudence as right reason applied to action. When encountering complex cases, we need prudence to discern correctly what is good versus bad, right versus wrong, and then act on it. The intellectual virtue of prudence *itself*, however, presupposes being oriented toward the correct goals in the first place.[9] To reason "prudently" about how best to achieve an evil end would constitute "false prudence" rather than true prudence.[10] According to Aquinas, the overarching ends or goals sought by the person are not appointed by prudence per se; they naturally flow from that person's character—from whether they possess moral virtues or not—and this sets the trajectory for everything that follows.[11]

The most important moral virtue is charity (love for God and love for one's neighbor in God). All baptized Catholics who have accepted their baptism in faith and are in a state of grace (rather than mortal sin) possess the virtue of charity. Charity has been infused in us by God through grace. Possessing this virtue empowers us to love our neighbors as God loves them. Our hearts are inflamed with the desire to help them, especially those who are weak and vulnerable to being harmed by others. If we begin existentially with love for all human beings, this sets the trajectory to make prudent judgments about them.

---

[9] Thomas Aquinas, *Summa Theologiae*, II–II 47.6.

[10] Aquinas, *Summa Theologiae*, II–II 47.13.

[11] Prudence does not appoint the ends to moral virtues; it only regulates the means. Aquinas, *Summa Theologiae* II–II 47.6.

But what if we lack charity altogether? Or what if we possess charity but also possess a vice (like vainglory or intemperance) that interferes with charity? Then we would be impeded in our ability to make a prudent judgment before reasoning even commences. For example, consider the vice of vainglory.[12] If the primary goal of a person's life is to be honored and esteemed by others, then naturally he will prioritize actions that enhance his likability in the eyes of others. If being a whistleblower in the face of injustice would make her appear heroic, then she subsequently will reason about how best to disclose bad behavior to the responsible parties, thereby objectively advancing the cause of justice, albeit for self-centered reasons. If, however, he conjectures that exposing immorality would earn him the disdain or even censure of those he wants to impress, then he either will stand by and do nothing or, worse, participate in a cover-up. Excessive concern for the praise of others also would make her more susceptible to being blackmailed by evildoers who wish to persist in their wrongdoing. Combatting injustice, even if desired on some level, ultimately would be deemed too costly to pursue, resulting in paralysis and inaction.

A second example: the vice of intemperance in any of its forms (gluttony, drunkenness, or lust). For anyone engaged in a ministerial role (either salaried or as a volunteer), if that individual's primordial focus is the pursuit of sensual pleasures (such as food, drink, or sex), this too can corrupt his or her moral judgment from the outset. For example, if he not only lacks the virtue of chastity but is enslaved to the vice of lust, then he is more likely to take sexual advantage of staff members, adults under his pastoral care (which would constitute an abuse of power even if mutual consent is present), or children (or anyone who is too young to give consent).

But even if she does not act out herself, if the lustful person acquires inside knowledge about other church leaders who are acting unchastely—or covering up for others who do—then she is highly unlikely to classify their behavior as a moral or pastoral problem to be solved. At the very least, it will not be viewed as *her* problem to solve, resulting in her inaction.

Only the person who loves his neighbor *more* than he loves sensual pleasures and who loves his neighbor *more* than he loves the honor

---

[12] See Aquinas, *Summa Theologiae*, II–II 132.

and esteem of other people can reliably *perceive* injustices against them and be *motivated* to act to remedy the infraction, or at least to prevent it from recurring. Only if charity remains unimpeded can prudential reasoning commence, as a person endeavors to discern the best means to attain this good end.

The virtue of prudence is cultivated through practice, but as an intellectual virtue, it also requires learning and experience over time. Ideally, this process of development should occur in the context of family life, as one grows into adulthood guided by the strong moral witness and patient explanations of one's parents and other trusted adults in the broader community. Where gaps still exist later in life, however, or where fine tuning is needed, then professional counselors, spiritual directors, and trusted friends (who are patient, supportive, and wise) can adopt the role of adviser to help bring this task to completion.

Most of us find it easy to tell other people what to do (when asked for our opinion) or to chastise them for what we believe they should have done in the past. But providing such feedback constitutes only one piece of the puzzle. Although prudent decision-making does involve taking counsel from others where necessary, individuals also need to become adept at making good judgments themselves—and then trusting those good judgments—rather than allowing their moral sense to be eclipsed entirely by the charismatic allure of a powerful authority figure who instills self-doubt and then leads them astray.

What might such formation involve? First, as a prerequisite for learning to occur, the individual must be willing to openly discuss various challenges that have confronted him in the past, present, or foreseeable future: what happened and how he responded (or plans to respond). Aquinas thus classifies docility—the readiness to be taught—as integral to prudence.[13]

Second, the adviser should acknowledge and affirm any steps of the individual's reasoning process that were undertaken correctly. Following Aquinas's model, this includes the following: (1) taking counsel from any relevant authorities regarding the best means to attain the good end being sought; (2) making a practical judgment by discerning which general moral principles are applicable to the

---

[13] Aquinas, *Summa Theologiae*, II–II 49.3.

particular case, and then applying them correctly in order to make a good decision; and (3) commanding oneself to execute the good decision that was made.[14] The individual should be commended for correctly naming what is occurring—especially when calling out evil as evil—rather than simply deferring to the language games of political correctness that dominate her social or ecclesial milieu.

Third, the adviser should gently but firmly point out any examples of imprudence and then assess whether the root causes were cognitive or indicative of a moral vice. For example, if the individual failed to seek counsel prior to making his own judgment, was it due to rashness (being in a hurry) or pride (not wanting to depend on anyone but himself)? If she failed to apply the relevant moral principles to the particular case, was it due to a lack of conscience formation? If so, then the appropriate remedy would be adult catechesis concerning what the church teaches about morality and why. Or is he already well-catechized, but failed to judge the situation correctly due to thoughtlessness (not thinking through something carefully) or to a vicious habit—like gluttony, alcoholism, lust, addiction to gaming, or excessive desire for honor from others—that caused him to engage in self-deception because he needed to see the situation in a certain way to obtain the desired outcome?[15] Finally, if she made a good decision but then failed to execute it, was that due to inconstancy (backing off because she felt uncertain about the conclusion she had reached) or negligence (laziness, perhaps rooted in spiritual apathy)?[16]

The church leader (or church member) therefore must love the people of God, intend a good end (to protect them from harm, provide healing for victims, and hold perpetrators accountable, even when

---

[14] As theologian Daniel Westberg has argued, for Aquinas the intellect and the will are closely intertwined in decision making, because each stage contains both a cognitive aspect and a volitional aspect: (1) the agent apprehends the end (*apprehensio*) and intends it (*intentio*); (2) the agent takes counsel from the relevant authorities (*consilium*) but must consent to doing so (*consensus*); (3) the agent makes a practical judgment (*iudicium practicum*) but also must choose it (*electio*); and (4) the agent commands himself to do it (*imperium*) and then carries it out (*usus*). Prudence refers to the cognitive aspects of stages 2–4: *consilium, judicium, imperium*. Daniel Westberg, *Right Practical Reason: Aristotle, Action, and Prudence in Aquinas* (Oxford: Clarendon Press, 1994), 130–31. See also Aquinas, *Summa Theologiae*, I–II 12–17.

[15] See Westberg, *Right Practical Reason*, 203 and 206–7.

[16] For Aquinas on imprudence, see *Summa Theologiae*, II–II 53. See also Westberg, *Right Practical Reason*, 214–15 (on inconstancy, negligence, and acedia).

higher ecclesial authorities have failed to do so), and reason prudently about how best to accomplish this (without being hindered by vices like vainglory or lust). His morally upright action plan still could be short-circuited in practice, however, if he is overwhelmed by fear of the harmful consequences he might suffer personally as a result of such righteous actions. Accordingly, both charity and prudence must be coupled with fortitude (the virtue of courage) and its connected virtues of patience and perseverance. This will empower the individual to endure difficulties for the sake of a greater good.

How does a timid or cowardly person become courageous? As the philosopher Aristotle taught (and Aquinas affirms), the timid person must intentionally place herself in situations that provoke fear (on account of the danger involved) and then force herself to stay there: rather than being so overwhelmed by fear that she flees entirely.[17] Of course, one should never voluntarily endure *irrational* dangers, such as drag racing; that would be reckless rather than courageous. But any fearful situation in which reason weighs goods versus dangers and recommends endurance rather than escape is fair game. The same goes for patience and perseverance; one must place oneself in challenging situations and endure them. Rather than looking to our secular culture of entitlement—which applauds self-expression, enjoyment of pleasurable activities, and avoidance of all suffering as the highest good—we should take our cues from Christ's alternative vision of happiness, "Blessed are those who are persecuted for the sake of righteousness, for theirs is the kingdom of heaven" (Matt 5:10), and form ourselves accordingly. By practicing patience, perseverance, and fortitude amid minor difficulties, we will be empowered to endure major difficulties for our neighbor's sake.

---

[17] According to Aristotle, "We become brave by accustoming ourselves to despise and endure terrors, and having become brave we are very capable of enduring terrors." Aquinas similarly affirms this. See Aristotle, *Nicomachean Ethics* 2.1104b; and Aquinas, *Commentary on the Nicomachean Ethics* 2.50.2: C264, trans. C. I. Litzinger, vol. 1 (Chicago: Henry Regnery, 1964), 121. Aquinas builds upon Aristotle's theory of habituation in his explanation of how all the natural virtues, including courage (fortitude), are cultivated. See, for example, Aquinas, *Summa Theologiae*, I–II 63.2: "Human virtue directed to the good which is defined according to the rule of human reason can be caused by human acts."

15

Safety and Mercy:
Challenges and Opportunities for the Education of Young People during the Abuse Crisis

David A. Clairmont

What do young people make of the clergy sexual abuse crisis in the Roman Catholic Church? What do young Catholics make of it? How has Catholic education—in Catholic schools and in parish religious education programs—changed in response to the abuse crisis? How have the social and spiritual lives of young people in the United States changed and how, if at all, do these changes relate to their response to the abuse crisis?

All these questions deserve attention, but this chapter focuses primarily on the third of these questions, which concerns the kind of young person who encounters the abuse crisis. Its sources are both sociological and theological, drawing on recent work on the social and spiritual lives of young people and Catholic theological engagement with ethical themes.[1] This chapter offers some preliminary

---

[1] While this chapter offers a contribution drawn primarily from the scholarly conversations in Christian ethics with some resources from sociology of religion, its intended audience is those engaged in ministry in the Christian churches—primarily but not only the Roman Catholic Church. It is also offered, however, from the perspective of a parent of children in Catholic schools and as an educator at a Catholic university. I claim neither a background in ministry nor a specific research competence in the abuse crisis but rather offer some resources from Christian ethics and sociology

observations about the challenges the abuse crisis poses to young people—from those in the later grades preparing for the sacrament of confirmation, to high school students in their religion/theology courses, to those pursuing their college-level education but who have, despite years spent in Catholic education, never been offered an opportunity to discuss the abuse crisis.

I argue that ministerial responses to the abuse crisis, while they may be well intentioned, will ultimately be insufficient if they do not emerge from a deep knowledge of and sensitivity to the social and spiritual context of young people. Because the protocols for addressing abuse in Catholic parishes, schools, and other church-sponsored organizations focus rightly on safety and protection of the young, they tend to miss an important counterpart: transparency and connection with the young. While these priorities of transparency and connection are particularly important for young people whose environments— particularly their digital environments—are profoundly shaped by the influence of stylized self-presentations that lack transparency and undermine real human connection, thinking about the effects of the abuse crisis on young people provides an opportunity for those working in Catholic ministry to rethink how to approach the abuse crisis with their wounded but largely silent adult populations as well. It is an easy but ultimately futile defense against a culture of abuse for the church to present itself as one more stylized, optimistic option for those who wish to retreat from the pain and confusion of the world rather than as a community of the wounded who have bravely committed to maintain their search for God in and with the church.

The remainder of the chapter is divided into three parts. First, I offer a few preliminary observations about young people in these ecclesial environments, focusing especially on sociological studies of the spiritual experience of young people and their digitally saturated social context. Second, I explore briefly one theme that has become

---

that could be helpful in thinking about the situation of young people who are themselves trying to make sense of their place in the church and to deepen their faith in the context not only of the abuse crisis but also within their own social practices as young people in a digital age. This chapter is an adaptation of a paper given as part of a panel that also included contributions by Mary Catherine McDonald and Marcus Mescher, to whom I offer thanks for their papers and for our conversations about the topic of our panel, which explored the moral and spiritual formation of young people in the age of the abuse crisis.

central when talk about the abuse crisis does happen in the church: the theme of a safe environment. Third, I suggest a way of shifting the conversation away from the exclusive focus on safety and toward two themes that, while not replacing due attention to safe environments, offer an important counterpoint to discussions of safety: justice and mercy. I conclude with a suggestion about the importance of mercy in relation to justice as a topic that can be introduced to students gradually in the late grade school years and nurtured as a meaningful topic for discussion through high school and into years of college and young adulthood.

Preliminary Observations

While it is difficult to draw any kind of generalizations about young Catholics from diverse backgrounds across a substantial age range (for example, those in the age range of twelve to twenty-one years old), recent sociological studies do offer some promising points of departure. First, young Catholics live within a culture that has some discernable features that they are constantly being forced to navigate. These challenges are not only moral but religious as well. As the sociologist Christian Smith has described in his study of the religious and moral views of young people through the National Study of Youth and Religion (NSYR),

> Very many Americans, including teenagers, appear to hold a primarily instrumentalist view of religious faith. For many parents in the United States, religion is good and valuable because it produces good outcomes for their kids. . . . Promoting an instrumentalist legitimation of religious faith may be effective in attracting adherents in the short and medium run. But it certainly comes at a long-term religious cost: faith and practice become redefined as instrumental therapeutic mechanisms to achieve personal goals that are probably not themselves formed by the religious traditions.[2]

---

[2] Christian Smith, "Is Moralistic Therapeutic Deism the New Religion of American Youth? Implications for the Challenge of Religious Socialization and Reproduction," in *Passing on the Faith: Transforming Traditions for the Next Generation of Jews, Christians, and Muslims*, ed. James L. Helft (New York: Fordham University Press, 2007), 61.

This does not mean that there is no concern among young people about the truth of religious claims (quite the opposite); rather, young people tend to see their religious lives in terms of that which is either "good for me" or "bad for me"—body and soul—and so there is little sense in being involved in the church or affiliated with a church-sponsored organization if it is not somehow good for me, especially (given the abuse that is going on in religious communities) if it might even be a risk to me. Smith's research focuses on religious affiliation and practice, but these are certainly not the only things about which young people adopt an instrumental mode of thinking. It may be easy to see the problem of instrumentalization of religion as indicative of a broad collection of social ills attributed to a purported secularization of society and to think of the church as providing a better and safer spiritual alternative, through its teachings and through the witness of Christians in the world. I suggest, however, that it is harder to convince young people to think of the church as an institution, or even a family of faith, that provides a model for living in service to God and neighbor when the abuse crisis has made care of self an important counterpoint to care for neighbor in an environment that can look profoundly risky, even dangerous.[3]

Second, young people in the church are growing up in a time of profound social, cultural, and political change and confusion, and this confusion is mediated not primarily by conversations with other flesh-and-blood creatures but through digital communication technologies that encourage both quick affirmations or denials of people and events ("likes" and "dislikes") and promise very few chances for ongoing, in-depth discussions about anything. The sociologist Douglas Rushkoff has examined this phenomenon under the label of "narrative collapse," by which he means that the onset and proliferation of digital technologies have made it more difficult for us to think about our lives as gradually unfolding stories. They incline us, rather, to see ourselves as a series of momentary interactions, connected sequentially rather than laterally through communities and through networks of affirmations or denials of other people's life

---

[3] I am indebted to the comments made by Elizabeth Pulido Hernandez on the twofold role of one's family of origin and one's family of faith as two necessary pillars for navigating the abuse crisis.

events and stylized self-presentations.[4] This has produced, Rushkoff argues, a phenomenon he calls "digiphrenia" as a way of explaining both the desire for individual narrative coherence over time and the simultaneous pulling away from that narrative coherence when we are drawn into an unrelenting focus on present moments. "By dividing our attention between our digital extensions, we sacrifice our connection to the truer present in which we are living. The tension between the faux present of digital bombardment and the true now of a coherently living human generates [a kind of] present shock."[5] It is hardly news that digital technology has profoundly changed us and our world, but perhaps it is worth considering that narrative collapse and digiphrenia mean something different for young people in the context of Catholic institutions—parishes, schools, and other organizations—where their religious traditions no less than their social networks exist within the wider shared cultural context of narrative collapse and digiphrenia. It is more difficult to see our lives as existing within and perhaps even *as* a significant part of God's story—creation, incarnation, redemption—if the very possibility of experiencing one's life as a story is being digitally shredded and delivered in fragments.

Third, young people in the church today have not known a church without an abuse crisis, and they have watched the church, including their parents and grandparents, wrestle with the meaning of the abuse crisis and how to respond. That our young people have never known a church without an abuse crisis is, however, part of but certainly not the whole picture. This is the generation whose grandparents lived through the changes of the Second Vatican Council and both the expectations and uncertainty that surrounded the post–Vatican II church. The oldest college-age students today (twenty-one years old) were born the year before the *Boston Globe* Spotlight team published its first stories on the abuse crisis in Boston.[6] These are young people whose parents learned the extent of clergy sexual abuse and the subsequent cover-up in real time, and they have been uncertain how

---

[4] Douglas Rushkoff, *Present Shock: When Everything Happens Now* (New York: Current, 2013), 16–18.

[5] Rushkoff, *Present Shock*, 75.

[6] The material from this investigation is collected in The Investigative Staff of *The Boston Globe, Betrayal: The Crisis in the Catholic Church* (New York: Back Bay Books, 2003).

to respond or to what extent they could trust church leaders to offer a fitting response to the gravity of the occurrence. Their grandparents had a somewhat different experience of the abuse crisis because their experience of the church includes something else that their children's and grandchildren's experiences do not: a lived experience of the pre–Vatican II church and the trust in religious authorities that the leaders of the church assumed. In a recent study commissioned by *America* magazine and conducted by Georgetown University's Center for Applied Research in the Apostolate (CARA), Mark Gray and Thomas Gaunt, SJ, summarize that "Millennial respondents (born in 1982 or later) were more likely than older Catholics to believe abuse happens 'often' these days. Twenty-three percent of these young Catholics responded as such, compared with 12 percent of Vatican II Catholics (born between 1943 and 1960) and 9 percent of pre–Vatican II Catholics (born before 1943)."[7] As Marisa Iati reports, "In an era when the church is frequently perceived as behind the times on matters of importance to them, some young Catholics have responded to the latest setbacks by pulling further away from the beleaguered institution, while others have drawn closer." Yet, however young people choose to respond, Iati notes that "this generation of Catholic college students has grown up amid the stain of the sexual abuse crisis, which was first exposed by the *Boston Globe* in 2002 and has since implicated clergy around the world. Most can't even remember a pre-scandal church."[8] Pope Francis himself seemed to acknowledge the abuse-clouded mood of Catholic youth as he spoke to an ecumenical youth gathering in Tallinn, Estonia: "They are outraged by sexual and economic scandals that do not meet with clear condemnation, by our unpreparedness to really appreciate the lives and sensibilities of the young, and simply by the passive role we assign them."[9]

---

[7] Mark M. Gray and Thomas P. Gaunt, "Three Years after the 2018 'Summer of Shame,' What Do American Catholics Think about the Sex Abuse Crisis?," *America*, July 15, 2021, https://www.americamagazine.org/mediasurvey. The full CARA survey is available at https://www.americamagazine.org/mediasurvey.

[8] Marisa Iati, "What It's Like to Be a Young Catholic in a New Era of Clergy Sex Abuse Scandals," *Washington Post*, October 21, 2018, https://www.washingtonpost.com/local/social-issues/what-its-like-to-be-a-young-catholic-in-a-new-era-of-clergy-sex-abuse-scandals/2018/10/21/6f327f4c-d307-11e8-8c22-fa2ef74bd6d6_story.html.

[9] Nicole Winfield and Jari Tanner, "Pope: Priestly Abuse Scandals Driving Catholic Faithful Away," Associated Press, September 25, 2018, https://apnews.com/article/8e627156352a4d9fb2ad95c4353882e3.

Fourth, on the matter of religious education, these young people who "can't even remember a pre-scandal church" are also the same ones who have, in many cases, been the first to learn about church teaching on matters of human sexuality, marriage, and family from a new approach to catechesis focusing strongly on themes of self-gift and the linguistic character of bodies. The introduction of Pope John Paul II's "Theology of the Body" through diocesan religion curricula across the country is widespread. Although John Paul II's homilies on Genesis occurred mostly in the early 1980s, their popularizations by Christopher West and others in books such as *Theology of the Body for Beginners* were first published in 2004—two years after the *Boston Globe* story—and the integration of John Paul II's thought into religious education curriculum began soon after.[10] I mention this because I think it is important to keep in mind how certain curricula and pedagogical strategies meet different contexts: in this case, the rise of a religion and ethics curriculum in Catholic schools that focuses in an intense way on the meaning of love and the meaning (or are there meanings?) of bodies—the *language* even of love and bodies— coincides with a time when students are hyper-aware of the instrumentalization of bodies *in* the church. Would it escape their notice, even if they cannot quite thematize it, that not only is there an

---

[10] While I have been not been able to locate national statistics, it seems safe to say that John Paul II's Theology of the Body is prominent in religion curricula in Catholic primary schools and high schools in the United States. While the selection (or development) and implementation of religious education curricula occurs in each diocese according to the requirements set by the local ordinary, they follow in structure and content the Doctrinal Elements of a Curriculum Framework for the Development of Catechetical Materials for Young People of High School Age developed by the United States Conference of Catholic Bishops (https://www.usccb.org/resources/high -school-curriculum-framework.pdf). Within that curriculum, Theology of the Body appears in part 6 ("Life in Jesus Christ") in the required portion and in election option D ("Responding to the Call of Jesus Christ"). High school–level curricula, such as the Ave Maria Press Encountering Jesus series, draw heavily on this approach. Some in the church think that a deeper education in this approach to human sexuality is an answer to the abuse crisis and, in some cases, even would have prevented it had John Paul II's insights about the meaning of the body and human sexuality been more widely available earlier. For example, on the USCCB website, we find linked a paper by Sr. Mary Timothy Prokes, FSE, delivered at the 2015 Anglophone Conference, Pontifical Gregorian University, arguing this position: https://www.usccb.org/issues -and-action/child-and-youth-protection/upload/Anglophone-Presentation-2015 -Prokes.pdf.

inconsistency between this prominent approach in their religion curriculum on respect for human dignity and their bodies' ability to communicate or fail to communicate love, and the fact that the bodies of their grandparents, parents, siblings, and friends may have been abused, but also an absence of any place to talk about this disconnect precisely where they ought to be able to share their honest concerns?

Fifth, this is a group for whom their primary exposure to the abuse crisis has been through the recent preventive measures taken to establish safe environment training that has become widely used in parishes, Catholic schools, and youth ministry programs. Such programs are vital, of course, for preventing occasions of abuse in the future, but these programs are (quite understandably) not designed to give young people an opportunity to discuss what has happened in the church. In reference to Rushkoff's point about the coincidence of digiphrenia and narrative collapse, safe environments are not likely to be narratively inviting environments. Young people today have learned that safe environment training is to be expected in the church; meaningful discussion of their questions about the abuse crisis is not. Neither, interestingly, have we seen any significant volume of work on how Catholic education, whether weekend religious education, religious education in Catholic schools, or Catholic youth ministry, has addressed the abuse crisis either in its curricular resources or in its classroom discussions.[11] As Chris Miller suggests, not only has the abuse crisis drained resources that could have been used to further develop youth ministry programs and produced a baseline of ecclesial mistrust with which youth ministers need to contend, but so too have safe environments frustrated building the kinds of relationships between ministers and youth through which youth might actually be open to sharing their deepest questions and worries.[12] Moreover, there has been little recognition in official ecclesial documents of the need for a deep and challenging discussion about the abuse crisis among Catholic youth.[13] Young people, no less so than

---

[11] See, for example, Chris Miller, "The Sexual Abuse Crisis in the US, Its Effect on Catholic Youth Ministry, and a Way Forward Through Relational Ministry Utilizing the Developmental Relationships Framework," *Religions* 11, no. 572 (November 2, 2020), https://www.mdpi.com/2077-1444/11/11/572.

[12] Miller, "Sexual Abuse Crisis," 4.

[13] For example, the 2018 Synod on Young People Preparatory Document has only one mention of abuse (https://press.vatican.va/content/salastampa/it/bollettino

adults, are acutely aware of dismissiveness, condescension, misdirection, and overly simplistic answers to the difficult questions that the abuse crisis often raises. They can be vulnerable and in need of protection, but they can also see with remarkable clarity when their questions are being ignored.

Safe Environments: Two Senses

Is it possible to strengthen policies and training programs that ensure a safe environment while also opening up a space for young people to talk about the abuse crisis in a way that is not reducible to safety? I suggest that one of the greatest challenges we face in the church today, especially with our young people but with adults as well, is encouraging them to a growth in maturity of faith that allows them to abide with ongoing difficult questions—including questions about their own church—in a way that holds the adult faithful (including but not only adult church leaders) accountable for what has happened in the church.

A safe environment is, in one sense, a place where we cannot be hurt, in body or mind or spirit. It is a place where we can trust the people around us and know that they want nothing from us except our own deepest personal and communal flourishing. This is one sense of safety. Another sense of safety is having the emotional space where we have the freedom to be vulnerable in the presence of another person, in the sense that we can share our deepest questions and doubts and not have those questions met with ridicule, dismissiveness, or simple answers, no matter how well-intentioned or insightful those answers might be. In Catholic social teaching, solidarity denotes a firm and abiding commitment to be with another person, through time and in the place where that person is in all its pain and uncertainty, to not abandoning them when things get uncomfortable, to not running away when we are unable to solve their problems or take away their pain, even when that pain becomes nearly unbearable

---

/pubblico/2017/01/13/0021/00050.html#EN), and the USCCB document Renewing the Vision: A Framework for Catholic Youth Ministry, written in 1997, has not been updated to address the effects of the abuse crisis on Catholic youth (https://www .usccb.org/topics/youth-and-young-adult-ministries/renewing-vision).

to share. As Pope John Paul II explained, "[Solidarity] is not a feeling of vague compassion or shallow distress at the misfortunes of so many people, both near and far. On the contrary, it is a firm and persevering determination to commit oneself to the common good; that is to say, to the good of all and of each individual, because we are all really responsible for all."[14] This is another kind of safe environment, but one that is perhaps even more difficult to provide to young people.

Mercy and Justice

How might we begin to provide the kind of safe environment that will protect not only the bodies of young people but the dignity of their most difficult questions? Certainly there is no easy answer to this, but if I were to offer one place in the Catholic tradition that might hold resources for providing young people a safe space to talk about the abuse crisis it would be in the biblical and theological traditions of justice and mercy. In her contribution to this volume, Anselma Dolcich-Ashley argues that the church's thinking about justice emphasizes giving each their due and in so doing facilitating right relations among people and between people and God. In this way, a sin against the sixth commandment is not only a sin against chastity but also a sin against justice.[15]

The works of mercy, which the *Catechism of the Catholic Church* discusses as part of its examination of the seventh commandment, prohibiting theft, deal not only with the prohibition of theft but more basically with the unlawful removal of that to which a human being is entitled: respect for another person's goods that are important for a life of authentic human flourishing (par. 2401).[16] The discussion of

---

[14] Pope John Paul II, *Sollicitudo Rei Socialis* (Vatican City: Libreria Editrice Vaticana, December 30, 1987), 38, https://www.vatican.va/content/john-paul-ii/en/encyclicals/documents/hf_jp-ii_enc_30121987_sollicitudo-rei-socialis.html.

[15] See Anselma Dolcich-Ashley's chapter in this book, "The Catholic Sexual Abuse Crisis and the Synodal Church: Insights from the Sixth Commandment," above, esp. p. 65.

[16] *Catechism of the Catholic Church* (1992), https://www.vatican.va/archive/ENG0015/_INDEX.HTM.

the works of mercy occurs in part 5 of that section within an examination of love for the poor.[17]

Typically, the works of mercy are linked in Catholic education to works of direct service that are part of preparation to enter more fully into the life of the church, such as the service hours offered by children preparing for the sacrament of confirmation. The works of mercy, as these are commonly understood, are directed to meet the needs of the poor—those who lack something in body or spirit that, in justice, they ought to have. The works of mercy are linked to justice because it is through such work that we restore to a person what they are due, that is, we restore them to right relation with their neighbor by helping to provide what they need for a good life—in short, to justice. The challenge, however, is that we tend to think of mercy as act-centered (the "works" of mercy) and don't often speak with young people about what mercy is. As James Keenan describes in his book *Moral Wisdom,*

> Mercy calls us to meet human beings in need. By meeting them, often we realize that their situation is compromised. . . . In the real merciful engagement, we realize that by entering into the chaos of others we eventually have to face the causes of that chaos. But usually we cannot know about those needs until we have a merciful engagement first. I think people who work for justice without knowing and meeting those who are suffering often have presumptions for action that are not helpful. I think that acting from mercy allows us to meet people in need and in turn we are moved to justice.[18]

Keenan's point is that when we enter into the chaos of another through mercy, we begin to see how unjust situations arose in the first place and what we might do to rectify them. If we want to fix a

---

[17] "The works of mercy are charitable actions by which we come to the aid of our neighbor in his spiritual and bodily necessities. Instructing, advising, consoling, comforting are spiritual works of mercy, as are forgiving and bearing wrongs patiently; the corporal works of mercy consist especially in feeding the hungry, sheltering the homeless, clothing the naked, visiting the sick and imprisoned, and burying the dead. Among all these, giving alms to the poor is one of the chief witnesses to fraternal charity: it is also a work of justice pleasing to God" (CCC 2447).

[18] James F. Keenan, *Moral Wisdom: Lessons and Texts from the Catholic Tradition,* 3rd ed. (Lanham, MD: Rowman & Littlefield, 2017), 103–4.

broken system, we first need to be in solidarity with those who have suffered the effects of that brokenness.

Would it be so hard to think about our young people, growing up in a church profoundly marked by the abuse crisis, as in need of mercy and as potential ministers of mercy to those who have suffered so greatly from clergy sexual abuse? What would allow us to enter into the chaos of young people—to return to our earlier point, to the chaos of a world where religion is viewed as profoundly instrumental to human ends, to the chaos of finding one's way in a world of disembodied images outpacing real communities of conversation, to the chaos of parents reeling and disoriented from suspicion and mistrust, to the chaos of being guarded in body and left with a homeless vulnerability of the mind and heart? Our young people know that there must exist the most profound chaos for survivors of abuse. How can we meet young people who have been abused or who one day might encounter, perhaps even marry, one who has survived abuse or one who is confronting abuse long covered over in one's own family?[19] I suggest that these are the questions we must keep in mind when thinking about the moral and spiritual development of young people in our time in the context of ministry. Of course, the model of mercy is Jesus himself, for who else has entered in the chaos of human life more than he? Did he not both listen deeply to us and also counsel us not to be afraid? As we put our trust in Jesus to help us envision how to respond to the abuse crisis in the church, we must not be afraid to trust our young people with the chaos we the church now carry.

---

[19] Some well-meaning Catholics and Catholic ministers might suggest that what I am calling for here is already available through sacramental reconciliation. To such suggestions, I would offer two responses. First, those who have been abused are often still so traumatized by the experience that they find it difficult even to approach the confessional, if they even consider doing so at all. Second, even those who have not been directly abused but are living with those who have suffered abuse will not find the context to discuss what they are feeling in sacramental reconciliation and often are even discouraged from doing so if it will take too much time.

16

Composing *The Passion*:
Empowering Young People to Be Ministerial Protagonists through Creativity in the Face of Suffering, Distrust, and Despair

Tristan Cooley and J. J. Wright

Introduction: Learning to "Dream Together" with Young People

At the end of Mass on the Solemnity of Christ the King on November 22, 2020, Pope Francis called for a renewal of the global celebration of young people in local churches in every diocese and eparchy. Every Catholic faith community around the world is encouraged to celebrate and reflect on youth and young adults annually on Christ the King Sunday. In the United States Conference of Catholic Bishops' National Pastoral Guidebook for the Global Celebration of Young People, four main priorities are outlined for the celebration of this event:

1. that the Catholic community draw closer to youth and young adults and their realities

2. that young people experience a sincere concern for their lives from the church and the community

3. that Catholics of all generations have a greater understanding, awareness, and appreciation of youth and young adults in the local area and of the church's ministerial work with them

4. that there be a renewed call for all people in the community
   to accompany and celebrate young people[1]

It is this call and yearly commemoration, which is an outgrowth
of Pope Francis's post-synodal apostolic exhortation *Christus Vivit*,[2]
that inspired us to create an original setting of Christ's final days, *The
Passion*. Francis speaks of the idea of "dreaming together," which for
us is akin to artistic formation, that is, cultivating holistic practices
(spiritual, emotional, physical integration), as a means for generating
artistic output.[3] Recognizing this, we hear Francis's call as particularly
empowering for translating this artistic formation into a process for
young people, so that they might imagine themselves within the
Scriptures and thereby their relationship with Jesus. This imaginative
posture becomes transformational because it connects and integrates
the lived experiences of the new generation with the ancient tradition,
stories, and practices of Christian faith. Our desire to build *The Passion*
comes out of the "passion play" (and, more broadly, the morality/
ethics play) tradition, which has historically been a source of cultural
expression of a given community of believers.[4] Passion plays, as
expressions of a collective need to perform Christ's suffering, body-
forth the values outlined in *Christus Vivit*, and have, across cultures,
occasioned the opportunity for an intergenerational Christ-centered
experience that allows each participant to learn to see one another
through the eyes of the Gospel.

Christus Vivit tells us that "the community has an important role
in the accompaniment of young people; it should feel collectively

---

[1] United States Conference of Catholic Bishops, National Pastoral Guidebook for
the Global Celebration of Young People (Washington, DC: USCCB, 2021), 7, https:
//www.usccb.org/resources/usccb-christ-the-king-guidebook.pdf.

[2] Pope Francis, *Christus Vivit* (Vatican City: Libreria Editrice Vaticana, March 25,
2019), https://www.vatican.va/content/francesco/en/apost_exhortations/documents
/papa-francesco_esortazione-ap_20190325_christus-vivit.html.

[3] "How important it is to dream together. . . . By ourselves, we risk seeing mirages,
things that are not there. Dreams, on the other hand, are built together." Francis
frames the act of collective dreaming as "adventure." Pope Francis, Address at the
Ecumenical and Interreligious Meeting with Young People, Skopje, North Macedonia,
L'Osservatore Romano (May 9, 2019): 9, http://www.vatican.va/content/francesco
/en/speeches/2019/may/documents/papa-francesco_20190507_macedoniadelnord
-giovani.html.

[4] The Passion Play of Oberammergau, Germany, is the most famous example.

responsible for accepting, motivating, encouraging, and challenging them" (CV 243). Therefore, the annual celebration is not solely the responsibility or focus of the person or persons at the parish, diocese, campus, apostolate, or movement who have oversight of ministry with young people; rather, it is strongly recommended that this occasion is something that should be engaged by the entire community. This is important because the responsibility for encouraging and maintaining active dialogue and creativity with the younger generation, the "preferential option for the youth," is the responsibility for all of us within the church.

Christus Vivit emphasizes that this type of engagement must rely on the "protagonism," or the energy and ingenuity, of the young people themselves (CV 174). And to channel this vital energy, the engagement "needs to be done in a synodal-missionary style and to make the most of the creativity, language, and methods that are typical of that age bracket."[5] Because "young people themselves are agents" (CV 203) of ministry with other young people, the church must be open to following their advice and supporting their initiatives. As Pope Francis noted, when we accompany young "protagonists," the resulting effort "goes out to those places where real young people are active and fosters the natural leadership qualities and charisms sown by the Holy Spirit" (CV 230).

Background and Initial Development

We were first commissioned to compose a passion in October 2018 by the Notre Dame Children's Choir (NDCC). The request came out of our shared desire with Dr. Mark Doerries, director of NDCC, to create a sacred and safe space where young people could share their struggles of faith through sacred music pedagogy and performance. We originally conceived of a setting of the passion as a large-scale sacred work focused on challenging themes, which we hoped would allow for an environment where it would be socially acceptable for young people to share their struggles within their peer group. The performing forces would be intergenerational in nature: the Notre Dame Children's Choir (ages ten to thirteen), the Notre Dame Folk

---

[5] USCCB, National Pastoral Guidebook, part 5.

Choir (undergraduate and graduate university students), and professional musicians. Around this time, the University of Notre Dame announced that the topic of the annual Notre Dame Forum for 2019 and 2020 would be the clergy sexual abuse crisis and welcomed proposals for a pilot grant from the president's office for new research and creative pursuits around the crisis. In our estimation, we believed there had to be a way to link these two stories in an artwork that could speak to and contextualize the evil of the world within God's merciful love.

We started researching the clergy sexual abuse crisis and contemplated the deep hurt and betrayal that was perpetrated by both the actions of abusers and the ensuing cover-up scandal. We found many parallels between the difficulties of the passion and the abuse crisis. The initial stages included difficult conversations with survivors of clergy sexual abuse and child psychologists to better contextualize, in particular, the startling revelations of the Pennsylvania grand jury report, which detailed the abuses of more than three hundred priests of over one thousand victims over the course of seventy years and was released just months before we began our research.[6] We kept coming back to a central question: how can we expect a new generation of Catholics to wholeheartedly enter into a church where such horrific evils were perpetrated? In response to this question, our desire was to cocreate an artwork that would allow for a cathartic and sacred expression of these seemingly intractable difficulties. This work would provide the opportunity for deepening the relationship with God for all participants by working through the "hard stuff" in a safe, trusted, and faith-based communal environment. The passion narratives and the clergy sexual abuse crisis would provide the material for scriptural and devotional prompts and become invitations to the students to articulate their creative impressions through words and/or music. In this earliest iteration of the project, we planned to gather parents of students in the NDCC to learn about how we might engage them and their families. We recognized that because of the sensitivity of the topics, we would need to build a sense of shared responsibility with parents so that we could walk together in our pursuit of tackling this difficult issue. We named the project *Passion of the Innocents.*

---

[6] "Fortieth Statewide Investigating Grand Jury Report 1, Redacted" (Harrisburg, PA: 2018), https://www.attorneygeneral.gov/report/.

While the church sexual abuse crisis has received attention from adults and church leadership, rarely are the voices of young people heard on this particular issue. The youngest generation of Catholics is growing up in the wake of the clergy sexual abuse crisis without the tools to safely and honestly engage with this issue. *Passion of the Innocents'* engagement with young people was meant to represent the central role that these voices should have in discussions of reform. Furthermore, the multigenerational performing forces would signify the broad community needed to share the responsibility for the protection of church members and for church reforms.

In March 2020, the COVID-19 pandemic interrupted life as we knew it and derailed all further efforts that we had envisioned for this project. Given the operational difficulty for a community-based organization during this time, outside of an organized school setting, the children's choir had to close their doors indefinitely. The university, meanwhile, looked for ways to finish the semester using alternative virtual meeting places and measures. Though the original libretto and music were essentially completed, we set them aside and began to organize small groups within the Folk Choir to discern if the ministerial framework we were developing could continue to thrive but in a new and reimagined context.

In these earliest small groups, the conversations were passionate and animated, and it was clear to us that continuing this work with the Folk Choir would be even more fruitful than we initially imagined, albeit with new and unforeseen challenges.

Expanding *The Passion*: From Clergy Sexual Abuse Crisis to COVID-19, Black Lives Matter, and *Laudato Si'*

In retrospect, we came to understand that we were building an iterative process over time that eventually culminated in *The Passion*. In making this artwork, we formed a preliturgical habitus wherein students in the Folk Choir could understand themselves as cocreators with the Holy Spirit in the unfolding life of the ensemble and of the church. The tools we used to establish this new habitus were largely drawn from our backgrounds in liturgical music ministry and creative writing, e.g., workshopping, music composition, and the various practices of improvisation native to those disciplines.

In the summer of 2020, we piloted our emergent methodology with one student, then a sophomore in the Folk Choir, Anna Staud.[7] In regular virtual meetings, we tested different strategies for working collaboratively with students through a creative practice, all while learning to frame the hardships of life through the passion Scriptures, particularly the stories set in the Garden of Gethsemane. In this same season, George Floyd was murdered, inciting a nationwide reckoning with racial justice, which weighed heavily on the minds of our students. This confluence of events—the pandemic and the George Floyd murder—opened our perspective to the broader idea that the passion could be a hermeneutic for encountering all types of suffering. Once this line was crossed, students were invited to see the passion through a diverse set of lenses. We began to notice that the lenses students were most interested in involved racial justice, care for our common home, and the mental health effects of COVID isolation.

A basic summary of the initial collaborative workflow will be helpful in establishing how the spirit of the project emerged and what it eventually taught us about Christian formational pedagogy. Following a successful start with one student, we broadened the scope of the collaboration to form a writing group, which we tasked with generating lyrics for a suite of songs based on the passion narrative. Students would respond to writing prompts, workshop them in group, and, over time, distill their individual offerings into one coherent text. These texts were then sent off to another group of students who composed music using those texts, and then that would be workshopped in large group rehearsals by the full choir. We deployed this rough, three-part process until we had ten to twelve songs, with each song corresponding to a different scene from the passion narrative.

To better connect the songs to the story of the passion, we then adapted the original libretto and expanded it, drawing more text directly from Scripture, while incorporating these newly written songs and a more deliberate dramatic conceit. At this stage we followed the same creative steps that we used to write the songs, that is, students in writing groups generating dramatic scenes around their songs and then workshopping them in rehearsal and review sessions with the whole choir. Once we had a working script, we held

---

[7] Anna Staud, "Writing Music for the Women of the Passion Helped Me Embrace the Contradictions of Being Catholic," *America*, April 6, 2023, https://www.america magazine.org/arts-culture/2023/04/06/notre-dame-choir-passion-holy-land-245048.

a weeklong rehearsal/retreat in January 2021 to workshop and ultimately perform the first version of *The Passion*. It was during this retreat that we began to identify and codify the spiritual and creative exercises that would propel the project into its future realization.

The rehearsal/retreat was a breakthrough moment for the liturgical life of the Folk Choir because it scaled the emergent habitus of our small groups to include the rest of the members of the group, many of whom had been less intensively involved in the composition of *The Passion*. We borrow our notion of habitus from Pierre Bourdieu, who defines it as

> the product of the work of inculturation and appropriation necessary in order for those products of collective history, the objective structures (e.g., of language, economy, etc.) to succeed in reproducing themselves more or less completely, in the form of durable dispositions, in the organisms (which one can, if one wishes, call individuals) lastingly subjected to the same conditionings, and hence placed in the same conditions of existence.[8]

The culture that emerged around making *The Passion* formed new habits of creative engagement with Scripture amid the structures of collective history native to the Folk Choir (e.g., providing music for weekly campus Mass). Meeting regularly to write, revise, and workshop original poetry and music was a departure from the students' historical experience of Folk Choir. This new practice required time and a gradual introduction to the established culture for it to "take" as a valid experience of being a member of the Folk Choir. By the time of the retreat, enough "durable dispositions" had been formed among the students to sufficiently attract the remaining choir community to the project.

The retreat/rehearsal helped formalize the creative habitus we'd been developing because it framed that development within a structure already recognizable to the Folk Choir, that is, a campus ministry retreat. The recognizability of the retreat form allowed us to fold novel participatory modes, like drama and improvisation, into the evolving scope of the project more easily. Through association with the spirituality of a retreat, students were able to extend their devotional experience to include the new dramatic exercises they'd been

---

[8] Pierre Bourdieu, *Outline of a Theory of Practice* (Cambridge: Cambridge University Press, 1977), 85.

using to develop *The Passion*. Throughout the week, students practiced inhabiting the thoughts, feelings, and struggles of the disciples on Good Friday through a combination of Ignatian spiritual exercises, structured improvisations, and guided conversations in small groups.

Based on the insights gained from these exercises and conversations, student leaders with professional collaborators designed the blocking for performance. As students learned to move with the libretto and the music, they established their own rituals for *getting into* the scene. Collectively devising the blocking in this way allowed students to embody the passion story. For those students accustomed to a relatively static mode of liturgical participation, this was a new species of creative expression and mode of relating to the gospels. As a result, the line between the disciples in the upper room and the students in the Folk Choir grew thinner, and this had fresh implications for the formational potential of our collaborative creative process.

What We Learned: Moving beyond Black-and-White Thinking Is Essential to the Creative Process

Developing the dramatic and theatrical dimensions of *The Passion* helped reform the Folk Choir's experience of aesthetic and ethical "goodness." That is, what could be considered "good" within a given student's experience of Folk Choir grew to include our sustained creative practices. James Alison provides the theoretical model for this orientation, noting how Jesus's death on the cross frees us from either/or thinking because it differentiates righteousness through obeying the law from righteousness through relationship to God.[9] Translating this concept to *The Passion*, we observed that as students went through the process of writing, workshopping, and revision, they grew in their understanding of what constituted "right" and "wrong" with respect to their creative choices. Early on, for example, even small poetic deviations from scriptural texts in the creation of a song or dramatic scene required patient catechesis and dialogue. Students expressed the reasonable concern that creative interpretation of the gospels could detract, distract, or even do harm to God's Word.

---

[9] James Alison, *Undergoing God: Dispatches from the Scene of a Break-In* (New York: Bloomsbury Academic, 2006), 200–203.

Allaying these fears, which ranged from the level of character crisis ("this is not what the Folk Choir is") to the soteriological ("this is blasphemy"), took time, but eventually it built a communal understanding of the significance of our shared work. Everyone was accountable to everyone else, regardless of their level of contribution, and the project could not be realized until we had found a way for everyone to contribute. Eventually, what was "good" in a given scene was less predicated on maintaining fidelity to received liturgical traditions of passion narratives, e.g., Palm Sunday, Good Friday, Stations of the Cross, etc., and more reliant on whether or not a dramatic moment captured the spirit of the communal process that produced it. In other words, because their relationship to the story of Jesus's passion had become intimately connected to their own histories—and had, in a sense, become their own unfolding story—the categories of right/wrong or good/bad became irrelevant. Creative choices were choices between multiple goods. The ones that ultimately stuck were those that honored the relationships the students had formed with Jesus and the disciples during the creative process.

Building *The Passion* according to our processual and grassroots model of radical inclusion facilitated the conversion necessary for students to recognize that we do not create our own Christian identities. Instead, as Brian Robinette observes, it is the ecclesial body *in memoria* that creates the believing subject through the invitation to know Jesus.[10] It is our hope that this process will find life beyond the Folk Choir, particularly among college-aged and even high school students. As Francis reminds us, it is their dreams, hopes, and desires for justice and peace that the church needs "as much as the earth needs rain."[11]

---

[10] Brian DuWayne Robinette, *Grammars of Resurrection: A Christian Theology of Presence and Absence* (New York: Crossroad, 2009), 112–13. He goes on to say, "If we can appreciate the conversion process that witnesses to the resurrection were invited to undertake, we will find that affirming 'He is risen; he is not here' or 'Jesus is Lord' is far more like learning a new language and acquiring a new set of skills within a communal context than it is assenting to a single proposition."

[11] Apostolic Journey of His Holiness Pope Francis to Portugal on the Occasion of the Thirty-Seventh World Youth Day (2023), https://www.vatican.va/content/francesco/en/homilies/2023/documents/20230806-portogallo-omelia-gmg.html.

Appendixes

Liturgical Resources to Promote
Accountability, Healing, and Trust

"I Will Put My Spirit Within You":
A *Visio Divina* Liturgy for Accountability and Healing

Kimberly Hope Belcher, Julia Canonico, and Eric T. Styles

At the conference, this liturgy was performed in a small, intimate chapel full of strong colors but with lighting on the dim side. The liturgical ministers were from groups with less ecclesial power: most were Native American, Black, immigrant, lay, or students.[1] The image used was "Valley of the Dry Bones" from The Saint John's Bible, *which illustrates Ezekiel 37 and 38. The image was displayed from the Heritage Edition of* The Saint John's Bible,[2] *which was held up for contemplation by participants, while a lector proclaimed the reading. The Heritage Edition lay on the altar when not displayed, and was available for viewing after the liturgy. The heft of the Heritage Edition of* The Saint John's Bible *gave an undeniable weightiness to the liturgical experience. The instructions for* visio divina *are inspired by those in* Voices Together: Worship Leader Edition.[3] *All texts, rubrics, and instructions are meant to be adapted to the particular assemblies among which you are ministering. It is sometimes helpful to let the assembly know how* visio divina *works at the outset.*

Greeting

Friends, welcome to this place and to this moment. Today we will be connecting with God through a practice called *visio divina. Visio divina*

---

[1] On the importance of choosing liturgical ministers, see chapter 8, page 102.

[2] *The Saint John's Bible* Heritage Program (Collegeville, MN: Saint John's University), https://heritage.saintjohnsbible.org/heritage-edition/volumes/.

[3] *Voices Together: Worship Leader Edition* (Harrisonburg, VA: MennoMedia, 2020), no. 45.

is rooted in the ancient practice of *lectio divina*, and invites us to encounter God through God's creation and visual art. Throughout the process of *visio divina*, we trust that God's creative Spirit was at work in the artist, is at work within us now, and will guide us through our sense of sight. We will be using Donald Jackson's image "Valley of the Dry Bones" from *The Saint John's Bible*. We will experience it in two stages: first, in an extended look at the one part of the image that first catches your eye, and then, later, in a broader look at the whole image.

Let us ask our loving God to strengthen us as we reflect together on the challenge of ministry in the church today.

Collect

O God of a just peace,
You have commissioned your people to become ambassadors for
    you in the world,
But too often, your ambassadors have failed to speak for you,
And your ministers have served only themselves.
Send your Holy Spirit among us as we gather for lament and for hope.
Teach us how to be accountable to the most vulnerable among us.
Show us how to promote healing among your people.
And inspire us with your truth.
We ask this through Jesus Christ, our Lord.
Amen.

Invitation

Having called down the Holy Spirit upon us, let us remain open to the working of the Holy Spirit as we engage in the practice of *visio divina*.

As we begin, I invite you all to close your eyes and breathe together, inviting God's presence with us.

Optional: instrumental music.

Breathe in . . . Holy Spirit . . .
Breathe out . . . come among us . . .
Pause for a few seconds.

First Look

Our ministers will now unveil the image. Please stand, if you're able, to encounter the Word of God.

When you look at the image, let your eyes rest on the first part of the image that catches your eye.[4] *Pause.*

Try to keep your gaze from wandering to other parts of the image for now. *Pause.*

Breathe deeply and let yourself gaze at that part of the image, reflecting on these questions:

- What emotions does this image evoke in you?
- What words, phrases, or sensations does it stir up?
- What response to God does it invite? Praise, lament, thanksgiving, wonder, or another response?

Pause for one minute. When the presider begins to speak, the instrumentalist should stop playing.

I invite you to express your meditations in a word or phrase, silently to God or aloud for the assembly.

This process may take up to two minutes, and some assemblies will not speak aloud. If you wish, one person may be prepared to offer the first word. At this point, the ministers who are holding the book may return it to the altar and sit down.

You may be seated for the reading.

Reading

The lector reads, slowly and warmly, from a biblical passage that complements the image chosen. If the image used is "Valley of the Dry Bones," Ezekiel 37:1-14 might be the reading. The reading should be followed by one to two minutes of silence.

---

[4] The scripts for the leader in "First Look" and "Second Look" are adapted from the *visio divina* instructions in *Voices Together.*

Second Look

Instrumental music may again be used.

Our ministers will now display the image again. You may stand if you are able.

Now, you may let your eyes gaze at the whole image . . . *Pause.*
- This time, what emotions, associations, and thoughts does this image evoke in you?
- Has anything changed since the first time you looked at the image?

Pause for one minute.

When the presider begins to speak, the instrumentalist should stop playing. If the assembly did not respond aloud in the first silent period, this may be adapted to permit sharing with one partner or in a small group, either now or after the close of the liturgy.

I invite you once more to express your meditations in a word or phrase, silently to God or aloud for the assembly.

The ministers who are holding the book may return it to the altar and sit down.

Take with you the gift of God's presence you encountered today through this image and offer it to God in prayer.

In the name of God, our creator, we pray for new life.
Amen.

Let us stand to raise our voices together in hope, and then we will go in peace.

A closing song suited to the assembly's musical capabilities and tastes may be used here. See, for instance, "Drawn Back to the Table (Through Him, With Him, in Him)" at the end of the next Appendix.

Prayer in the Morning/Evening

Kimberly Hope Belcher, Julia Canonico, and Eric T. Styles

Invitatory and Hymn

*This liturgy may begin with the invitatory ("O God, come to my assistance"
. . .) and an appropriate hymn or piece of music. At the conference, we used
a chant invitatory and the penitential litany "Hold Us in Your Mercy."[1]
We used this structure for morning prayer two days in a row, and options
are suggested based on that experience. Of course, adaptations to fit a local
assembly are encouraged.*

Psalmody

Psalm 51 or Psalm 130

*Recited antiphonally (sides alternating) in full or set to music. We used
an antiphonal arrangement of Psalm 51 and Clarence Joseph Rivers's
unpublished setting of Psalm 130, sung a cappella.*

Psalm Prayer

Father,
he who knew no sin was made sin for us,
to save us and restore us to your friendship.
Look upon our contrite heart and afflicted spirit
and heal our troubled conscience,

---

[1] Rory Cooney and Gary Daigle, "Hold Us in Your Mercy," *Gathering Rite* (Chicago: GIA Publications, 1997).

so that in the joy and strength of the Holy Spirit
we may proclaim your praise and glory before all the nations.
Amen.

Psalm 63, Another Psalm, or a Nonbiblical Poem

Recited antiphonally or set to music. We used Rawn Harbor's setting of Psalm 63 and an excerpt from Maya Angelou's On the Pulse of Morning.[2]

Canticle

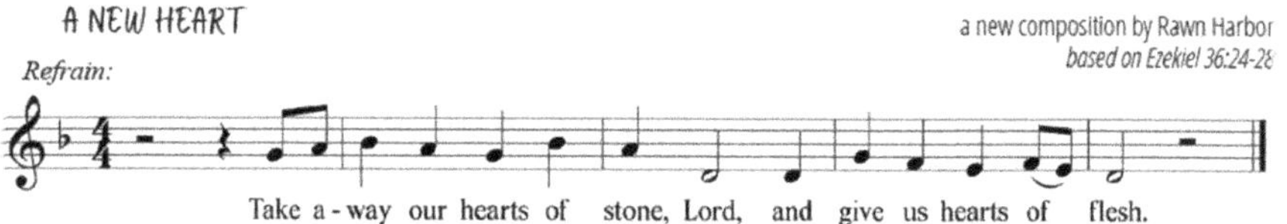

Text and music of "A New Heart" by Rawn Harbor. Printed with permission. All rights reserved.

Scripture

Isaiah 58:5-9a; Isaiah 58:9b-12

Because we held morning prayer on successive days, we were able to read contiguous portions of Isaiah 58. Of course, many other readings could be chosen.

Sermon

Gospel Canticle

An appropriate setting of the Benedictus *or* Magnificat *may be used.*

---

[2] Maya Angelou, *On the Pulse of Morning* (New York: Random House, 1993).

Intercessions

This ancient structure for intercessions provides time for reflection on each petition.

Presider:
Let us ask our merciful God for help addressing the devastating effects of the sexual abuse crisis.

For survivors of clergy sexual abuse and all survivors of abuse.
Pause.
Lord, empower and heal them, bringing your new life to light in
their lives.
We pray to the Lord.
Lord, hear our prayer.

For abuse survivors who have died.
Pause.
Welcome them into the heavenly kingdom, and grant them divine
justice.
We pray to the Lord.
Lord, hear our prayer.

For survivor advocates and other professional specialists who support survivors.
Pause.
Inspire your people who support survivors and grant them a spirit
of discernment.
We pray to the Lord.
Lord, hear our prayer.

For ministers, both lay and ordained, in parishes and educational institutions.
Pause.
Grant them wisdom and compassion in their work surrounded by
the consequences of abuse, both for survivors and for their
communities.
We pray to the Lord.
Lord, hear our prayer.

For scholars and students.

Pause.

Bring your truth to light in their work, so that your justice may
    be done.
We pray to the Lord.
Lord, hear our prayer.

For artists, musicians, and writers.

Pause.

Let their work be a revelation of your love that stands against the
    haze of secrecy and lies.
We pray to the Lord.
Lord, hear our prayer.

For bishops and other church leaders.

Pause.

May they become true witnesses to your passion for the most
    vulnerable.
We pray to the Lord.
Lord, hear our prayer.

For all God's people.

Pause.

As we do penance this Lent, reconcile us in justice and peace, that
    we may bear witness to the risen Christ.
We pray to the Lord.
Lord, hear our prayer.

Presider:
Lord, we bring these prayers before you as your baptized and broken-
hearted people. We beg your grace on your shattered church. Bring
true repentance and lament to the halls of power; light a flame of
hope in the hearts of those who suffer. We ask this through Christ,
our Lord.

And now let us pray as Jesus taught us.

The Lord's Prayer

Our Father . . .

Concluding Prayer

Lord,
with your loving care
guide the penance we have begun.
Help us to persevere with love and sincerity.
Grant this through our Lord Jesus Christ, your Son,
who lives and reigns with you and the Holy Spirit,
God, for ever and ever.
Amen.

OR
God of our hope,
look upon our weakness
and reach out to help us with your loving power.
We ask this through our Lord Jesus Christ, your Son,
who lives and reigns with you and the Holy Spirit,
one God, for ever and ever.
Amen.

Dismissal

May the Lord bless us,
protect us from all evil,
and bring us to everlasting life.
Amen.

Concluding Song

"Drawn Back to the Table (Through Him, With Him, in Him)," J. J. Wright, Tristan Cooley, and the Notre Dame Folk Choir

Drawn Back to the Table

Tristan Cooley and J.J. Wright

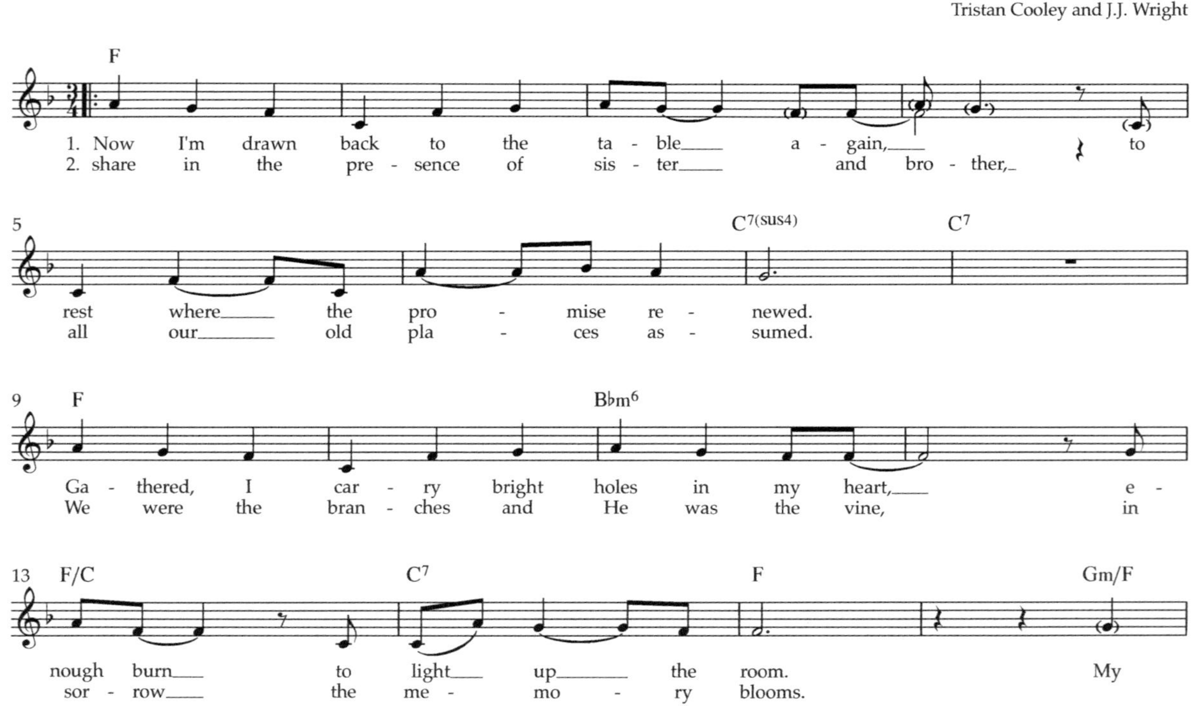

Text and music of "Drawn Back to the Table" by Tristan Cooley, J. J. Wright, and the Notre Dame Folk Choir. Printed with permission. All rights reserved.

Litany of Prayer:
From Anguish, Toward Justice

Ronald Patrick Raab, CSC

Response: Receive our lives, O God.

From our stories of fear . . .
From our silent panic . . .
From our abandonment and abuse . . .
From our weariness and exhaustion . . .

When our hearts feel dirty and worthless . . .
When our trust is broken and lost . . .
When our identities become confused . . .
When our pasts become dark and secret . . .

When the church leaves us in anguish . . .
When we can no longer pray . . .
When we feel abandoned by believers . . .
When clergy resist responsibility . . .

For in our shame, show us a new path . . .
For in our misery, heal our stories in love . . .
For in our forgetfulness, help us find forgiveness . . .
For in our darkness, lead us into new light . . .

May we discover our authentic gifts and talents . . .
May we learn to listen with acceptance and delight . . .
May we unearth joy and contentment in all relationships . . .
May we open our eyes to the beauty of the earth . . .

May we discern Christ's healing love . . .
May we thrive in our daily search for justice . . .
May we forgive and flourish in every moment of life . . .
May we walk in freedom toward God's healing and mercy . . .

Contributors

Melanie Susan Barrett serves as professor and chair of the Department of Moral Theology at the University of Saint Mary of the Lake/Mundelein Seminary. She teaches graduate-level courses on Catholic social doctrine, the ethics of sex and marriage, virtue theory, philosophical ethics, and Reformation- and medieval-era theologians. She has published one book (on the ethics of theologian Hans Urs von Balthasar) and numerous articles and book chapters (on various topics). Currently, she is completing a second book on suffering and the moral life in the work of Thomas Aquinas.

Kimberly Hope Belcher is associate professor of theology at the University of Notre Dame, where she specializes in liturgy and sacramental theology. After earning a bachelor's degree in math and chemistry at the University of Florida, she did her doctoral work at Notre Dame. She is coauthor of *One Baptism—One Church?: A History and Theology of the Reception of Baptized Christians* (Liturgical Press) and author of *Eucharist and Receptive Ecumenism: From Thanksgiving to Communion* (Cambridge University Press). Her current research focuses on the impact of ritual practice on healing from crisis. She has three children and teaches the 5th and 6th grade catechesis class at St. Joseph Parish in South Bend, Indiana.

Jennifer Beste is the College of Saint Benedict Koch Chair in Catholic Thought and Culture and professor of theology at the College of Saint Benedict and Saint John's University. She is author of *College Hookup Culture and Christian Ethics: The Lives and Longings of Emerging Adults* and *God and the Victim: Traumatic Intrusions on Grace and Freedom* (both from Oxford University Press). Beste is currently under contract with Georgetown University Press to write a book re-envisioning what constitutes justice for Catholic children in light of the church's historical and present global child sexual abuse crisis.

Julia Canonico is a doctoral candidate in the Liturgical Studies program at the University of Notre Dame. Her research interests include sacramental theology, popular piety, ecclesiology, and inculturation. These themes are explored in her dissertation, which is titled "Beholding and Becoming: A Renewed Theology of Eucharistic Adoration."

Peter Capretto is assistant professor of pastoral care in religion and culture at Phillips Theological Seminary in Tulsa, Oklahoma. His research explores how social experiences such as empathy shape the ethics and politics of care—specifically around trauma, disability, and race. His writings on politics and theology have appeared in the *Journal of the American Academy of Religion, Los Angeles Review of Books, The Heythrop Journal,* and various scholarly anthologies. He is coeditor of *Trauma and Transcendence: Suffering and the Limits of Theory* (Fordham University Press). Trained clinically as a hospice chaplain, pastoral counselor, and crisis counselor, Dr. Capretto uses his teaching and writing to situate theories of care in close proximity to cultured and lived experiences of psychic trauma, loss, and mourning. He holds a PhD in religion, psychology, and culture from Vanderbilt University.

David A. Clairmont teaches in the Department of Theology at the University of Notre Dame. His research focuses on comparative religious ethics, particularly the moral thought of Roman Catholicism and Theravada Buddhism, professional ethics (particularly in business contexts), and the connection between ethics and spirituality. He is the author of *Moral Struggle and Religious Ethics: On the Person as Classic in Comparative Theological Contexts* and (with William Schweiker) *Religious Ethics: Meaning and Method* (both from Wiley-Blackwell).

Tristan Cooley is a theologian and writer from Vermont, where he works growing fruit trees.

Anselma Dolcich-Ashley, after a career in campus ministry, completed her PhD in moral theology at the University of Notre Dame with a dissertation on the sexual abuse crisis in the Catholic Church in 2002–2007, and served as a theology instructor and adviser for Notre Dame's Glynn Family Honors Program. Currently, she is studying for certification in spiritual direction in the spirituality program at Benet Hill Monastery in Colorado Springs, Colorado, and devotes herself to writing and art projects.

Sarah Gallagher served as a Jesuit Volunteer for two years in Ashland, Montana, at St. Labre Indian School. Following her time in Ashland, Sarah completed a master of divinity degree at the University of Notre Dame, where she also worked with the American Indian Catholic School Network (AICSN). Sarah and her husband have two children, and she continues her involvement with AICSN.

Rev. Kevin G. Grove, CSC, is a Holy Cross priest, associate professor of theology, and director of the master of divinity program at the University of Notre Dame. His academic work treats memory, Christology, St. Augustine, and Blessed Basil Moreau.

Gerard J. McGlone, SJ, PhD, is a research fellow at Georgetown University's Berkley Center for Religion, Peace, and World Affairs, where he leads a project on "Towards a Global Culture of Safeguarding." Currently, he resides in Port of Spain, Trinidad and Tobago, directing trauma services for the archdiocese and the Caribbean region. He has written several award-winning books and articles, and has been at the forefront in designing, researching, and implementing evidenced-based child abuse prevention programming, trauma-informed education, and formation programming.

Marcus Mescher is associate professor of Christian ethics at Xavier University in Cincinnati, Ohio. Dr. Mescher specializes in Catholic social teaching and moral formation. He is the author of *The Ethics of Encounter: Christian Neighbor Love as a Practice of Solidarity* (Orbis Books) and a forthcoming book addressing the psychological, spiritual, moral, and relational harm caused by clergy sexual abuse entitled *A Body of Broken Bones: A Morally Injured Church* (Paulist Press).

Bruce T. Morrill, SJ, holds the Edward A. Malloy Chair in Roman Catholic Studies at Vanderbilt University, where he is distinguished professor of theology in the Divinity School and Graduate Department of Religion. A prolific author of academic and popular articles, his several books include *Divine Worship and Human Healing* and *Anamnesis as Dangerous Memory* (both from Liturgical Press), as well as *Practical Sacramental Theology: At the Intersection of Liturgy and Ethics* (Cascade Books).

Stacey Noem, MDiv, serves in the theology department at the University of Notre Dame as a professor of the practice and director of human and spiritual formation. She has worked professionally in, with, and for the Catholic Church since 2001, most recently as a formator for lay students and religious for the Congregation of Holy Cross for the last thirteen years.

Ronald Patrick Raab, CSC, was ordained a priest in the Congregation of Holy Cross in 1983. Ron ministers among the vulnerable and marginalized of society and the church. He is active as a retreat director, blogger, award-winning author, and visual artist. Fr. Ron serves as religious superior at Holy Cross House, a retirement and medical facility in Notre Dame, Indiana.

Hilary Jerome Scarsella is assistant professor of ethics and director of Women and Gender Studies in Church and Society at Colgate Rochester Crozer Divinity School and director of Theological Integrity at Into Account. She is a scholar, speaker, and advocate with expertise in trauma, theology, ethics, religious practice, and policies relevant to sexual violence. She is committed to an intersectional approach to resisting sexual violence, one that centers racial justice. Her work at Into Account focuses on direct partnership with and advocacy for survivors. She is the primary point person on the IA team for assessing the implicit and explicit theological dimensions of community practices, policies, social patterns, modes of communication, etc., so that the religious dimensions of survivors' experiences can be named, validated, and addressed in the communities that produced them. In addition to working directly with survivors, Hilary develops resources to support high-quality theological education on the subject of sexual violence. As a part of that work, she consults with religious leaders and communities who want to develop a culture that is more trauma-informed, mindful of sexualized violence survivors who are members of the community, and wise with respect to members who are perpetrators.

Rev. Kenneth W. Schmidt is a priest of the Diocese of Kalamazoo, where he serves as judicial vicar and as the advocate for priestly ministry and support. He is a licensed professional counselor and a cofounder of the Trauma Recovery Program in his diocese. He educates and fosters the development of organizational leaders, human service providers, and trauma survivors themselves to respond more effectively to the impact of childhood trauma.

Eric T. Styles, since 2016, has served as the rector of Carroll Hall, an intentional undergraduate residential community at the University of Notre Dame. A Chicago native, he holds degrees from the University of Cincinnati and Loyola University Chicago. Eric worked as a parish liturgy coordinator at Saint Benedict the African Catholic Church in Chicago and as a house manager for the Theatre School of DePaul University. He discerned religious life for seven years with the Society of Jesus, during which time he prayed the thirty-day retreat designed by St. Ignatius Loyola and received formal training in spiritual direction. He later left the Jesuits and eventually found his way to Saint Mary's University of Minnesota, where he worked as a campus minister for liturgy and faith formation. Now at Notre Dame, he continues to assist as a retreat leader and an occasional spiritual director. Eric remains active in the performing arts as a collaborator with Afro House, a Baltimore-based music driven performance art ensemble. Eric writes about theology, liturgy, and contemporary culture for publications like *America*, *Church Life Journal*, and *U.S. Catholic*.

Patrick J. Wall is a former Roman Catholic priest and Benedictine monk from Saint John's Abbey. Mr. Wall earned degrees in philosophy (BA), theology (MDiv), and canon law (LLM). As a priest, he served in the Archdiocese of Saint Paul and Minneapolis parishes, the tribunal and finance council. As an advocate, Patrick has assisted criminal prosecutors, civil lawyers, bankruptcy attorneys, professors, journalists, and is a subject-matter expert on artificial intelligence and stem cell projects. Coauthor of *Sex, Priests, and Secret Codes: The Catholic Church's 2,000-Year Paper Trail of Sexual Abuse* (Taylor Trade), Mr. Wall has lectured at the University of California, Irvine; California State University, Fullerton; University of Notre Dame; and University of Toronto, Evasion Lab. He assists Grant & Eisenhofer attorneys in several practice areas that represent survivors of sexual assault.

J. J. Wright is the director of the University of Notre Dame Folk Choir. As a conductor, pianist, composer, and producer, his interests lie at the convergence of the creative process, music-making, spirituality, and liturgy. J. J.'s work has appeared on Grammy-award winning and #1 Billboard Classical albums.